INTERNATIONAL BUSINESS MANAGEMENT:
The Essentials for MBAs and Executives

2022 Edition

Farok J. Contractor, Ph.D.
Distinguished Professor, Management and Global Business
Rutgers Business School

Farok J. Contractor, Distinguished Professor of Management and Global Business at Rutgers Business School and author of ten books and over 150 scholarly articles, holds a Ph.D. (Managerial Science and Applied Economics) and an M.B.A. from the Wharton School, as well as two engineering degrees, M.S. (Michigan) and B.S.E. (Bombay). A Fellow of the Academy of International Business (AIB), a worldwide association of 3,500 academics and consultants, he is also on the AIB Board, currently serving as President (2021–2022). Professor Contractor is the recipient of a Silver Medal for the number of contributions to the *Journal of International Business Studies*, a leading management journal. His research focuses on key issues in International Business, such as corporate alliances, emerging markets, outsourcing and offshoring, valuation of intangible assets, the technology transfer process, licensing, and foreign direct investment.

Professor Contractor's website for managers, students, policymakers, and educated laypeople covering International Business issues has been read over time in 174 countries: https://GlobalBusiness.blog.

For more details on the author's background, see his curriculum vitae on the Rutgers Faculty Page: https://www.business.rutgers.edu/sites/default/files/documents/faculty/cv-farok-contractor-long.pdf.

ISBN: 979-8-8219-3023-1

ELLIPSIS EDUCATION
NEW JERSEY, USA

A GLOBALBUSINESS© PUBLICATION

COVER IMAGE: SHUTTERSTOCK

NET PROFITS FROM THIS BOOK WILL BE DONATED TO A CHARITABLE ORGANIZATION

TABLE OF CONTENTS

INTERNATIONAL BUSINESS MANAGEMENT:
The Essentials for MBAs and Executives

Part III. Foreign Exchange Rates: Their Impact on International Operations

Section A. Hedging Foreign Currency Receivables and Payables

Section B. Interest Rates and Foreign Exchange Rates

Part IV. Foreign Exchange Rates and Pricing in International Markets

Includes Discussion of Additional Problems from Chapter 13, Part III

Section A. Economic Exposure and Operational Planning

Section B. Optimal Pricing as a Function of Exchange Rates

Part V. Global Management in a Still-Fragmented World:
Local vs. International

PREFACE AND INTRODUCTION

International Business Is Vastly More Complex Than Domestic Operations

The successful practice of management, at middle to senior levels, requires managers to understand a large variety of topics, from finance to marketing to supply chain management, as well as many others. They also need to be widely read persons and be proactively aware of external influences on their firms.

International Business adds an additional level of complexity on top of managing domestic businesses because the 193 nations on our planet exhibit dramatically different and diverse cultures, income levels, costs, and risks of doing business, multiple currencies, marketing practices, regulations, and institutions.

This book is designed for a short course. It does not focus on the environment of international business – its geography, politics, or cultures, *per se*. It assumes that the educated reader or manager has already picked up, or will become aware of, this background. Instead, this textbook focuses on tools and strategies that are essential to the practice of cross-border management. At the same time, it touches on a few theories that have practical import.

Essentials for Understanding International Business Management Covered in This Textbook

The art of international management consists of bridging and arbitraging differences. The bridging function entails determining how and where to expand operations abroad and by what method. A company can serve a foreign customer by exporting to that nation, or it can create a foreign subsidiary inside the country, or it can form an alliance and collaborate with a "partner" in the foreign nation. Part I of this textbook focuses on the advantages, drawbacks, and risks of different strategies of "doing business abroad."

The scanning ability of multinational companies also enables them to spot and seize arbitrage opportunities. Because of the large diversity across nations, the multinational firm can arbitrage and take advantage of differences in labor costs, regulations, and resources across countries. By accessing these in nations where such costs are lower, the multinational gains an advantage over purely domestic rivals. At the same time, reorganizing global operations and transferring resources across borders can also increase risks. Global supply chains are organized on the idea of splitting and fine-slicing the "value chain" (whether it be raw materials, components, or steps in production, or even after-sales service) over countries where each function can be best performed at lower cost. An Apple iPhone may have components sourced in more than 18 nations, be assembled in China, and be sold as a finished product in over 100 countries. Such fine slicing of the value chain reduces overall cost. However, it also heightens risks (such as floods, volcanos, blockage of transportation channels) which can cause major disruption across the entire procurement chain and end-markets.

We are still in a world with more than 175 national moneys or currencies. By definition, therefore, doing international business necessarily entails the conversion of one currency into another. Each 24-hour period sees the worldwide exchange of over $5 trillion of currencies. What is critical is the exchange rate. Competitive transactions may have a profit margin of less than 5 percent, a margin that can be wiped out in days or hours if the exchange rate shifts by more than 5 percent – a not uncommon occurrence. Part II of this book covers two theories, the idea of "Comparative Advantage" of nations, which forms the basis for international trade competitiveness, and "Purchasing Power Parity Theory," which gives the reader some sense of why currency values change – both across nations and over time. Theories are not covered merely as an academic exercise. Rather after reviewing each theory, this book is more concerned with its practical, real-life uses and relevance.

Part III of the book is not concerned with *why* currency values change, but with *how* the manager can protect her/his company from the possibility – almost the certainty – that exchange rates will fluctuate over time. In the short run, for, say, exporters and importers whose contracts span a few months between order acceptance and execution or shipment, banks can provide "forward cover"; or, using so-called money market operations, the outcome can be fixed in the exporter or importer's currency in advance. On the other hand, foreign subsidiaries of multinational corporations or licensing agreements can last for years. For a long-run purview, the only protection against currency risk is to adopt proactive strategies covered in Part III B and Part IV of the book. Note that the Foreign Exchange Risk Management Problems are included in Chapter 13, but many (including Case 2) are listed in reading order in Part IV.

Part V returns to the themes of managing across cultures and finding the optimal middle ground between the extremes of global standardization (which can lower costs worldwide) and local or country-by-country adaptation of products and processes (which can increase revenues in each nation and hence worldwide). This tension between global standardization and local adaptation is accompanied by the strains of managing multicultural and multilingual workforces, as well as differences in ethics and regulations across nations. Over the past quarter-century, more than 3,000 workers in Bangladesh's garment factories have suffered fatalities and injuries because of poor work conditions. Recently, companies such as H&M have come under fire in China because they have adopted "ethical sourcing" standards that are offensive to certain sections of the Chinese public, whereas publics in advanced nations demand more stringent labor and ethical standards. The art of global management includes managing regulatory, cultural, and other differences.

This book, while designed for a short course to cover the essentials of international management, does offer a sufficiently deep dive into the complexities of cross-border strategies.

Note that suggested readings that are not part of this textbook are accessible via the internet and/or university libraries as listed in the Appendix: Additional Suggested Readings.

Part I. Overseas Expansion:

Strategies to Reach Foreign Markets

NOTE TO READERS:

**For Relevant Materials Not Included in This Textbook,
Refer to the Appendix: Additional Suggested Readings**

CHAPTER 1

International Expansion Strategies:
Classic Ways of Reaching Foreign Markets and Assessing Benefits, Risks, and Costs

Overview

This chapter is about how a firm may expand its operations to other countries. There are many ways to enter foreign markets. Each presents a strategic choice to the manager. Let us suppose a company wishes to deliver a product or service to customers in a new market abroad. The first choice is whether to produce inside that country, or whether to produce the service or item in the company's existing plants and ship it to the new market. The first decision, then, is between local production and exports. Several economic and strategy criteria affect this choice. To export the item to a foreign market means additional costs of freight, customs duties, insurance, special packing, and other taxes, which may be avoided if the item were to be produced in the foreign country itself. On the other hand, setting up production in a foreign nation involves additional capital investment, risks of foreign production, and higher or lower production costs compared to the company's existing facilities (especially when we take exports from the latter on a variable cost basis). The manager also has to consider the risks and organizational issues associated with setting up a new foreign investment, such as political instability, an unfamiliar environment, currency fluctuations, training new management and staff to fit in with the company's existing procedures, hierarchy, and operating specifications, and on-going control and communication costs.

A contractual alliance, such as licensing the company's expertise, patents, or brands to another firm in the foreign market, and to have this firm produce the good or service for customers there, is another option. The foreign alliance partner or licensee company receives training and the rights to intellectual property, and in turn pays fees and royalties to the company as licensor. This is more or less a "hands-off" approach to international expansion, involving less control over the foreign operation than an equity investment. Since it is the foreign partner or licensee company that makes the investment and assumes the risk of developing the market in their country, the royalties and technical fees they are willing to pay the licensor are often inferior to the dividends and growth in equity value the company could have earned if it had made the foreign investment by itself. A hybrid option, also involving a partner, is to form an equity joint venture company in the foreign nation whose shares are owned by our company and a local investing partner. Managers from both allied firms – foreign and local – then jointly run the operation.

Each option involves different levels of investment, expected return, control, risk, duration, competitive threat, and tax and strategy implications. There is no single optimal choice. The decision depends on the product and market in question, on the company's financial and managerial resources, its risk averseness, and its overall global strategy.

This chapter has two major parts. First, the "classic" foreign market entry choices of exporting, licensing (contractual alliance), and foreign direct investment are presented and compared as strategy alternatives. How a firm may choose a particular mode in developing a particular country market is shown. Reality, however, is often far more complicated. For one thing, risk, tax, and strategy often call for *combining* some of the options rather than treating them as substitutes for each other. The second part of this chapter describes how and why the classic strategy options are often combined in large, mature global companies. Globalization calls for treating a foreign market not as a compartmentalized operation, but as one that is integrated with the rest of the global firm's activities. For instance, a foreign affiliate (equity investment) may also have received technology or intellectual property from the parent (under an auxiliary license agreement), while at the same time its inputs are supplied by an affiliate from another nation (this is called a global supply chain, or global value chain (GVC) or intra-firm exports). In this example, direct equity investment, licensing, and trade are not substitutes, but are combined into one foreign operation. Firms beginning their international expansion are more likely to view them as substitutes. The mature globalizing firm may view them as concurrent strategies.

1. The Classic Strategy Options

The three classic international expansion options are shown in Table 1 which indicates that cash returns under each type are likely to be very different in magnitude, timing, duration, various risks, and tax liability. In exporting, profit margins are earned immediately, shipment by shipment, under control of the company; risks are those associated with the exporting location, and the profits are immediately taxable in the exporting nation.

In foreign direct investment (FDI) a new company is acquired or created abroad with a substantial investment, and the investing company owns (all or some of) its shares. If the parent company owns *all* of the foreign affiliate's shares it is called a "fully owned subsidiary". If the shareholding is less than 100percent then it is still called an equity "affiliate," or "equity joint venture." If the shareholding is above 50 percent the affiliate may be called "majority-owned affiliate" in some nations. If some of the affiliate's shares are held by a local partner, then it is called a "joint venture" affiliate. In some cases, the multinational parent's shareholding may be well below 100 percent, but if the balance of the shares is widely held by small investors in the foreign nation, then effective control still rests with the parent multinational company.

In the term "foreign direct investment" the word "direct" reminds us that the investor directly controls, or has some influence over, the management of the foreign company. A shareholding under 10 percent is generally considered passive or portfolio investment. Shareholding above 10 percent is considered "foreign direct investment" or FDI. The degree of control is, of course, only very loosely correlated with the percentage of shares held. By value, most international direct investment takes the form of fully owned subsidiaries or majority (over 50 percent shareholding) affiliates. The cash returns under a capital investment are usually considerably delayed compared to exporting (immediate profit margin on the export) or royalty returns (since royalties as a percentage of sales are payable even if the licensee makes no profit). But all in all, returns from a company's own equity investment are likely to be far bigger and lead to eventual growth in equity value as well. Unlike contractual alliances which are often time-limited, for equity investment (FDI) there is usually no time limit. Capital investments do, of course, face the risk of failure and eventual termination. The investment is also subject to political and foreign exchange risk in the foreign country. Dividend returns are a partial distribution after the corporate tax bite in the country, and remittances are subject to an additional withholding tax in several nations.

In licensing or contractual alliances, the returns are under an agreement (between two more or less independent, or arm's-length firms. This is our assumption in the first part of this chapter). Agreements usually have a limited life, of between two and ten years generally, unless renewed. Some agreements call for a significant lump sum payment at the inception, plus running royalties, usually expressed as a percentage of the sales value of the licensed item in the licensee's market.

Table 1. Classic Strategy Options and Type of Income from Each

Strategy	Type of Return
1. Exporting the product, that is to say, International Trade	Immediate direct profit mark-up on item sold; taxable in exporting country. Short-term planning horizon because of uncertainty over receiving orders from abroad.
2. Foreign direct investment (FDI)	Profits and equity growth declared by foreign affiliate; taxable in foreign country. Long-term planning horizon.
3. Contractual alliance / Licensing to independent party	Royalties (and technical fees) over life of the agreement; royalties are tax-deductible to licensee firm. Intermediate planning horizon.

Most governments (within limits) allow licensing fees and royalties to be counted as deductible expenses to the payer, that is, the licensee. This means that, unlike dividends, remittance of licensing payments legally escapes the foreign country's corporate income tax altogether. This confers a marginal to significant advantage to the licensing option.

Key Decisions in International Expansion: Location, Ownership, and Control

Among the key variables in choosing a foreign market entry mode are location, ownership, and control, as shown in Figure 1.

The location question relates to where the product is to be made, or the service created – inside the foreign nation, or made in the company's home or other production locations? The decision is affected by production cost in each place, transport costs (if the item is produced in one location and sent to another), tariffs, non-tariff barriers, and other factors. Immediate cost comparisons should be modified by *long-run* forecasts of relative exchange rates when calculating import costs, just as local production cost estimates are to be tempered by forecasts of input costs of local labor, materials, and finance. Costs are sometimes not the crucial factor because marketing success may be predicated on speedy and effective delivery and quality, rather than on price. In terms of overall strategy, criteria other than simple direct cost comparisons, such as political risk considerations, may dominate the location decision.

If the decision is made to produce inside the foreign market, this can be done by a foreign direct investment, either fully owned, or in a strategic alliance with a local firm (i) as an equity joint venture, or (ii) as a licensing arrangement. In the latter two cases when a partner firm is involved, designing the arrangement to exercise "control" over the operation becomes important.

In a fully owned subsidiary or a majority foreign affiliate, managers obey the wishes of the multinational parent firm even if they are nationals of the country. But in alliances, when other interests are involved, such as local joint venture partners or licensees, their aims, methods, and behavior may not always conform to the investor company's objectives. The term "control" should not appear sinister or manipulative. In any good business arrangement involving two or more parties, mutual checks and balances should be built in. In international business, this is all the more important because of economic, legal, and cultural differences. For example, a foreign partner or licensee, having acquired a technology, may then become a competitor with its licensor in other countries. There are several historical examples involving US firms, which licensed technology to Japanese or Chinese companies. In the early years, they provided good income to the US licensors, but later, the Chinese or Japanese became competitors in Asia, and even in the "home" market of the US licensors.

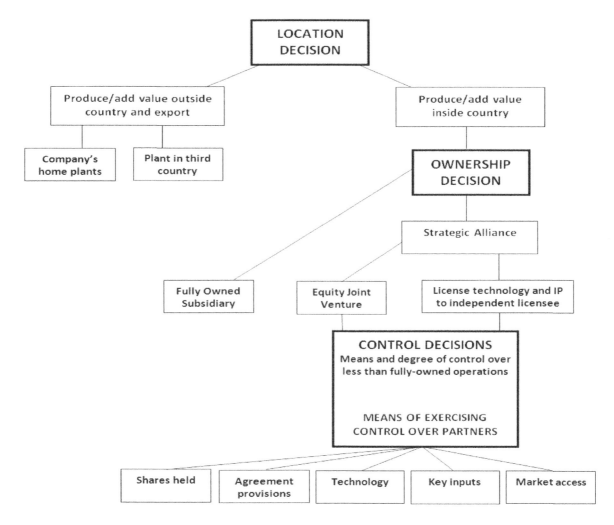

Figure 1 Three Key Decision Domains: location, ownership and control

Alliances may present other issues. In a joint venture, one partner may want a high dividend declaration or a quick "payout," whereas the other may have a long-term strategy preferring reinvestment of most of the joint venture's earnings in the early years. The local licensee or ally may wish to export to neighboring nations, but the multinational firm may already supply that country directly and not want their profits in that third nation diminished. Such differences can be serious, and they should be anticipated, with mutual checks and balances structured into the arrangement from the beginning.

How Control Can Be Wielded (See the five lower boxes in Figure 1)

These checks and controls could be structured into the agreement. In an equity joint venture, it is assumed that the majority shareholder makes all the ultimate decisions. But this does not always work out, if the other minority partner has other "bargaining chips" such as political connections, needed market contacts, or if legal recourse in that nation is ineffective. All alliances are governed by an initial agreement between the parties whose provisions are subject to negotiation. An agreement may confer the majority of seats on the Board of Directors, or certain decision rights to one partner -- even though they hold less than 50 percent of the shares. Some agreements give one of the partners veto power over certain key managerial appointments or specify which production method will be used. An agreement could specify maximum and minimum dividend payouts in each year, and so on.

Control can also be wielded by means other than a written agreement, by holding out the lure of new technology or improvements which the other partner desires; by one partner controlling the supply of key materials, components, or ingredients; by the threat of withdrawing a valuable brand; or by controlling access to international markets for the output of the joint venture or licensee. The ongoing dependence of one partner over the other would temper their behavior in the interest of mutual gain. Some of the longest-lived strategic alliances are those where the partners continue to be mutually dependent.

In strategic alliances the two firms, while remaining separate organizations, coordinate activities for a common purpose. Beginning in the year 2000, there has been a proliferation, not only in the common forms of strategic alliance such as joint ventures and licensing agreements, but also in other modes of cooperation between firms. Examples include research consortia, long-term supply chain and service agreements, joint marketing arrangements, and co-production agreements. However, since much of the strategy discussion about licensing and joint ventures also applies to these other forms, we will not treat them separately here.

2. Exporting as an International Strategy

Advantages of Exporting

Exporting is a logical means of serving a foreign market when the exporting country or location has a comparative production advantage, or when the foreign market is too small, or too risky, to justify its own factory. For an initial expansion into a foreign market, exporting from existing plants means no new investment may be needed in the foreign location, with its capital investment and risk. The company merely uses its slack capacity by increasing plant running hours or adding shifts. Plant managers love export orders, especially if domestic demand is slack, as they utilize existing equipment and employees. (See Table 2 for a summary of the advantages.) For some industries, there are considerable economies of a large scale derived by combining production in one location and operation.

Table 2. **Pros and Cons of an Export Strategy**

Pros	*Cons*
No new investment (true for small foreign orders)	Existing slack production capacity may be used up (by growing demand)
Very profitable on variable cost basis	Can face formidable "non-tariff," transport, tariff, and other barriers
Utilizes existing capacity and employees	
Economies of large-scale production	High exposure to foreign exchange risk (in long-term strategic sense)
Familiar production environment	
Very low (short-term) foreign exchange risk exposure	Just-in-time fast delivery and customer (short-term) relations difficult

Assuming that the fixed costs of the plant are covered by domestic sales and existing export sales, any *incremental* order adds handsomely to profit, since any revenue above variable cost goes directly to profits. An export order, even at a price *less* than the domestic price, can still be profitable – that is to say, as long as variable costs are covered by the export revenues, however low. (This may subject the firm to "dumping" allegations as we will see later. The domestic price may cover all costs - fixed and variable. The export price can be lower than the domestic price if the foreign market is price sensitive, very competitive, or consumers are poor. Of course, the export price can also be higher than the domestic price in other markets). Serving several countries from one plant enables a company to charge different prices for the same item in different nations.

In general, when fixed costs are very high and variable costs per unit are low, this favors concentrating production in a few giant plants (from which exports are shipped to various markets). For example, a semiconductor factory may cost five billion dollars to set up. But once constructed and the large R&D costs are already incurred, the variable cost of producing a chip may be less than one dollar or a few dollars. Automated plants have few workers and so labor costs are not a major consideration. Moreover, chips are light weight and transport cost is very low. This scenario favors producing at a large scale and exporting from a few large factories to several nations. Other "high-tech" industries with a similar economic structure (high R&D and fixed costs with low variable costs), such as pharmaceuticals, could also prefer an export strategy. Alas, exporting is not often possible because of other obstacles and pressures.

Drawbacks of Exporting

The drawbacks of an export strategy are also indicated in Table 2. The additional costs of freight, insurance, special packing, and customs tariffs sometimes make the delivered or landed cost in the foreign market prohibitively high, even with the cost base near to the variable cost floor.

International freight costs, on average, are 5 percent of value, or below. However, this is an average with huge variation, depending on the foreign location and the ratio of transport cost to product value. Because of the country's location, Australian consumers pay a higher price for many goods. Being light in relation to value, (i.e., a high value-to-weight ratio) a diamond may be mined in South Africa, cut in Israel, set in jewelry in China, and the finished piece sold in the USA – all of this without too much of a freight penalty, as a percentage of the high value of the item. Other bulk goods, (with a low value-to-weight ratio) however, such as construction materials, are restricted by freight costs to a certain radius around their manufacturing location. Software is exported from India to the USA at the click of a key on a computer in Bangalore. This appears to have low marginal "transport" cost, but this is a bit misleading since we cannot ignore the huge, fixed cost outlays for satellites and transponders.

After fifty years of the General Agreement on Tariffs and Trade (GATT) talks, later renamed the World Trade Organization (WTO), customs tariffs in the major industrialized nations are down to an average of below 3 percent. So, on average, in the rich nations of the world at least, tariffs are not a significant obstacle to international trade, anymore. (Incidentally, averages mask a big variation from zero to over 100 percent on some items). Today, far more than tariffs, it is "non-tariff barriers" that remain a principal obstacle to trade. Non-tariff barriers impede trade, not by adding on an extra tariff element, but by imposing regulations, bureaucracy, tough or unreasonable inspection requirements, and quantitative restrictions on imports. As average tariff barriers have reduced over the decades, thanks to WTO, there has been a proliferation in industry regulations introduced by each government. Typically, these may involve such tough inspection rules and certification requirements for certain items to preclude their import. Restrictive quotas have been imposed on a wide range of items from clothing to cauliflowers to cars. A government may force another country to restrict its shipments, and impose an unwritten quota. These are sometimes called "Voluntary Trade Restraints," but the restriction is far from voluntary and is undertaken because of strong, behind-the-scenes political pressure. A "buy local" mentality in some nations may produce a similar *de facto* limitation on imports. Many markets simply cannot be served by exports because of such "non-tariff" restrictions.

An exporting strategy faces other problems in some sectors. By definition, exporting means doing business (or at least locating production) at a distance from the customer. This means "just-in-time" delivery and customer relations are more difficult, and riskier, compared with the option of producing within the foreign market (in the company's own foreign subsidiary, for example). With unexpected events such as floods and volcanos, or pandemics and blockage of the Suez Canal which occurred in 2021, the importer may be left without goods, or a factory importing key components may be forced to idle for a while.

In many industries such as fashion garments, fickle or seasonal demand requires a fast reorder, or response, to surges in demand. Shipping from Asia to the US or Europe may take four to seven weeks. This explains why some garment factories remain in the USA despite labor costing four to eight times the level in low-wage nations. In other manufacturing supply chains, components may be needed "just-in-time," within days, to meet the shifting demand of assembly lines switching over from one model to another. Co-location of the component manufacturer near the assembly operation – not just in the same country but often in the same municipality – enables production scheduling flexibility and also, importantly, greatly reduces inventory carrying costs. This rules out exporting as a viable strategy.

Another limitation to exporting is that while utilizing existing spare capacity is desirable, that argument can only be carried up to the capacity limit of the factory. Up to a point the existing plant can handle foreign demand by adding second or third shifts. But there are only 24 hours in a day. After that, if foreign demand is bigger still, how does the firm handle further growth? Even adding shifts escalates costs: on night shifts workers have to be paid higher wages, quality is often poorer and the reject rate higher. The time comes when the company will have to contemplate adding another factory or line, which requires additional millions in capital investment. Then the firm can no longer treat its incremental export sales on a variable cost basis. Additional capital investment means additional fixed costs, which then have to be covered from the export price.

Exporting as an Evolutionary Stage

At this stage in the evolution of a company's international business, when another plant must be added because of growing foreign demand, some companies conclude that they may as well build an additional plant inside the foreign market. This would eliminate transport costs and customs duties, reduce non-tariff barriers and logistics, shorten delivery times and improve customer contacts. This is how firms most often make their first overseas investment.

Of course, in some cases, companies may conclude that the foreign market is too small or uncertain, or the required capital investment too massive to justify such a step. Such companies must then restrict their international business to a level based on available capacity or consider the licensing option.

Foreign Exchange Risks in Exporting

In Table 2 there seems to be a contradiction between foreign exchange risks in the left versus right columns. In the short-run, each shipment can usually be hedged against foreign exchange risk. The easiest approach is for exporters to ask for payment in their own currency. However, this does not eliminate the exchange risk but transfers it to the importer. So, this approach can work at the risk of annoying the buyer. It depends on whether it is the buyer or seller that holds the dominant negotiating position. At any rate, for major currencies (such as the US dollar, Japanese yen, euro, or pound sterling in which most exports are denominated), forward cover is easily obtained, whereby a bank guarantees the foreign exchange rate well before the shipment date. Or an "option" can be bought. Thus, currency risk for each shipment can be reduced or eliminated in advance.

However, while the exchange rate for each shipment can be fixed in advance (at least up to a year or so), the forward rate or option price itself will change over time as the spot rate changes for a currency (appreciation or devaluation). Hence in the long run, with repeated future shipments, there is no escape from foreign exchange risks associated with exporting.

Plants dedicated to export markets are therefore fundamentally exposed to shifts in the exchange rate over the long term. Consider a Japanese plant selling cameras or mobile phones to the USA. What if the Japanese yen moves from a rate of yen 120 = $1 to say yen 100 = $1 over time? If the camera price is kept the same in dollars, the company loses, as one dollar would earn it only yen 100 instead of yen 120. One possible solution for the Japanese firm would be to increase the dollar price for their cameras by 20 percent, so as to retain the same yen revenue per mobile phone or camera. However, this may not work. In very competitive markets like the US (aided by open-market policies of the US government for most items), the dollar unit price of phones or cameras cannot be raised significantly. As a result, the last time the dollar weakened (i.e., the yen strengthened) Japanese exporters could not increase their dollar prices by much. They saw, not just their profits eliminated, but their gross yen revenues were dramatically reduced. A difficult situation for such foreign companies can be a happy situation for the US consumer. Thus, while exporting has minimal exchange risk in the short term (shipment by shipment), this strategy leaves the company exposed in the long term.

A Numerical Case Study

The numerical example below illustrates the concepts of (1) variable and average cost pricing, (2) economies of scale, (3) tariff barriers, and (4) transfer pricing and "dumping," which enter into export pricing decisions.

A US video game manufacturer sells 200,000 units of a video game to a mature domestic US market. Variable cost per game is $9 each and fixed costs amount to $2,200,000 per year. The game is sold in the US at a wholesale price of $22 each, involving a profit mark-up of 10 percent – or $2 over the average cost of $20 per game. Maximum capacity of the factory is 250,000 video games per year. We see in Table 3 that there are strong economies of scale – from a prohibitively

Table 3 Scale economies in video game production

Quantity	Variable cost total	Fixed cost	Total costs	Average cost
10000	90000	2200000	2290000	$ 229
100000	900000	2200000	3100000	$ 31
200000	1800000	2200000	4000000	$ 20
210000	1890000	2200000	4090000	$ 19.48
250000	2250000	2200000	4450000	$ 17.8

Variable cost per unit	= $9
Domestic sakes Q	= 200000 games per year
Trial export order	= 10000 games
Domestic wholesale price	= $22 (10 per cent above average cost)
Maximum factory capacity	= 250000 games per year

high cost of $229 per unit for a small volume of 10,000 units to a reasonable $20 per unit at a volume of 200,000 games.

Let us suppose that the company receives an e-mail one day, indicating that there may be a nascent demand for the video game in a foreign market. Would the company please quote for a trial export shipment of 10,000 units, on a "landed cost" basis (meaning that the exporter bears all costs including freight, insurance, and import tariff), to the foreign market? Investigation reveals freight and insurance costs to be $1 per game, and the tariff in the import nation will be 50 percent on the "Free on Board" (FOB) value. (FOB in international trade refers to the exporter bearing the cost of goods, including delivery and loading on board a vessel or aircraft in the exporter's port.)

The most common reaction of small US exporters is to reason thus: "We charge $22 to our domestic customers. Why should we treat our foreign clients any better or worse? We will charge them the same $22 plus whatever freight and tariff costs are incurred – that is their responsibility." This is quote No. 3 in Table 4, which amounts to a landed cost of $34 in the foreign market. Quote No. 2 is similar, with only a slight difference. Since the export order adds to domestic volume, making the total 210,000 units, this lowers the average cost to $19.48 (in Table 3). Add to $19.48 the customary $2 profit margin, and we get $21.48 as the FOB value. This makes for a landed cost of $33.22 in the foreign market, as shown in Table 4.

Table 4 Possible export quotations for video game (delivered to foreign market)

Quote	FOB US Port	Freight and insurance	Customs Duty at 50% on FOB	Total landed cost in foreign market
1	$9.00	+ 1	+ 0.50(9)	= $14.5
2	$21.48	+ 1	+ 0.50(21.48)	= $33.22
3	$22.00	+ 1	+ 0.50(22)	= $34
4	$38.00	+ 1	+ 0.50(38)	= $58

However, both quotes 2 and 3 may be wildly off the mark. Foreign markets are likely to be very different from the domestic market in consumer tastes, income, product cycle maturity, competition, and price elasticity. To make an export quote based on the domestic price is nothing more than a shot in the dark. Unfortunately, this is what some exporters do (particularly small ones), either because of ignorance or because the costs of overseas market research are too high. Several foreign markets may be able to sustain a price much *higher* than the domestic price. Customers there might be affluent, or the video game, being new, might attract a coterie of fanatics willing to pay a high price. Alternatively, the foreign market may only be able to sustain a price much *lower* than the domestic US price, because income levels are low or because the culture does not appreciate video games, or because of intense competition. What the manager needs to do is to calculate a minimum and a maximum.

What is the minimum? If fixed costs are said to be covered by domestic US or other existing sales, any quote above the US variable manufacturing cost floor plus international delivery, logistics, and tariffs (i.e., a $14.50 landed cost, with international delivery to the foreign market) would make some additional contribution towards profit. Rather than ignoring poor or very price-competitive markets, the firm can make some additional profits there. The $4.50 in Quote No. 1 in Table 4, thus constitutes a floor price.

What is the maximum price? (This is especially useful to remember when the foreign market is affluent). Here we cannot work upwards from FOB cost, but must work downwards from whatever price the market can bear. Let us suppose in this scenario that the market is affluent, and competition is weak, and that 10,000 video games can be sold to teenage fanatics at a wholesale price of $58 each (Quote No. 4 in Table 4). The export executive works backward from the expression:

$$\text{Put} \quad X + 1 + 0.50X = 58.00, \text{ i.e., } X = 38.$$

This calculation derives an FOB value of $38 which is much higher than the US price of $22. So, in Calculation No. 4 in Table 4, the exporter types on their invoice an FOB value of $38. If a foreign market can bear a higher price, it would be foolish for the company not to charge it. Why lose potential profit and give the product away too cheaply? (As long as conditions in the foreign market allow higher prices, and the company itself is not using monopolistic tactics to reduce competition, its higher price is generally considered legal).

Profit Maximization in Global Marketing

The essential point is that the price charged in one territory (domestic), often has little bearing on the price to be charged in another territory (export). This is especially true in international business when the territories are separated by borders, oceans, and large cultural and income differences. In international business, to maximize its global total profit, the company should charge a different price in different nations – even for the exact same product. The same video game that is sold for $22 wholesale in the US domestic market, may sell for $58 in an affluent country, and nearly as low as near $14.50 in a poor or price-sensitive nation – and still yield an incremental profit on each item sold.

When the Fixed Costs of an item are very high (billions) and the Variable Cost is relatively minor (few dollars per item), the easier it is for the multinational firm to play the marketing game of global price discrimination. In most nations it is legal. Affluent customers may not know, or care, that they are being charged more. But this policy benefits customers in middle-income or poorer nations. A drug or computer chip may sell for only a few dollars in one nation, but may command hundreds or thousands of dollars in another nation whose customers are able, willing, or forced, to pay a higher price. All the pharmaceutical or semiconductor firm needs to ensure is – that for all customers worldwide and over all nations – worldwide revenues over the product cycle cover the R&D and high fixed costs. If the company can get away with it, it should play the game of setting different prices in different nations. This is not just a theory. In real life practice, price differentiation is what international companies do – charge different prices for the same item.

The "Grey Market" or "Parallel Imports"

But the above strategic recommendations may cause some problems that the global firm will have to deal with, and try to minimize. If an item is easily transportable, and encounters low tariffs, in that case, unauthorized third parties may buy the item in the cheaper price country and ship it to a higher price nation, thus undercutting the company's own distribution channels and undermining its price discrimination policy. Companies respond to this "grey market" problem by attempting to differentiate products, using different designs, packaging, branding, or warranties for different nations. The same consumer electronic item – say a video game player – may be given different model numbers, or a different color, and in some cases a few extra control buttons may be added, or a few features disabled – adapting the product to make it look different. But it is the same product. However, sometimes adaptation is costly to the company, and adaptation may not work for commodity items. Thus, there are such things as globally standard prices for copper, wheat and oil. The price variation across countries for small, easily transported items like watch batteries also tends to be lower. Pan-European regulatory scrutiny of drug prices has reduced price disparities for drugs within the European Union (EU). However, the vast majority of manufactured goods and services are not standardized, but remain differentiated – by design, technology, brand names and the uses they are put to in different nations. So, the "grey market" problem affects some industries, but not others.

Other Reactions to Global Price Discrimination

Besides the grey market, other adverse reactions to a company's price discrimination policy include (i) governments forcing down prices for so-called essential products such as pharmaceuticals (ii) large global buyers who have discovered the price differences across nations and now demand that the supplier quote one lower "global price" to all their subsidiaries worldwide. (iii) adverse public reaction from a public that increasingly travels abroad and learns about prices in different nations, (iv) accusations of "dumping." (See below.)

E-Commerce, the Internet, and Eventual Price Convergence?

The introduction of e-commerce and a common currency such as the Euro have, over time, begun to reduce price disparities, as gaps in price across countries become more obvious to buyers. But transport costs, tariffs, taxes, delivery times, the desire for quick gratification, buyer search costs, and other impediments prevent complete price convergence, except in items close to being generic or being commodities. Indeed, in many sectors, ranging from garments to electronics, affluent customers seem to value speed and variety over low price. For such products, where customers value variety and speed over cost, mass production is being replaced by mass-customization, flexible production, and smaller but varied batches.

The overall conclusion is that for the foreseeable future, the world will remain a fragmented marketing landscape for a majority of items sold. There is therefore currently no need, and moreover it is globally sub-optimal, for a company to charge identical prices in the different countries it sells in. The very attempt is foolish and doomed in a world of floating exchange rates. The Euro exchange rate fluctuates against the US dollar every millisecond. The EU and US cover less than one-tenth of humankind, the rest of the world is comprised of nations with distinct currencies which swing even more dramatically in the long run. Even if prices were set equal in two different countries, they would soon drift apart as the rate of exchange varies.

Dumping and International Trade

Historically, the Japanese were the first to digest this important lesson and apply its potential to international marketing. In competitive markets they showed flexibility by setting prices low (a bit above variable cost – like quote No. 1 in Table 4, but below average cost – Quote No. 2). A company cannot sell at low prices in all countries, because it would go bankrupt if average costs were not covered over all territories taken together. However, the "below-global-average-cost" price in competitive territories can be made up by charging "above-global-average-cost" prices in other countries where the market can sustain a high price (Quote No. 4).

But charging low prices in some nations can invite accusations of "dumping." The question of "dumping" products has been an especially sensitive issue in the US. The US has relatively open policies towards imports. But the US is also one of the most price competitive markets in the world for many industries, in part because of its openness. Foreign producers exporting a product to the USA are often *forced* to accept low prices. They make up for this by charging higher prices for the same item in "other countries." The "other country" is often the company's own home market. The company's home consumers often pay higher prices than their US counterparts for a wide range of items, although as Japan opens itself to imports, this trend is diminishing.

The same music or video player sold in the US for $150, may cost a Japanese teenager the yen equivalent of $250. (This is especially true when a weak Dollar makes the price charged in the US much lower than the same product's price in other nations). There are thousands of similar examples, in many countries. The explanation is that the US is an open, low-tariff, fiercely competitive market for consumer electronics. Companies from all over the world try and sell their products. Other countries, by contrast, may have a sheltered market and the competition is generally among fewer companies who then set a higher price.

The US public at large does not understand this aspect of dumping. Most consider dumping nasty and predatory, designed to drive competition out of business after which the dumping firm would raise prices. In actual fact, the overwhelming majority of dumping cases do not involve predatory behavior, but prices reflect local market conditions and are above the variable cost floor. Moreover, if the dumping company were to raise prices later on after eliminating competitors, at least in a relatively free and entrepreneurial market like the US, new competition would emerge once again.

Looking at it one way, the foreigner who pays a higher price is subsidizing the US buyer. If the US buyer understood this fact of international business, they would probably say, "If this is dumping, then please dump more products on me at a low price." Unfortunately, things are not so simple or neat. The US consumer's gain may be offset by the loss of American jobs. The importing society must balance the consumer gain against possible losses to the domestic producer, and their employees and shareholders.

"Under-Invoicing" (or Tariff Avoidance) in Exporting

The observant reader may have found something curious going on in Table 4. Notice that the customs duty is not constant. It varies depending on the FOB price. Who sets the FOB price? The exporting company, of course. The customs official will look at the FOB figure typed on the manufacturer's invoice and compute the duty owed, at 50 per cent of the FOB figure. In quote No. 1, it would amount to 0.50(9) = $4.50. If invoice or quote No. 4 were used instead, the duty would be 0.50(38) = $19.00. This is a huge variation.

Let us change our story a little, just to make a point. In Scenario A an independent US exporter and an independent foreign importer are at "arm's-length" to each other. In Scenario B the multinational exports to its own subsidiary or foreign affiliate. (Incidentally, it is estimated that as much as 40 percent of world trade is intra-firm, i.e., Scenario B).

Scenario A, where the importer and exporter collude with each other.

Scenario B, where the US company exports to its own sales office abroad – i.e., the importer and exporter are one and the same company.

In the above two scenarios, there is a strong temptation to declare (type) an artificially lower FOB price on the invoice, in order to pay less customs duty. Remember that the landed cost abroad is a cost calculation. The ultimate retail customer would pay the same price, regardless of the landed cost. The gain from a lower customs duty would be pocketed by the company in scenario B or shared between the importer and exporter in scenario A, with a rebate, or a perhaps illegal "kickback," or extra under-the-table payment.

This can be illegal! If the customs authorities can prove an intent to defraud by "under-invoicing," i.e., deliberately putting a lower price on the invoice, that is clearly illegal. Regrettably, this is a widespread practice, especially in some developing nations. There are countries whose total export figure as reported in International Monetary Fund (IMF) statistics is suspect. We have no option but to consider such practices reprehensible.

Alas, things are not always so clear-cut. Many times, companies have honest motivations, but are still accused of malpractices. Suppose the foreign market for the video games was very competitive and our company set a low FOB price *for that reason*, merely to penetrate the market. If customs authorities investigated, they would find the company selling the game for $22 in the USA, but at a lower price in their country. They may accuse the company of under-invoicing and cheating – even though the FOB price was not set low in order to cheat, but because business conditions required it. International company executives have to be vigilant about the possibility that, even although their motives are honest, their company could be accused of under-invoicing, dumping and price discrimination.

The Evolution from Exporting to Foreign Direct Investment

In our video game example in Table 3, the US factory has a maximum production capacity of 250,000 video games. With US domestic sales of 200,000 units, the most that can be produced, from the existing factory, for exports is an additional 50,000. Although the foreign demand for this particular video game is only 10,000 units at present, in time it could become as great as the US sales of 200,000 units. Another factory will be needed to serve mature foreign demand. If so, it may as well be established abroad. Foreign production avoids the cost of freight and the import tariff. For these reasons many companies decide to make a foreign direct investment in or near their foreign customers' country, despite the uncertainties of operating in a strange environment. Thus, exporting may evolve, over time, to a foreign direct investment strategy.

3. Foreign Direct Investment

For the world as a whole, foreign direct investment (FDI) is a far more important means of serving foreign customers than exporting to them, or licensing firms in their nations. For example, in 2019 the sales made by the foreign affiliates of multinational companies (outside their home nation) were approximately $30,000 billion. By contrast, all exports of goods and services totaled only about $23,000 billion. This means a typical customer was far more likely to receive a so-called "foreign" product or service from a foreign firm operating inside the customer's nation, than receiving a foreign product via importation. (Because of the pandemic, 2020 sales from both methods of international business, FDI and trade, were understandably a bit lower).

Since the 1990s, FDI has been the top method of international business. The reasons for investing abroad and the advantages which accrue to a multinational firm are shown in Table 5.

Table 5. Strategy Motivations for Foreign Direct Investment (FDI)

Market-driven investment
- To develop a ripe or untapped foreign market based on differentiated product, brand or proprietary firm technology
- Oligopolistic or defensive counter-moves
- Overcoming trade barriers

Resource-seeking investment
- Multinational company efficiency in natural resource exploration, extraction, refining, and global distribution
- Investment for the purpose of seeking local knowledge

Global rationalization and cost reduction
- Access to cheapest sources of inputs and resources
- Economies of global scale
- Building global value chains

Risk diversification
- Taking advantage of non-synchronous business cycles
- Reduction in foreign exchange risk exposure
- Reduction in total political risk exposure

Market-Seeking Investments

By far the most common motivation for foreign investment is to exploit an untapped potential market. Through its past research, product development and advertising expenditures, the firm may possess a distinctive technology, product and brand equity which local companies in the country may not have. The international dominance of pharmaceutical firms, such as Pfizer, or Information Technology companies is based on proprietary high technology. But there are also humbler and less technology-intensive products that have led their firms to develop untapped foreign markets. Coca Cola drinks or Kellogg's corn flakes and breakfast cereals are not high technology products, but the companies made several investments in Europe, Japan, Australia, South Africa and other emerging countries based on brand recognition. Dietary habits among the middle and upper classes in those countries were changing, or could be changed by advertising. Attractively packaged cereal boxes and the internationally recognized Kellogg or Coca Cola brand name meant that buyers were enjoying not just the cereal or drink, but also identifying themselves with new modern ideas.

Resource-Seeking Investments

Firms may invest abroad to seek resources − either natural resources or knowledge. In natural resource investments, global firms are most sensitive to criticism that they are exploiting the country's natural "patrimony." However, large multinational firms also provide proprietary expertise in all stages from exploration to extraction to distribution − advantages that cannot be easily replicated by local companies in one nation. Oil and gas companies have proprietary drilling and "fracking" knowhow which can be used to greatly increase the amount drawn from wells.

Internal knowledge or technology aside, a large multinational has an advantage simply because of its sheer size and global scope, which confers on it network advantages that are difficult to match by a smaller rival. An example of the global network advantage that a major oil companies possess is found in their quantitative production scheduling models. Crude oil, being an organic substance, is found in an astonishing variety of specific gravities, hydrocarbon mixes, impurities, etc. No two wells produce the same crude. Refineries have different capabilities. Some can handle light crudes, others heavy. Some can tolerate a sulfur content, others not, and so on. Furthermore, within each refinery, the company can take the same crude oil and decide what kind of refined petroleum product it needs, depending on market demand, spot prices and inventory. In some cases, they may want more aviation fuel, or heating oil or kerosene. The operating cost, scale and capacities of refineries vary, of course. The final set of variables relate to transport and tariff costs. They arise from the location of the wells in n countries, with oil tankers going to p refineries, from which the finished products are shipped to m markets. Additionally, the price paid by the company for the crude, and the price it gets for each refined product vary over time and have a bearing on the optimal plant allocation decision. This makes for a gigantic, global optimization problem needing Artificial Intelligence (AI) or algorithms.

The problem is insoluble in its detailed form, even using the best analysts and computers. But proprietary algorithms exist inside the large energy, trading and shipping companies, and are used. The fact that the major oil companies have this flexibility to route their crude from many sources to refineries worldwide gives them a considerable cost advantage over purely national or smaller oil firms. A commodity shipping company may have scores of vessels in mid-ocean which can be redirected to different ports, as the algorithm calculates changes in prices, inventories and demand across different markets. This global network advantage cannot be replicated by a one-nation or smaller rival firm.

These days, corporate knowledge is as much a resource as are oil or minerals. For example, many small Taiwanese and Chinese firms have a FDI affiliate in Silicon Valley mainly to learn about US technologies and tap into local networks of knowledgeable personnel and engineers.

Global Rationalization: The Search for Low Cost and Efficient Location of Production

Global rationalization is based on finding the country locations where an input can be obtained more cheaply. In fact, the oil companies are using some of the concepts listed in Table 5 under global rationalization and cost reduction. Compared to purely national firms, the global firm has knowledge of the cheapest sources, not just for natural resources, but also for capital and personnel. There is widespread borrowing by companies in international financial markets. (Even a domestic company can do the same, but it is less likely to do so, and its information is likely to be poorer.) Some international shipping companies or hotel chains make it a point to recruit in nations like the Philippines or India, where skilled, English-speaking staff are available at modest salaries. Immigration laws do not easily allow foreign personnel to enter other nations to work. But increasingly after 2021, some work has shifted online. For functions that cannot be performed online, several nations allow an influx of skilled workers, especially when there is a labor shortage in their countries. Global firms are constantly asking governments to permit the entry of specialist managerial and technical personnel, or even farm workers. Regional integration, such as the EU, necessarily involves the relaxation of barriers to expatriate employment.

The concepts of vertical integration, "production rationalization" and scale economies are separate, but intertwined in many global operations. If an automobile company designs a car for sale in many countries, it need not then produce all the components in each market. By eliminating duplicative facilities - for example, by producing the transmission/axle sub-assembly in only three global locations instead of ten, the company gains in two ways. First, there is a cost saving per unit at the lower cost global locations – merely by eliminating the more expensive locations. Second, there is an additional cost saving because the scale of operation in the remaining global locations is now larger. The component plants are vertically integrated with the assembly operations and the markets. However, this means that the company must now undertake a far larger volume of shipments of components and sub-assemblies across national borders. This increases logistics, transport cost and risk since the plants are now more interdependent on each other. If a strike, flood or volcano affected the transmission plant, it would disrupt assembly in many countries. However, such risks, extra transport costs and increased coordination and logistics costs must be outweighed by the overall cost savings in the automobile industry which is moving towards a greater degree of global or cross-border integration.

Risk-Reduction from Geographical Diversification

There are obvious political and currency risks in making direct investments abroad. But how can multinational investment *reduce* a company's risk? The answer is that geographical diversification naturally reduces risk. One reason is that countries do not go through recession and booms together – the "business cycles" of different nations are not synchronized. While Europe may still be in a recession, North America may be in an expansionary stage, or *vice versa*.

The concept is also applicable in currencies. If a company believes the US Dollar and the Euro will fluctuate against each other substantially, then it may wish to locate its operations in both sets of countries, since the net exposure in their cash flows and accounts can be greatly reduced by carefully structuring their liabilities and assets in the two currencies. This is not to say that investments are made purely for risk-reduction reasons, but these could be important *secondary* considerations.

When it comes to reducing so-called "political" risk, the history of the Japanese auto industry provides a good illustration. Protectionism is manifested in two ways – by official government actions such as tariffs or quotas, but also by a "buy-local" sentiment. If Honda and Toyota hedge their bets by having assembly operations in the USA and the EU as well as importing cars to those markets, they are less vulnerable to future shifts in US or EU policy, compared to other firms which do not yet have this multiple source capability. This also gives them the flexibility to switch output from one location to another as the yen goes up or down against the Euro or Dollar. Transport costs in automobiles have also been reduced with special ships specifically designed to bulk-carry cars. The cost of shipping an automobile across the Pacific to California is no higher than sending a car from Detroit to California.

The most dramatic example of "political" risk is a *coup d'etat* or the outbreak of war in a country. If the country has a critical component sourced from that nation, the problem can affect global operations. But if it is a local-market-driven operation, the risk can be confined mainly to that nation, while operations continue elsewhere. Having operations in multiple countries therefore reduces overall risk for the international company. "Political" risk can also be unexpected changes in regulations, for example tariffs, such as the ones levied against Chinese imports by the Trump and Biden administrations. Protectionism is also manifested by a "buy-local" sentiment, or local-value-added mandate. Honda and Toyota hedge their bets by having assembly operations in the

USA, Mexico, and the EU, as well as importing cars to those markets. This makes them less vulnerable to future shifts in US or EU policy, compared with other firms that do not yet have this multiple-source capability. This also gives them the flexibility to switch output from one location to another as the yen goes up or down against the euro or dollar. Transport costs in automobiles have also been reduced with special ships specifically designed to bulk-carry cars. The cost of shipping an automobile across the Pacific to California is no higher than sending a car from Detroit to California.

4. Licensing and Contractual Alliances

The third "classic" foreign market strategy is licensing to an independent local firm in the other country. (Here we are not referring to business to end user licensing as in packaged software, but to business-to-business licensing of technology and brands). Instead of undertaking to manufacture or sell on its own in a foreign nation, a company that has a proprietary technology, design, patent, or brand (let us call it the licensor firm) transfers those intellectual property rights and production capability to a foreign partner company (called a licensee company). The licensee pays it royalties and other fees including lump sum fees. Usually, under the agreement, the licensee has exclusive rights to use the licensed asset in thir market for the duration of the agreement.

How does this strategy compare with the other two international strategy options? In choosing any option, the manager must balance its advantages and drawbacks vis-à-vis the alternatives. This balance is described in Table 6 below.

As listed in Table 6, contractual alliances have unquestionably the highest return on incremental investment (ROI), that is, if we consider the research and development (R&D) costs of a particular product as "sunk" or already expended. Then the *incremental* costs of negotiating an agreement, transferring drawings, codes, and specifications, and training the licensee's or partner's personnel can be very small – in the region of tens of thousands of dollars to a few hundred thousand dollars at the most – compared with the millions needed for an FDI capital investment in a foreign subsidiary's factories, buildings and personnel. In licensing, the capital investment and its risks are borne by the local partner or licensee. The licensor only grants the licensee rights to use its intellectual property (patents or brands) and knowhow. Once the agreement is signed and the licensee is trained, subsequent licensing income is pure profit to the licensor. One study shows that over the life of international agreements, more than 95 per cent of licensing income earned by US multinational companies goes directly to the "bottom line" – that is to say, the costs of setting up and negotiating an agreement average below 5 per cent of revenues, a fabulous ROII (return on incremental investment, or setup cost of an additional contractual alliance) indeed.

Table 6. Contractual Alliance / Licensing Compared with Other Strategies
(Licensor Perspective)

Advantages	*Drawbacks*
Very high ROI (not counting R&D costs)	Often lower NPV compared with other strategies
No new capital investment	Royalties alone may be a poor income source (unless other income types included in agreement)
Low negotiation/implementation costs	Agreements may have a limited life(unless renewed)
Most income goes directly to profits	Lack of control over licensee's quality may hurt licensor's reputation
Very low political risk	Licensee can become a competitor after agreement expires, or even before
Could have lower tax rate to licensor if licensing income treated as return on capital. (Also, most nations permit licensees to deduct royalties as an expense item.)	
Company can license in many worthwhile markets closed to exports or investment	
Quicker way to enter foreign market compared to investment	
Licensee may be used as a guinea pig to test market	
Return of technical information from licensee	
Low cyclical fluctuation in income (compared to dividends)	

A substantial benefit of licensing or a contractual alliance is that it is a lower-risk strategy for two reasons:

(i)   All risk, and particularly political risk, is lower in licensing because it is the licensee, not the licensor, who has made the big capital investment in the foreign nation. The licensor has few or no assets stuck in the ground in the foreign nation (compared to setting up a FDI subsidiary or affiliate worth millions, which may then be subject to the vagaries of foreign politics, or events in the foreign nation). The stakes are much lower for a licensor than a foreign direct investor.

(ii)   Licensing income is also more stable, and less volatile than the FDI alternative of the multinational company relying on the dividends or profits received from foreign affiliates. The reason for this is simple: most contractual alliance agreements specify that the licensee pays royalties as a percentage of sales achieved for the licensed items (regardless of the licensee company's profit or loss). And for all companies anywhere, top-line sales revenue is axiomatically more stable than bottom-line profits. Hence a formula where royalties are based on a percentage of sales (licensing) is axiomatically less volatile than a dependence on profits from foreign affiliates (FDI).

Moreover, if the product is patented and foreign markets can be segmented by strong patents in each nation, or territorial limits placed on each licensee, or products hard to ship from one country to another, in theory the company could sign separate license agreements in each worthwhile foreign market, thus increasing total global licensing income. Other advantages of licensing include the possibility that foreign market entry can be quicker than the FDI alternative, since the local partner (licensee) typically already has in place some production capacity, knowledge of the local market and contacts with their buyers and government. When speed of foreign market entry is of strategic importance, sometimes licensing is preferred even if the FDI alternative is available.

In a few instances, a deliberately short license agreement can serve the licensor as a tactic to test the viability of the foreign market without committing significant resources up-front.

Finally, while this is not frequent, technical improvements made by the licensee and fed back to the licensor, can be valuable to the latter.

Contractual alliances such as licensing have many advantages, but Table 6 also lists several drawbacks. While ROII from licensing is very high, net present value (NPV) – or the absolute amount of money earned from a foreign country – is usually much lower compared with the other strategies of direct investment or exporting. After all, companies are not in the business of maximizing ROI, but NPV. This is perhaps the main drawback to licensing - inadequate total income from royalties alone compared with FDI or exporting. Why? By tradition, if not theory, most royalty rates are less than 8 or 10 per cent of the licensee's sales, and the average is perhaps 4 to 5 per cent. From the foreign partner's point of view this is correct because they are bearing all the capital investment, political and other risks. From the licensor's point of view, considering how little they spend in merely negotiating and setting-up the agreement and transferring the technology (without any capital investment) this is attractive – or an excellent return on incremental investment. But if the company were to invest (do an FDI) in the foreign nation and sell the product itself, the total income could be much higher (except in mature or very competitive industries where return on capital investment is low already). That is to say, foreign direct investment (FDI), for all its risks and high investment costs, can also yield a much higher *absolute* magnitude of total profit compared with the absolute magnitude of foreign licensing income.

When comparing licensing with other alternatives, one cannot overlook the fact that agreements have a limited life, ranging from two to twelve years typically, although they are frequently renewed if the foreign partner still depends on, and benefits from, the link. By contrast, a FDI investment has a theoretically unlimited life, and the company at least hopes that it will continue to earn dividends on its foreign investment indefinitely.

The tax advantage of licensing is that whereas dividends declared by foreign direct investment affiliates are subject to corporate income tax in the foreign nation, most governments allow the payment of royalties by the licensee to be treated as a deductible expense. This means that remittance of royalties across national borders legally escapes corporate tax. (See an example in Table 9.) This favors the licensee, but in so doing boosts the ability of the licensee/payer to promise higher royalties to the technology supplier. Even for the technology-supplying alliance partner, or licensor, unlike receiving dividends from an FDI affiliate, receiving royalty income may attract a lower, capital returns rate of tax in some home nations.

Although licensing (to independent foreign parties) runs a distant third as an overseas strategy in the minds of many executives, in recent years its use has been growing faster than FDI. Contractual alliances are growing fast both internationally and domestically because of four reasons: (a) the growth of high-tech sectors with licensable intellectual property, (b) improvements worldwide in the protection of intellectual property (IP) rights lessens the fear of prospective licensors that they might lose control of their IP, (c) engineers and technicians in foreign partner companies in emerging nations are better able to receive foreign technology and use it effectively on their own. Recall that in licensing, after perhaps a bit of training of the foreign partner, then the licensee has to operate on their own in their assigned territory or markets, and (d) in recent years, there has been a much greater "codification" or "writing down" of corporate knowledge into manuals, drawings, algorithms, and artificial intelligence programs – which enhances the transferability of technology and its usability by the technology recipient or licensee.

For start-ups, for smaller multinational companies, and for many firms based outside the USA that lack "deep-pockets" or capital to invest in FDI affiliates, licensing can be an important alternative global strategy because it does not involve significant up-front investment. An extension of this logic is the phenomenon of franchising, which is nothing more than multiple contractual alliances or licensing on a mass scale, with the franchisor minimizing their own investment risk.

Another factor that powerfully affects any strategy choice is the relative risk of the two options. For the same projected cash flow, the lower the risk, the lower the discount rate, and the higher the consequent net present value calculation. Licensing has inherently lower risks compared to a company's own investment because:

I.   Royalties are usually a percentage of sales. Sales fluctuate over a business cycle or recession much less than FDI dividends, which are declared out of profits, if any. In a bad year there may be no foreign dividends; however, a licensee still pays the royalty.

II.   There is little "political" risk in licensing. Agreements are almost always honored by all governments.

III. Licensing is a low-risk method of testing the viability of a foreign market. The licensee as a "guinea pig" makes the investment and tests the waters of the marketplace. (There have been cases where a successful licensee has been brushed aside by a more powerful licensor moving into their country once the agreement has expired.)

On the other hand, as summarized in Table 6, licensees may become so successful and entrenched that they may become competitors with the original licensor not only in that country, but other countries as well. In the worst scenario the foreign licensee comes back to compete in the licensor's home market. Several Chinese partners of US firms did exactly that – learned from their

European and US partners or collaborators to later become rivals. In 2019, the US and European governments express great concern about mobile phone companies like Huawei or Xiaomi who have assimilated foreign technology, improved on it in their own R&D labs, and now compete successfully against their rivals such as Apple or Samsung. An old classic example involves RCA which, licensed color television technology to Japanese companies, only to find them competing years later with RCA in the US market itself. Long ago, RCA disappeared as a company and lapsed into being only an "also-ran" brand name. Mattel licensed the "Barbie" doll's trademark and copyright to Estrela in Brazil and to Takara in Japan, only to find at the end of those agreements that the licensees refused to renew the agreements and introduced their own copycat dolls under the "Susi" name in Brazil and "Jenny" in Japan. Susi and Jenny were sufficiently differentiated from Barbie that there was no legal recourse. Even in a developed legal system like the USA, the dimensions of a mechanical component can be slightly changed, or its alloy composition slightly altered, so that the original patent holder's rights cannot be upheld (or litigating is too complicated and costly) – even though the functionality of the copycat component is the same.

However, in the majority of cases, the licensee remains, to some degree, technologically and organizationally inferior, and sometimes dependent on the licensor for materials or trademarks. In most cases the licensee is bound under the purview of the agreement to the assigned territory. On average, executives do not show an excessive concern with the issue of licensee competitiveness in third markets. In specific industries, however, such as semi-conductors, mobile telephony, biosciences and some chemical processes, the fear is so dominant as to preclude partnering with non-affiliated firms.

All said and done, in an increasingly diverse global environment, firms can no longer afford a strategy which ignores the option of contractual alliances and licensing. That licensing in many selected situations is not only very profitable, but superior in a net risk-adjusted comparison with alternatives, is an idea gaining ground. Some of the largest companies already have far more global licensees than subsidiaries; and cases exist where the more stable licensing income via royalties related to licensee sales has helped to smooth out the greater volatility of foreign dividend income, since profits are, by definition, more variable than output volume.

5. Comparing the Three Classic Strategy Options

How do we compare the three international expansion strategies? By estimating the *foreign sales* achieved by each method of international business. As noted earlier, the total sales revenues of the foreign affiliates of all multinational companies (*not* counting sales in the home nation of each firm) are estimated at around $30 trillion in 2019. The sum total of exports (goods and services) from all nations put together amounted to between $23 – 24 trillion. The sales achieved by foreign licensees as a result of receiving intellectual assets and knowledge from foreign licensors can be estimated at around 7 trillion worth of revenue. Of the classic alternatives, FDI, exporting and contractual alliances, licensing is number three in importance, but is still huge in absolute magnitude. While foreign sales achieved through licensing are a distant number three, this method of international business has exhibited the fastest growth rate in the past quarter century.

A caveat: as we shall see in Section 6 below, large multinationals *combine* exporting, FDI and licensing as integrated approaches for strategic and tax reasons, so that there is more than a little double-counting and tax biases in the above numbers. Nevertheless, it is correct to conclude

Table 7 Factors involved in choosing a strategy

	Majority/fully-owned investment	Exporting	Licensing
Total returns	high	moderate	moderate to low
Financial resource costs	high	low	negligible
Managerial resource costs	high	moderate	small
Control over foreign operation	high	high	low
Ordinary commercial risk	high	low	almost zero
Political risk	high (depends on country)	low	zero
Foreign exchange or convertability risk	high (depends on country	low	lowest
Effective tax rate	high	highest	lower
Threat of creating competition	very low	low	can be high

that in the 2020s decade, FDI is by far the biggest type of international business, followed by exporting or trade, and followed distantly by contractual alliances.

Table 7 and Figure 2 list the principal factors affecting the choice of strategy. Please note that such generalizations cannot possibly apply to all companies or all countries. However, these concepts are a useful overview for a manager to consider when choosing an appropriate international strategy for their firm.

Direct investment in majority controlled or fully owned investments generally yield the highest total returns despite the high investment of capital and personnel. This is because the firm internalizes its advantages in technology, organizational learning, intangible proprietary assets such as patents or trademarks, and an international scope of operation. These give it control of strategy, as opposed to sharing decisions with other parties who could later become competitors or terminate the alliance. However, the risks are also greatest in an FDI strategy. Besides ordinary commercial risk of business failure, there is political risk in the host nation because changes in government policies may go against the interests of foreign investors.

Exporting can be highly profitable at very low risk, but this is only true to the extent that the company can use the slack capacity in their existing plants for exports. Assuming domestic or existing sales cover fixed costs – that is to say, as long as the firm uses the spare capacity in the existing plant – the incremental contribution of exports, over the variable costs thereof, is substantial. Risks and costs are much higher, however, if a factory is built especially for exports.

Figure 2 shows a spectrum of choices, from contractual or licensing type arrangements to increasing equity investment in equity joint ventures (which are a hybrid of contractual alliance and equity investment made by both partners), to a fully owned subsidiary at the other end. As a generalization, expected return and control increase as the firm increases its equity strike. However, the risk also increases. For each product/market combination, the strategist must decide which modal choice provides the optimum combination of return, control, and risk in the foreign market.

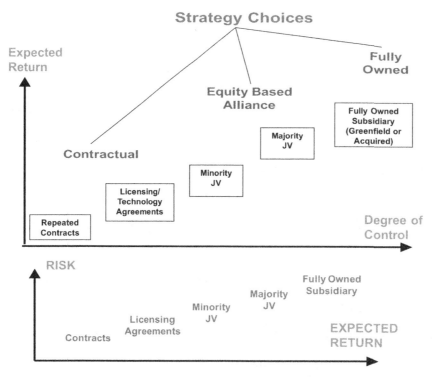

Figure 2: Comparing Returns, Control and Risk Across International Strategy Choices

Contractual alliances such as licensing involve negligible costs of execution compared with the revenues then earned from such agreements. Over 95 percent of licensing revenues are pure profit (in an incremental sense, if we ignore sunk R&D costs or the ongoing cost of developing brand equity through massive advertising. Disney is one of the biggest global licensors, but spends mega amounts to advertise its characters and images). In general, the absolute profit from licensing is smaller than profit which could be earned from direct investment or export sales -- but then, the risks are generally far lower also; there is little investment of financial or managerial resources, and commercial risk is borne by the licensees. Assuming that the global market is segmented by patents, tariffs, or by territorial agreement provisions, so that each country is a separate territory, then a licensing agreement can be signed in every viable market. This would make global total revenue from licensing very worthwhile. By comparison, even the largest of companies find it impossible to make an investment in every worthwhile foreign market. In selected cases, licensing has the drawback of creating a competitor in the licensee.

The effective tax rate is likely to be highest in exporting since profit margins on export sales go directly to that year's reportable income in the exporting nation (unless sheltered through a foreign sales corporation). The income of foreign affiliates and subsidiaries may be reinvested indefinitely, postponing the parent nation tax bite, if not taxes in the country of operation. It is not until foreign affiliates' dividends are actually repatriated to the parent that additional tax is owed. Even then, the taxes paid to the foreign nation can be used as a credit against parent firm tax liability. If a licensing agreement is properly structured, royalty and licensing income can be treated as a return on past R&D investment. This is taxed at a far lower rate than ordinary corporate income, in the licensor's nation.

Before making the decision as to how to earn income in a foreign territory, the strategist needs to consider all the factors of potential income; financial and managerial resource cost; commercial, political, and foreign exchange risk; the effective tax rate; and the potential for creating or reducing international competition.

6. Combining International Strategies

So far in this chapter we have examined how contractual methods such as licensing versus exporting or direct investment in the foreign market may be looked upon as substitute methods for serving the foreign customer. We next look at what some mature global companies are actually doing, which is *combining* the benefits of the foreign market entry modes, by using them *simultaneously* for strategy and tax reasons. Let us begin by seeing how trade and direct investment (FDI) are not just substitutes, but complement each other as well.

Exporting and Foreign Direct Investment as Complementary or Combined Strategies

Some 45 percent of all exports in the world are "intrafirm." That is to say, the export goes from a company in one nation to its own foreign equity affiliate acting as importer, or vice versa. Or the exports occur between the subsidiaries of the same multinational. Exporting then, is not a pure substitute for foreign direct investment, but the two are intermingled strategies. The trade deficit that the USA suffers against the rest of the world (for example China) has been the source of much concern to the public and breast-beating in American politics. But perhaps, to look at trade *only*, is to look at only half the overall international business picture.

Table 8 examines the case of a hypothetical nation called Fredonia, against which the US suffers a large trade deficit of $31.2 billion. (While this is a hypothetical example, Table 8 very roughly parallels the China-US international business situation until very recently. Substitute the word China for Fredonia and the overall China-US relationship will become clearer).

Looking only at the trade picture in Table 8, US exports to Fredonia are much smaller than Fredonian exports to the US. The US may therefore be seen as suffering a horrendous trade deficit of $342 billion. However, adding (A) exports from the USA to Fredonia to US multinational company production in Fredonia (B), the (A + B) total comes to $635 billion, from the perspective of the Fredonian consumer buying so-called "American products." For American consumers buying so-called Fredonian products, Exports from Fredonia to the USA (C), plus Fredonian company production in the US (D), or (C + D), adds up to $676 billion.

In short, from the eyes of the consumer in each country, comparing (A + B) with (C + D) is not as alarming an imbalance as would be suggested by looking only at the trade balance alone. After all, whether a Fredonian product is imported or made in the US by Fredonian firms, they are still labeled by the US consumer as "Fredonian" products. Similarly, Fredonian customers buy US products directly via imports, as well as indirectly, from the local production by US FDI affiliates in Fredonia. In terms of US "product presence" in Fredonia, the total of $35 billion in sales is very large and respectable, although not as large as the Fredonian "product presence" in the USA which adds up to 676 billion, as seen in the Table 8 illustration. This is despite what appears to be an alarming trade deficit.

Local production by foreign investment affiliates substitutes for imports into a nation. Therefore, from a jobs and employment perspective, the US position vis-à-vis Fredonia is even worse than that suggested by the trade statistics. (See comment No.1 in Table 8). There are other flaws and omissions in the logic, with a lot of double counting as a result of Global Supply Chains. Sales in Fredonia by US affiliates have components imported from their US parents. Consequently, part of [A] is double counted in B. Similarly, part of the value of Fredonian company production in the USA (D), is accounted for by part of [C], which is the exports from Fredonia to the USA. To compound the statistical spaghetti-mix, on the output side, part of B shows up in C. That is to say, some US company production in Fredonia is exported back to the USA, just as Fredonian affiliates may export part of their production in the USA (D), back to Fredonia (A).

Table 8. Combining Trade and Foreign Direct Investment ("Lies, Damn Lies, and Statistics" in Trade and Investment Figures)

For a particular year let us suppose that,

- **Exports from USA to Fredonia - Exports from Fredonia to USA = (US suffers a Trade Deficit of)**
  226   -   *568*   =   *342*

- But from the consumer's perspective in each country, combining Trade and FDI figures shows,

The Fredonian market for US items		vs	The US Market for Fredonian items	
Exports from USA to Fredonia	+ US company production in Fredonia	vs	Exports from Fredonia to USA	+ Fredonian company production in USA
[A]	**[B]**	vs	**[C]**	**[D]**
(226	+ *409)*		*(568*	+ *108)*
= 635		vs	= 676	

Some Additional Comments
1. The "Job Loss" Balance? *[409 + 568] vs [226 + 108] is unbalanced*
2. *Some double counting:*
   (i) Some sales in Fredonia by US affiliates have inputs from US exports. That is to say, some value is added in [B] with [A] inputs
   (ii) Similarly, some value is added in [D] from [C] inputs
   (iii) Part of [B] shows up in [C] , that is, Fredonian production by US affiliates is exported back to the USA
   (iv) Part of [D] is similarly exported from USA to Fredonia and shows up in [A]
3. Items produced in Fredonia under license from US firms also substitute for both US FDI in Fredonia, as well as US exports to Fredonia.

Because of the complementary way in which global companies use exports and direct investment simultaneously, these statistics did not give a complete or accurate picture.

Finally, even the labels "US firm" or "Fredonian firm" or "Chinese firm" will become inaccurate in the future. With large global firms having sales in many nations, their home market sales may have fallen below half of the global total. Can they be any longer identified with their "home base" from which the company started? Is Honda a Japanese or an American firm? A large part of the global sales of so-called "Japanese" companies like Honda already take place in the US market, with over 60 per cent value-added in the US for many models. A significant part of Honda's R&D and design operations are in the USA. The company exported US-made cars back to Japan, some components in the cars having made a ten-thousand-mile round trip back to Japan, while many of the other parts are US or Mexican. Some Honda models sold in the US market come from three simultaneous sources: (a) assembled in the US, or (b) assembled and imported from Japanese plants or (c) imported into the US from Honda's Mexican plants. Car buyers in the US may not know the difference, or care. Already, a fraction of the shares of many Japanese companies is owned by US and European investors, a fraction that will grow in the future.

At any rate, the purpose of the foregoing discussion was to show how trade and foreign direct investment are at once substitutes, as well as complements, to each other, in rather complex ways. Moreover, country-of-origin labels, already suspect, may mean even less in the future.

Direct Investment and Licensing in Combination

Most governments allow licensing fees and royalties to be considered a deductible expense, even when a fully owned subsidiary is paying royalties to its own parent. Governments offer this tax concession (illustrated in Table 9) in order to induce the transfer of technology and intellectual property to their countries. From the point of view of foreign investors, many of them would have transferred the expertise and intellectual property to their majority equity affiliates anyway, even without this concession. But governments have no way of distinguishing those that would have transferred the technology without the tax incentive, from companies that would not have done so. Hence the concession is offered to all.

As illustrated in Table 9 a Japanese subsidiary has established a fully owned subsidiary in the US. In the first column there is no licensing agreement between the Japanese parent and its US affiliate. In the second column, a licensing agreement is introduced whereby the US subsidiary has to pay a 5 percent royalty to its own Japanese parent. Because US law (and the laws of most nations) allows the deduction of reasonable royalties as a deductible expense item to the payer (in this case the US licensee firm), the remittance of royalty to the foreign (Japanese) parent legally escapes US corporate income tax altogether. The total tax liability to the US government is lowered in the second column of Table 9. Therefore, the after-tax profit remitted to Japan increases from 210 in the left-hand column to 225 in the right-side column. And this is legal. But there is a temptation to channel more and more of the remittance via the royalty channel, even if that means less is remitted under the "profit after local tax" category, because the *total* of the two cash flow channels is higher than after-tax profits alone. Some companies may indeed divert "too much" of their intra-corporate funds via higher royalty and intellectual property payments, in order to minimize tax liability in a nation. The royalty rate may be *un*reasonable and considered by the tax authority to be "too high." Then tax authorities' audits ask the company to justify the intra-corporate charge. But who is to say whether a 10 per cent royalty is unreasonable, where a 5 per cent royalty is reasonable? That depends on the value of the technology, the market, the R&D cost, and several complicated factors. What is an appropriate charge for global overheads levied against a subsidiary in another nation? What fee should a parent charge an affiliate for introducing a brand into the country? The valuation of intangibles and intellectual property, especially in international transactions, remains among the critical unresolved management and accounting issues of our day (Contractor, F.J., 2016 and 2000).

Table 9. **Tax Effect on Intra-Firm Royalty Payment**

• Sales by Japanese subsidiary in US	1000	Sales by Japanese subsidiary in US	1000
• Total costs (no royalties involved)	- 700	Royalty (at 5 percent on sales)	- 50
• Profit before tax	300	Total costs (excluding royalties)	- 700
• US tax (at 30 percent)	- 90	Profit before tax	250
• Profit after tax	210	US tax (at 30 percent)	- 75
		Profit after US tax	175
		Royalty remittance to Japanese parent	+ 50
		Total remittance to parent	225

The fact remains, however, that as a consequence of the deductibility of such intra-corporate payments, much of the royalty and licensing fees remitted across national borders are likely between foreign majority affiliates and their own parents, as opposed to licensing agreements between unrelated or quasi-arm's-length licensors and licensees (Contractor, F. J., 1999). Licensing is only one form of corporate alliance. Others include equity joint venture (two or more firms jointly holding the shares of another company). The discussion below role-plays negotiations to set up a Japanese-American joint venture company in the US, instead of being fully owned Japanese as in Table 9.

Table 10 indicates the effects of a licensing agreement *cum* joint venture – a hybrid of licensing and FDI. This is a common arrangement in international business. To extend the case from Table 9, let us suppose that, instead of a 100 percent subsidiary of a Japanese parent, the US company is now a joint venture where 60 per cent of shares are held by a Japanese partner and 40 per cent held by a US company. Distribution of the $210 after-tax profit (seen in Table 9), split proportionally to the shareholding would earn $126 for the Japanese and $84 for the US partner in Scenario 1. With the introduction of 5 per cent royalties payable to the Japanese partner by the joint venture corporation in Scenario 2, the Japanese partner's take (legally) jumps to $155. The US partner's after-tax distribution declines somewhat to $70. As a negotiating demand therefore, the US partner may ask for an increased 48 per cent shareholding in Scenario 3 in order to accommodate the Japanese partner's desire for a licensing agreement to avoid US tax. The 48 per cent shareholding given to the US partner restores their share to $84 in Scenario 3, while still leaving the Japanese partner better off than in Scenario 1 with a total take of $141 in Scenario 3.

Table 10 What if the above affiliate was a joint venture?

Why Companies Should Consider Combining Strategies for Global Integration

It has been shown in this chapter that licensing, foreign direct investment, and exporting are used in many cases as substitute methods for serving foreign markets. This is appropriate for all firms expanding into a new foreign nation, and in particular, for smaller companies who are beginning their internationalization process. But for a large, global company seeking global optimization and efficiency, an integrated strategy would combine the methods to achieve higher income and control, lower taxes, and reduce risk. Table 11 summarizes the advantages.

Agreement-defined fees and royalties have the tax advantage described above. The payer, whether an independent licensee, or an affiliate of the licensor, gets to deduct royalties paid as a deductible expense. The remittance of these fees then legally escapes the corporate income tax of the nation of the licensee. In addition, in some nations, there are also preferential tax advantages in the licensor's country for the licensor. In order to favor more R&D in some technical areas the government wishes to promote, some governments tax receipts of licensing income such as royalties at a lower rate than the receipt of foreign affiliate dividends. An obvious but critical factor in joint ventures is that while profits are shared, one of the partners, as licensor, gets *all* of the royalties and fees. Lump sum fees, if paid on signing the agreement, provide immediate and certain returns, in contrast with distant and uncertain dividends. Royalties are payable even if the venture's profits are zero. Moreover, a royalty linked to sales is axiomatically more stable over the business cycle than dividends. In recessions, many firms have found that royalties come in at almost the normal level, even when profits on their equity investment have disappeared.

On the other hand, there is no denying the fact that an equity stake (middle column in Table 11) is a direct claim on the future success and profits of a venture, and this is likely to be far more valuable, in the long run, than royalties which are usually capped at a fixed percentage of sales, and eventually expire when the agreement terminates.

In the case of a joint venture, a local partner may be unwilling to renew the joint venture's licensing agreement with the international company, because it reduces their share of dividends. They may feel that once they have learned the technology and business from their partner and paid royalties for several years, there is no need to keep paying – unless new technology or knowledge is to be transferred. A 100 percent equity ownership position, in a fully owned foreign subsidiary, by contrast, is at least in theory forever.

Finally, there are significant advantages in setting up an intra-corporate supply chain or trading relationship for the purchase of components or sale of finished products between the global firm and its affiliates in each nation. There are, of course, strategic imperatives in many businesses for this setting up a trading or supply relationship between the companies, mainly cost reduction and efficiency. There are other advantages. Margins on the supply of components, being linked to production, are a more stable profit flow to a global firm, compared to volatile dividends. Moreover, mark-ups can be high on proprietary, high-technology or branded items, and these mark-ups are earned outside the tax jurisdiction of the country. (There is often a thin line between

Farok J. Contractor, Ph.D.

the above strategy prescription and conscious tax evasion by transfer pricing abuses. The latter is illegal and immoral).

Table 11. **Strategic Advantages of Multiple Cash Flow Types**

Lumpsum Fees and Royalties	*Dividends/ Equity Share*	*Margins on Components or Product Traded with Affiliate or Licensee*
• Lumpsum fee provides immediate cash return	• Direct share in future success, growth, and profits of affiliate	• Margins can be high on proprietary, high-tech, or branded items
• Royalties are inherently less volatile compared to dividends paid out of uncertain profits	• More valuable as years pass than fixed percentage royalties	• Less affected by cyclical fluctuations compared to dividends
• Royalties earned even if affiliate/licensee's profits are zero	• No expiration (By comparison, a licensing or materiel supply agreement may terminate)	• Profit margins earned outside affiliate/licensee country jurisdiction. i.e., no convertability risk
• Licensing income legally escapes the local tax in the payer's nation		• Transfer pricing advantages
• Also possible lower tax to the licensor (compared to dividends)		
• All royalties kept by licensor (whereas dividends have to be shared with an equity joint venture partner)		

International Tax-Avoidance or Transfer Pricing Revisited

Figure 3 provides a simple example of transfer pricing. An affiliate A supplies 1,000 widgets per year to affiliate B, initially at $1 each, in scenario 1. The corporate tax rate in Country A is 30 per cent, and in Country B it is 50 per cent., with pre-tax profit levels in each affiliate as shown in Figure 3. Take the numbers in Scenario 1 as given, or the starting position.

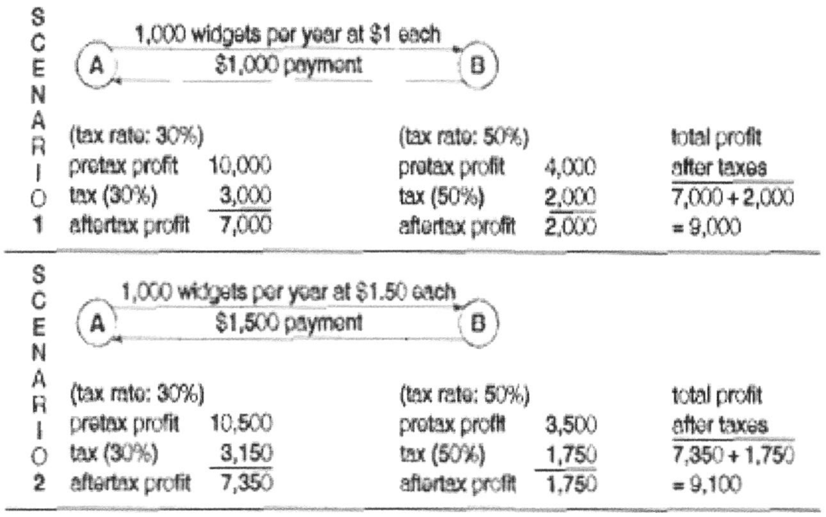

Figure 3

But there is an obvious temptation to declare less profit in the high-tax location B, and to declare more profit in the lower-tax country A. This is done in scenario 2 by raising the unit transfer price from $1.00 to, say, $1.50 per widget, as an example. In scenario 2 (compared with scenario 1) after-tax profits in B decline, but they decline by less than the amount by which after-tax profits in A increase. Consequently, the global total, after-tax profit of the global company, as a whole, increases from $9,000 in scenario 1, to $9,100 in scenario 2.

The above example in Figure 3 is the most common maneuver by multinational companies to shift taxable profits from a high tax nation to a lower tax country. However, this results in paying $250 less tax to country B, which may be illegal if the government can prove that the change from a unit price of $1.00 to $1.50 was for no other reason than to evade taxes. But that is difficult for governments to find out, let alone judge the company's intent. In the long run, no company or individual can survive or prosper on such a basis without being discovered. An honest company will attempt to follow "arms-length pricing" based on an estimation of what the transfer price would be if companies A and B were independent, arm's-length firms, and not related to each other. Alas, things are not always so clear-cut, since there are no "arm's-length equivalents" for much of the intra-corporate trade within global firms which is based on products and services which are highly differentiated, partially assembled or even unique. In many cases there is no similar item on the market. Consider another scenario. What if affiliate A has undertaken costly R&D to develop a new model, and for that legitimate reason wishes to raise the transfer price to $1.50 per unit? This illustrates how, even with honest motives, a company can be accused of cheating.

This form of international tax avoidance or transfer pricing manipulation is widespread. In 2021 the US and EU were increasingly scrutinizing multinational company tax filings and trying to negotiate a minimum corporate tax regime across America and Europe so that each country could earn at least some tax revenue). Notice how, in Figure 3, even with a fairly wide differential in tax rates between the nations, and although the unit transfer price was raised by as much as 50 per cent, the total after-tax profit of the global firm increased by a measly $100 or 1.1 percent. With converging tax rates in the major Organization for Economic Cooperation and Development (OECD) nations, the incentive is even less. Far more important is the fact that the intra-corporate trade was set up between affiliates A and B in the first place. Suppose that in years past B was sourcing this widget locally. Now A supplies B. That means that as much as $1,000 is being transferred to a lower tax jurisdiction – and done legally. Multinational companies thus enjoy advantages by setting up internal intra-corporate trade in components and finished products.

Another form of "transfer pricing," or shifting taxable profits from one nation to another, takes the form of intracorporate loans. Let us suppose that for a US-based multinational the effective US corporate tax rate is higher than for its German subsidiary paying tax to the German government. If the US parent company can borrow money from a bank at say 5 percent interest, but then extends credit it to its German subsidiary at say 2 percent, that means lower profit in the US but an extra profit to the German affiliate (because otherwise the German company borrowing from German banks would have paid a higher 4 percent interest). This shifts taxable profit from a higher to a lower tax jurisdiction or country.

Alternatively, the opposite can occur if the US parent has an effectively lower corporate tax rate than its German subsidiary. The US parent, having raised funds at 5 percent, charges its German subsidiary 7 percent, thereby increasing taxable profit in the US and lowering taxable profit in Germany. The German company could have borrowed money locally at only 4 percent interest. But recall that the subsidiary managers must do what the US parent asks. The US parent's finance or treasury department looks at the situation from the point of view of *global total tax reduction*.

7. Risk and Regulatory Considerations

A variety of risks affect exporters, importers, foreign direct investors, and allies in cross-border contractual alliances. Dealing with governments and various global risks, is the inevitable consequence of being a multinational firm. Indeed, some will regret that, in the 2021 decade, the long-term trend of privatization and easing of regulations between 1980 – 2016, is beginning to be reversed. Governments are scrutinizing foreign companies in more detail, and in a few cases expelling them from their nation.

Geopolitical Risks

In 2022, a relatively unanticipated risk was the invasion of Ukraine. Wars and *coups d'etat* obviously affect profits in the local market for the multinational firm. Some estimates put the 2022 shrinkage in the Ukrainian GDP at as much as 55 percent. But if the affected country is also a source of raw materials or components in an international supply chain, where the company's operations in other nations are dependent on the supply of the materials or components, then the risk "spills over" into other international markets. In 2022, the shortage of computer chips hitherto mainly sourced from the Far East has badly affected automobile assembly operations in the US and Europe. Ukraine used to produce 18.5 percent of the world's wheat. Ukraine's share in global wheat exports was 10 percent, and Russia's share was 19 percent. The invasion of Ukraine and embargos on Russian exports affects only a negligible fraction of multinational companies, such as Bunge, Cargill, or Orsett Trading, and shipping firms that handled Ukrainian wheat exports. However, the shortage of wheat in world markets is part of the story of escalating inflation in food prices worldwide. Tragically, it more seriously affects low-income populations in wheat importing nations ranging from Indonesia, Egypt, Bangladesh, and Philippines to Morocco and Tunisia – where most families may spend 40–60 percent of their disposable income on food. By contrast, until the invasion, American families spent only 5 or 6 percent of their disposable income on food at home.

Another example of "geopolitical risk" is the Chinese company Huawei, frozen out of the 5G mobile telephony market in 2021 by the US, Canada, UK Sweden, and Australia, with other nations from Libya to India to Vietnam, doing this informally. Other 2021 examples include the sharp drop in H&M's sales in China (with termination of store leases and virulent posts by Chinese social media trolls) because H&M's ethics policy stated that they would no longer source garments made with Xinjiang cotton. Turkey's purchase of Russian missiles increased the likelihood of US and NATO country sanctions, and further chilled the FDI and trade environment for that country.

A more common type of political risk is local, and it is based on an unexpected change in a nation's regulations, which results in a downturn in the expected cash flows from a foreign operation. Examples include new price controls on regulated industries, or a change in party politics in a country that changes or reneges on previous commitments. A multinational company, having sunk an investment worth millions into the ground of a foreign country, is then held "hostage" because the assets cannot be pulled back out of the nation. This particularly applies to infrastructural projects where, once built, a road or power plant cannot be picked up and brought back home from the foreign nation. Even service sector investments such as hotels or information technology face this issue, although to a less severe extent.

Increasingly, multinational companies that perceive political risk, especially in not-easily-reversible investments, ask for arbitration clauses in their agreements, which specify compensation in the case of certain contingencies occurring. All in all, however, political risk is not a major consideration, as a generalization across the huge scope and spectrum of international business operations.

Tax Scrutiny Risks

As we have seen above, most multinationals try to shift taxable profits from high-tax to low-tax countries, which risks increased regulations and scrutiny. (For further details, see Chapter 5 or Contractor, 2016). While such accounting maneuvers have been occurring for over 50 years, governments around the world have recently woken up to the need to examining the books of multinationals. Since the year 2000, it is estimated that over $ 500 billion in additional taxes and fines have been collected by governments, from companies especially in high-tech sectors. Multinationals consider this an area of increasing risk.

Partner Risks

Three recent trends have opened up a new area of risk management for companies. Alliances and inter-company collaborations are increasing at a faster rate than the growth of single-management companies, leading firms to formally assess "partner risk." An underlying reason is the growing importance of proprietary technology and intangible assets as the core competence of companies (Contractor, 2000 a and b). Secondly, technologies have become so complex that even giant firms cannot encompass all areas of development or distribution on their own and hence seek allies – especially in foreign markets. Third, leakage, or unintended spillover, of secrets to competitors (especially foreign competitors with fewer ethical scruples) is looming as an unfortunate management control issue in companies. This can occur through internet-based "hacking," or by employees who act as spies, or by the conscious act of entering into an alliance. We saw earlier that a big drawback to licensing or joint venture alliances is the possibility that the licensee or partner learns production of financial techniques, trade secrets, or marketing skills from the original technology developer – only to eventually become a competitor. This is a growing area of risk-management in companies. But if so, why do companies enter into tens of thousands of alliances each year? Because the benefits of partnership and collaborations are seen as outweighing the risks and costs.

Including alliance partners in any operation increases the risk of leakage of proprietary knowledge, compared with say a fully owned subsidiary where the multinational's own employees operate, presumably under headquarters control. But even there, employees can become spies, or can quit and join a competitor, carrying company secrets with them (Contractor, 2019). Even exporting a finished product carries a slight "reverse-engineering" risk, if the importer disassembles the product, analyzes its construction and materials, learns how to copy it, and introduces a rival product in their own country, or even in other markets.

Protectionism and Nationalism

For four decades since the year 1980, the pendulum swung in favor of more globalization. Countries mutually reduced their tariffs on imports, opened their doors wider to the FDI entry of multinational companies, and even offered them generous incentives to invest. International trade greatly expanded because tariffs, as well as non-tariff (regulatory) barriers, were reduced, and unified global standards facilitated the formation of multi-country markets and the salutary economies of a global scale of operations. This is still largely true. However, some argue that the globalization drive or pendulum has reached its zenith, and that a pullback may occur (Contractor, 2017a). There are small signs of this everywhere, from the US increasing tariffs in the Trump administration, to China's assertive push for localization, to India's new-old gospel of "*atmanirbhar,*" or "self-reliance." (Incidentally, just these three countries – the US, China, and India – already comprise 40 percent of the world's GDP and world population – with their share likely to increase to beyond 50 percent of the world economy and population by the 2030s.)

Nationalism and protectionism are indeed risks to be taken seriously by the strategic planning departments of multinationals, to prepare their firms for the contingencies of heightened trade barriers, stricter FDI entry regulations, or even outright bans or expropriation of assets. On the other hand, some scholars argue that the fundamental drivers of globalization remain strong, so that (apart from a partial decoupling of US-China commerce) the economic justification for continued international business will ensure that FDI, exports, licensing and other modes of collaboration will continue to grow, especially in an era where international cooperation on a range of issues from pandemics to climate change have heightened the need for a global consensus (Contractor, 2021).

Foreign Exchange Risk

International business necessarily entails the conversion of one currency for another. And the *rate* at which the currencies are exchanged fundamentally affects profitability. Consider a US importer who imports from France, with the shipment or cargo payable in Euros. In March 2020, the exchange rate was $1.12 per euro. A short while later in August 2020, it reached $1.18 – an appreciation of 5 percent. The US importer's profit margin, in a competitive business, may have been less than 5 percent, which means their entire profit would be wiped out, through no fault of their own. (One solution may sometimes be to raise US prices by more than 5percent, to compensate. But that is not often possible in as price-competitive a market like the US).

Currencies can also move in a company's favor, in the short or long run. The Euro was $1.58 in July 2008 but devalued to $1.10 by July 2015. This meant that the dollar cost of a European import fell dramatically for the US importer.

One can judge the importance of this topic, and its accompanying risks, with the following facts. Each 24 hours, over $5 trillion worth of all currencies changes hands worldwide. Of that, just one pair of currencies, the dollar-euro pair, comprises more than $1.2 trillion in traded value.

> As we will see in the chapter entitled "***Representative Problems (With Solutions) in Foreign Exchange Risk Management***," foreign exchange risk can be managed in the short run (up to say one or two years) by the use of Forward Market and Money Market methods. But in the longer run, there is no escape from currency risk.

For FDI and licensing, currency risk is more of a long-term risk, because dividends received from foreign affiliates, or licensing royalties are spread over many years. If the foreign currency of the FDI affiliate declaring dividends, or licensees who pay royalties in their local currency, devalues against the home currency of the multinational parent or licensor, then that cash stream converts into less money for the multinational or licensor. But in finance terms, "risk" can also simply mean "volatility" including up-side gain. If the currencies of foreign affiliates or licensees appreciates, then the multinational parent or licensor would benefit in terms of their currency.

Global Supply-Chain Risks

Another area of recent concern is the management of international supply chain risks. International supply chains, or global value chains, are common today in most industries and firms, for the simple reason that even giant companies do not have the internal capability or efficiency to produce all the raw materials or components, in-house. Even if they could be "vertically integrated" that would make no economic sense, to pay advanced nation wages of $30 – 60 per hour, when millions are happy to do the same work in Bangladesh, China, or Vietnam for between $2 – 5 per hour. Some auto components made in Mexico, may then be added to a sub-assembly in a Canadian plant, which then goes into the finished automobile assembled in the US.

Transport costs have shrunk to the point where an Apple iPhone can be shipped from its Chinese assembly point to the US for less than $1, and a t-shirt for around 0.30 each. As a result, splitting up the value chain over several nations, even thousands of miles apart, does not generally entail significant costs, but results in huge net savings.

The rationale for international supply chains is to lower the overall cost of production because of two underlying factors, (1) Taking advantage of foreign countries' comparative advantage in cheap labor or raw material access (in 2022, for example, China has an advantage in both reasonably low wages and rare-earth mines), and (2) Managing and coordinating the global value chain so tightly that inventory levels are reduced to only a few days' worth at various points. Carrying inventory is a huge cost element, because inventory is nothing more than dead capital sitting on a shelf, incurring interest, depreciation, real estate, insurance and obsolescence costs, and not earning anything. As a consequence, as long as a company can rely on its suppliers to deliver, as promised, "just-in-time" inventories can be held to a bare-bones minimum.

But the bare-bones minimum inventory carries the risk that if there is a delay, or disruption anywhere along the global supply chain, that can severely affect not just that operation, but all downstream sub-assembly and assembly operations around the world. This risk has increased significantly after 2021, with constraints on ship capacity, less predictable or volatile demand, a partial decoupling between the US and China, and other geopolitical risks.

In the chapter entitled ***"An Introduction to Managing Global Supply Chain Risks,"*** we will see how while international supply chain risk has increased, it can be managed with greater strategic direction and new technologies such as block-chain, artificial intelligence and 5G monitoring.

---

8. Conclusions

For many companies beginning their international expansion into a foreign market, the strategy options include exporting, foreign direct investment, and contractual arrangements (of which the most notable is the licensing of expertise and intellectual property to a firm in the foreign market). This chapter discussed the pros and cons of each and enumerated several criteria whereby a firm may choose between the foreign market entry methods. The choice of method will depend on the firm, the product, and the foreign market in question. There is no one optimum. Some of the important criteria influencing the choice include expected returns, intended duration of the strategy and product cycle, required degree of managerial control, the risk appetite of the company, availability of financial and managerial resources, applicable tax rules, political and foreign exchange risk, and the risk of future competition from former licensees and strategic allies.

In the second part of this chapter, it was shown that as firms mature, and integrate globally, they will not treat foreign market entry methods as merely separate options, but consider combining these methods, and have a trading and a licensing relationship with their affiliates and equity partners abroad. Exports, licensing, and foreign direct investment, in this view, are alternate channels for income extraction, as much as they are market-serving strategies. Moreover, this combined approach lowers volatility and risk, increases control, and strengthens ties with partners (if any) in the other nation. The globalization of business reached a peak in 2019, but many observers conclude that this is a temporary plateau, and that despite somewhat heightened nationalism, protectionism and global risks, the globalization of the world economy will become even more necessary and important in the future.

Further Reading

Contractor, F. J. (2021). "The world economy will need even more globalization in the post-pandemic 2021 decade," *Journal of International Business Studies*, 1-16. (as agains predictions of a plateauing or decline of globalization, this article argues that globalization will keep increasing in the long run, and why globalization is necessary for worldwide economic progress).

Contractor, F. J. (2019). Can a firm find the balance between openness and secrecy? Towards a theory of an optimum level of disclosure. *Journal of International Business Studies*, *50*(2), 261-274.

Contractor, F. (2018) "Ten Quick Facts about US Trade: Deficits, Dumping, and Discords," *Yale Global*, May 2018. (This piece explains specific issues in international trade such as dumping and deficits).

Contractor, F. (2017a) "Global Leadership in an Era of Growing Nationalism, Protectionism, and Anti-Globalization," *Rutgers Business Review*, 2(2): 163-185. (This article traces the increase of nationalism and protectionism in recent years, and the causes).

Contractor, F. (2017b) "What Is at Stake in China-US Relations? An Estimate of Jobs and Money Involved in the Bilateral Economic Tie," *Rutgers Business Review*, 2(1): 1 – 22. (This is one of the few papers that tries to estimate the number of jobs and money involved in the US-China commercial relationship, the biggest bilateral international business link in the world between two countries).

Contractor F. (2016) "Tax Avoidance by Multinational Companies," *Rutgers Business Review*, September. (This article illustrates various methods used in multinational companies to shift taxable profits to lower-tax countries. It also treats the ethical issues surrounding such practices).

Contractor, F. (2012) "Why Do Multinational Firms Exist? A Theory Note About The Effect of Multinational Expansion on Performance and Recent Methodological Critiques," *Global Strategy Journal,* November, pp. 318-331. (Reviews the advantages of multinationality).

Contractor, F., Kumar, V., Kundu, S. & Pedersen, T., (2010) "Reconceptualizing the Firm in a World of Outsourcing and Offshoring: The Organizational and Geographical Relocation of High-Value Company Functions," *Journal of Management Studies*, December, pp. 1417-1433. (Slicing of the value chain and dispersal of value-added activities worldwide by outsourcing and offshoring).

Contractor, F.J. (2000a) "Integrating Strategic Planning with Technology Management in the Global Firm," in Tayeb, M., (ed.), *International Business: Theories, Policies and Practices* (London: Pearson, 2000). (Describes how technology management can be integrated into multinational strategy.)

Contractor, F.J. (2000b) "Valuing Intangible Assets in Alliance Negotiations," in Contractor, F. (ed.), *The Valuation of Intangible Assets in Global Operations* (Cheltenham, UK: Edward Elgar, forthcoming). (Treats the issue of setting a price for technology and corporate knowledge).

Contractor, F.J. (1999) 'strategic Perspectives for International Licensing Managers: The Complementary Roles of Licensing, Investment and Trade in Global Operations," *Journal of the Licensing Executives Society*, June 1999, pp. 1- 12.

Contractor, F.J. (1986) *Licensing in International Strategy: A Guide for Planning and Negotiations,* Westport, CT: Quorum Books. (A comprehensive volume on the role of licensing in the international strategies of companies. The book contains considerable empirical data drawn from firms directly, as well as from secondary sources. Several cases illustrate what companies are doing.)

Frazzon, E., Albrecht, A., Pires, M., Israel, E., Kück, M., & Freitag, M. (2018). Hybrid approach for the integrated scheduling of production and transport processes along supply chains. *International Journal of Production Research*, 56(5), 2019-2035.

Kale, P. & Singh, H. (2009) "Managing Strategic Alliances: What Do We Know Now, and Where Do We Go from Here?" *Academy of Management Perspectives*, August, pp. 45 – 62. (Identifies the complexity, pros and cons of alliances).

Kano, L., & Oh, C.H. (2020). Global value chains in the post-COVID world: Governance for reliability. *Journal of Management Studies*. Published online 15 September 2020. https://doi.org/10.1111/joms.12626

Laker, B. (2020) "How Organizations Need to Manage Supply Chain Risk Today," *Forbes*, September 7.

Lund, S., Manyika, J., Woetzel, J., Barriball, E., Krishnan, M., Alicke, K., Birshan, M., George, K., Smit, S., Swan, D. and Hutzler, K. (2020). *Risk, Resilience, and Rebalancing in Global Value Chains*. McKinsey Global Institute. https://www.mckinsey.com/business-functions/operations/our-insights/risk-resilience-and-rebalancing-in-global-value-chains#

Petrova, M. (2018) "We traced what it takes to make an iPhone, from its initial design to the components and raw materials needed to make it a reality" *CNBC*. December 14. https://www.cnbc.com/2018/12/13/inside-apple-iphone-where-parts-and-materials-come-from.html

Reich, R. (1990) "Who is Us?" *Harvard Business Review* (January-February): 53-64. (The author describes how the affiliation of companies with their national or home base is becoming weaker.)

Reilly, R. (1995) "Economic Evaluation Techniques," *Les Nouvelles: Journal of the Licensing Executives Society*, June 1995, pp. 53 – 58. (Benchmarks for valuing intangible assets).

Rundle, J. (2020) 5G Promises Radical Overhaul for Supply Chains, *Wall Street Journal*, April 12, https://www.wsj.com/articles/5g-promises-radical-overhaul-for-supply-chains-11586556432

Schmidt, C. G., & Wagner, S. M. (2019). Blockchain and supply chain relations: A transaction cost theory perspective. *Journal of Purchasing and Supply Management*, 25(4), 100552.

Scott, S. (2013) "U.S. International transactions, Fourth Quarter and Year 2012," *Survey of Current Business*, April. (Statistics on US Investment and Trade).

United Nations (2020) *World Investment Report 2020,* New York: United Nations. (Annual comprehensive survey of multinational companies and their activities worldwide).

US Department of Commerce (2013) *A Basic Guide to Exporting: The Official Government Resource for Small and Medium-Sized Businesses*, (International Trade Administration). https://www.trade.gov/learn-how-export

Chapter 2

International Entry Strategies – Criteria for Choosing

Entering foreign markets, to reach foreign customers, involves choosing from a spectrum of strategic choices, as we saw in the previous chapter, ranging from exporting to contractual alliances to equity joint ventures and fully owned subsidiaries (whether by "greenfield" – established for the first time – or by "acquisition" – purchasing an already established company in the foreign nation).

For each of these choices, the expected returns, various costs, tax consequences, levels of risk, the degree of control maintained, the duration of the strategy and how easily the decision can be reversed, are important strategy criteria to be considered in making the final choice. The answers will, obviously vary from one company to the next. This chapter and the table below, serves as a summary reminder, or checklist for each company, in deciding on its foreign market entry strategy.

While the criteria will vary by company, we can with hesitation, make some generalizations. The planning horizon becomes longer (more years into the future) as we go from left to the right of the table. After all, a Foreign Direct Investment (FDI) subsidiary established in a foreign nation is at least in theory, forever, compared with exporting to that market. Similarly, financial and managerial costs are greatest in FDI, compare to just exporting or a contractual licensing alliance agreement. Equity joint ventures fall in between because they also entail capital investment and deputing managers abroad to run the joint venture.

On the other hand, negotiating costs are highest in alliances (either contractual or joint venture). At the same time any and all strategy choices need to be judged against the opportunity and consequential costs they precipitate. For example, in South Korea, forming an alliance with one "chaebol" or business group such as Samsung, may hurt existing business being done with its rival the LG group, creating a loss for that operation. Hence the loss of business caused by taking one decision, needs to be calculated and evaluated. By the same token, if a decision or strategy closes the door on another possible profitable strategic option, that is called an "opportunity cost."

Every strategic decision creates its tax consequences, which need to be evaluated, for both the foreign and home country of the multinational. The subject is highly complex, and also volatile as countries change their tax laws. However, Chapters 1 and 5 in this book give a sufficient idea of the complexities involved as well as tax-avoidance techniques used by companies.

In terms of risk, going from left to right in the table below entails both capital and managerial investment rising from left to right, i.e., greater risk from that perspective. Political risk also rises towards the right-hand side simply because in joint ventures and subsidiaries, assets are "stuck in the ground" in the foreign nation, and subject to political risk, as compared with exporting or licensing where the company has no irreversible investments there. However, a risk of growing importance in 2021, is the risk of losing proprietary intellectual technology or trade secrets that leak out to a partner. This risk is clearly highest in alliances such as licensing or joint ventures.

The need to maintain control over foreign operation again depends on the company in question. As compared to exporting or fully owned subsidiaries, alliances by definition involve the voluntary relinquishment of some control to partners. There is another angle to this question. In some companies that are either decentralized, or where one country operation is not strongly networked with other country operations, ceding some control in one nation is less worrisome. But for other multinationals where operations in one nation are tightly integrated with those in other nations, a problem in one country can ricochet and affect others. Hence the strategist needs to ask how globally integrated the company is.

Finally, broad criteria, or questions, to be thought of in adopting a strategy for a foreign country are "What is our anticipated duration for this country or operation – long or short?" and "How reversible do we want to make our commitment in the nation?" It is clear that strategies to the right side of the table below are more long-term, and less reversible. But the two questions above should trigger thinking about political and economic stability, and risks, in the foreign nation, to determine the degree of commitment the multinational company is willing to make there.

The Summary Table – "Criteria for Choosing Between Strategies" – follows on the next page.

Criteria for Choosing Between Strategies

EXPECTED RETURNS	Exporting	Contractual Alliance e.g., Licensing	Equity Joint Venture	Fully Owned Subsidiary
• Planning Horizon: Short-term				
• Planning Horizon: Long-term				
COSTS				
• Financial Costs (project related)				
• Managerial Costs (cost and opportunity cost of managers and technicians)				
• Cost of negotiating with allies and transferring knowledge (can be buried in overheads				
• Governance Costs (can be buried in central overhead)				
• Opportunity Costs (can sometimes be forgotten)				
• Consequential Costs (see below under Risk)				
TAX CONSIDERATIONS				
RISKS				
• Size of Assets at Stake				
• Ordinary Commercial Risk				
• Geopolitical Risk				
• Foreign Exchange Risk				
• Risk of Leakage of Proprietary Knowledge and Creating a Competitor (consequential cost)				
CONTROL				
• Degree of Control Needed over Management in That Nation (this is also related to the degree of centralization of global operations)				
• Day-to-Day vs. Long-term				
• Interdependence of Partners (overtime)				
REVERSIBILITY OF DECISION				
ANTICIPATED DURATION OF STRATEGY				

CHAPTER 3

An Introduction to Managing Global Supply Chain Risks – Summary and Excerpt from Chapter 4[*]

In the post-pandemic era with heightened awareness of risks, another area of recent concern is the management of international supply chain risks. Whether an Icelandic volcano disrupts airfreight in Europe, or a megaship blocks the Suez Canal causing months of disruption and port congestion everywhere, or floods stop production in Thailand's car-component factories, which idles automobile assembly plants in North America and Europe, or geopolitical tensions grow between China and the US, or an unexpected shortage of computer chips reduces the production of appliances and cars worldwide, these have been only a few recent examples of supply chain risks.

International supply chains are designed for efficiency or cost-reduction, by slicing production into discrete steps and spreading the production over many nations (Contractor, et al., 2010). One report has Apple sourcing raw materials and components for its iPhones from 43 countries in 6 continents (Petrova, 2018). (Apple itself does not "produce" anything. Rather, Apple is a global "'orchestrator," a brilliant designer, technologist, and a savvy marketing company, with most of its value in intangible assets (i.e., thought and ideas), while leaving the physical piece of its business to lower-cost component manufacturers and assemblers who then ship the finished and assembled products to country markets, also under Apple's supply chain direction).

But with sources for raw materials and components spread over dozens of countries, the level of risk increases. A jam, disruption or bottleneck in one part of the "global value chain" (GVC), or supply chain, can slow or idle operations and sales everywhere. The sensitivity to supply chain risk is now much greater in multinational companies after the 2020 pandemic, with rising nationalism, conflicts, and the possibility of a partial decoupling between the US and China. Happily, however, there are new measures and technologies that can mitigate these risks.

As illustrated in Figure 1 below, the vertical axis tracks "Cost Per Unit of Procured Item" as well as the company's "Risk," while the horizontal axis tracks increasing "Resilience" of a GVC (resilience is the enhanced ability to handle international supply chain risk; GVC is a composite index constructed from four sub-indicators).

---

[*] Summary and Excerpt from Farok J. Contractor (2021, February), The world economy will need *even more* globalization in the post-pandemic 2021 decade, *Journal of International Business Studies*, 1-16. See Chapter 4.

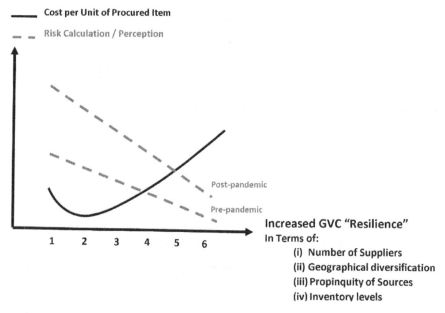

Figure 1: Tradeoffs Between Resilience and Efficiency (or Cost Reduction vs. Risk) in International Supply Chains

The Figure 1 framework enables a company to assess whether and how it should reconfigure its GVC to make it more risk-resistant or resilient. "Resilience" is greater (and risks lower) toward the right on the horizontal axis of the graph. Risk decreases toward the right because of four strategic decisions by the firm:

(i) Increasing the number of suppliers worldwide for the item,

(ii) Geographical diversification (spreading suppliers over more source countries),

(iii) Propinquity: Weighted average of the (a) political and (b) geographic distance from supply sources to the point of assembly or demand, and

(iv) Overall inventory levels maintained.

The cost per unit procured is a J-curve. Why? Often, a sole-supplier (being a quasi-monopoly) – number 1 on the x-axis – charges a higher cost per unit than a situation where competitive pressures between two or more suppliers reduces the cost. However, beyond two or three suppliers, the cost per unit is likely to increase simply because the multiplicity of supply sources increases (a) global logistics cost and (b) transaction plus management costs.

To summarize: Risk reduces from left to right in the graph. Resilience increases toward the right of the x-axis, as sources are diversified to more suppliers in more countries, the weighted average distance from sources to demand points is reduced (the extreme case being complete reshoring of supplies), and inventory/sales ratios carried for the item in question increase. The optimum position is neither close to the extreme left of the x-axis nor far to the right, but somewhere in the middle.

Optimizing the supply chain is a tradeoff between it being too lean on the above four indicators (in the interest of efficiency and low cost) and being too resilient or risk-averse (which increases cost per unit). For instance, being too risk averse and increasing inventory or numbers of suoppliers by more than a slight extent can put a firm at a competitive disadvantage. Firms that are overly cautious in the future and carry too much inventory compared to rivals, or increase the number of worldwide suppliers by more than a marginal extent, will suffer a worse performance, compared to competitors who are willing to assume higher risk. (The exact shape of the J-curve will vary from one subsector to another).

"Risk" can be a strategic perception, but can also be actually estimated by the multinational company's Supply Chain Department using probabilistic models that include the likelihood of "stock-outs" and their consequences for each GVC configuration, in terms of lost sales or profits, as well as reputation. This will of course vary firm by firm. Figure 1 is a schematic representation.

The World Is Now More Risk-Averse

Before 2020, when perceived risks were lower, a multinational could be content to have two or three suppliers worldwide. With higher nationalism, protectionism, and regional wars, the post-2022 risk curve lifts upward (the higher dashed line in Figure 1), which calls for, or allows, increased risk-aversion or resilience (e.g., more suppliers worldwide). But this shift can only occur to a limited extent because costs per unit also rise to the right of the x-axis. Sensitivity to risk has increased after 2021. But that can be offset by risk-reducing organizational and technical developments in GVCs, described below.

Risk-reducing Organizational and Technical Developments

Supply chain risks can (and will) be mitigated by three digital technologies still in their infancy, (i) Blockchain, (ii) Integration of Vendor-Buyer Computer Systems and (iii) Artificial Intelligence (AI) which produces predictive demand analytics (Lund et al., 2020; Kano & Oh, 2020). In general, over the past 30 years, information technology and closer communication between buyers and suppliers has led to the growth of GVCs. But even today, to a surprising extent, the computer systems of multinational buyers are only loosely integrated with those of their foreign suppliers, so that a procurement manager often does not exactly know the status of an order in the foreign factory or service provider.

Blockchain based contracts lead to greater contractual assurance, lower information asymmetry, and real-time information which reduces uncertainties, risks and transaction costs (Schmidt & Wagner, 2019). Integration of buyer-supplier computer systems, or the ability of the multinational company to monitor, any time, the status of the vendor's production by accessing their servers, reduces uncertainty and helps to better schedule its own own sales, inventories and other processes (Frazzon, et al., 2018). Systems integrated via 5G will further reduce GVC risks by providing real-time information in transportation pathways (Rundle, 2020). Finally, the use of artificial intelligence (AI) that incorporates data from weather, volcanoes, politics, economic cycles, competitor moves, wars, commodity and other price levels, etc., should lead to more accurate forecasting of demand and hence lower risk in the management of GVCs (Lund et al., 2020).

In conclusion, while sensitivity to GVC risk has increased, at the same time there will be countervailing risk-reducing effects from new technologies which will reduce risks by improving the management and coordination of foreign supplier systems.

REFERENCES

Contractor, F. J. (2021). "The world economy will need even more globalization in the post-pandemic 2021 decade," *Journal of International Business Studies*, 1-16. https://link.springer.com/article/10.1057/s41267-020-00394-y

Frazzon, E., Albrecht, A., Pires, M., Israel, E., Kück, M., & Freitag, M. (2018). Hybrid approach for the integrated scheduling of production and transport processes along supply chains. *International Journal of Production Research*, 56(5), 2019-2035.

Kano, L., & Oh, C.H. (2020). Global value chains in the post-COVID world: Governance for reliability. *Journal of Management Studies*. Published online 15 September 2020. https://doi.org/10.1111/joms.12626

Lund, S., Manyika, J., Woetzel, J., Barriball, E., Krishnan, M., Alicke, K., Birshan, M., George, K., Smit, S., Swan, D. and Hutzler, K. (2020). *Risk, Resilience, and Rebalancing in Global Value Chains*. McKinsey Global Institute. https://www.mckinsey.com/business-functions/operations/our-insights/risk-resilience-and-rebalancing-in-global-value-chains#

Petrova, M. (2018) "We traced what it takes to make an iPhone, from its initial design to the components and raw materials needed to make it a reality" *CNBC*. December 14. https://www.cnbc.com/2018/12/13/inside-apple-iphone-where-parts-and-materials-come-from.html

Rundle, J. (2020) 5G Promises Radical Overhaul for Supply Chains, *Wall Street Journal*, April 12, https://www.wsj.com/articles/5g-promises-radical-overhaul-for-supply-chains-11586556432

Schmidt, C. G., & Wagner, S. M. (2019). Blockchain and supply chain relations: A transaction cost theory perspective. *Journal of Purchasing and Supply Management*, 25(4), 100552.

CHAPTER 4

The World Economy Will Need *Even More* Globalization in the Post-Pandemic 2021 Decade[*]

Abstract

This chapter, originally published in the leading academic journal of the *Academy of International Business*, is a sweeping overview of likely changes in the global business environment post-2022. It gives reasons why the future world economy will need even more globalization, which, after a pause, will resume its growth. The predictions of a post-pandemic world characterized by decoupling of economies, shake-up of global value chains, and the retreat of globalization, will occur temporarily – but to a lesser extent, the author asserts. This chapter proposes that the changes induced by heightened nationalism and protectionism will be localized and marginal for the world as a whole, rather than fundamental in nature. These marginally higher risks can be handled and ameliorated by multinational enterprises through alternative cross-border business strategies and emerging technologies.

INTRODUCTION

Much has been written about how the global economy will change as a result of the Covid-19 pandemic, including the operations of multinational enterprises (MNEs), and patterns of trade (e.g., Baldwin & Tomiura, 2020). Particular attention has been focused on the reconfiguration of international supply chains (e.g., Ivanov & Dolgui, 2020; Verbeke, 2020) since it was reported, early in the pandemic, that 94percent of the Fortune 1000 companies were encountering coronavirus supply chain disruptions (Sherman, 2020). The importance and complexity of cross-border supply or value chains may be gauged from an UNCTAD report that estimated that 60percent of global trade consisted of intermediate goods and services (i.e., components and semi-finished items), with around a quarter re-crossing borders at least twice before final assembly or release as a finished product, software or service package (UNCTAD, 2013).

---

[*] Reprinted from: Farok J. Contractor (2021, February), *Journal of International Business Studies*, 1-16, https://link.springer.com/article/10.1057/s41267-020-00394-y; also available through Rutgers Libraries.

In a post-pandemic world, it is proposed that a fundamental shift in MNE strategies and managerial thinking will occur and will be skewed towards greater risk aversion, nationalism, and protectionism (Fontaine, 2020), pre-existing trends that they say the pandemic has now precipitated. Some go even further, presaging a "legitimacy crisis" for the post-war neoliberal economic order (Abdelal, 2020). Others even proclaim the coming "end of globalization" (Young, 2020).

This article instead proposes that the fundamental rationales for globalization have not eroded, and that, in a post-pandemic world, there will be an even greater need and utility for globalization. Certainly, the shifts proposed, such as rethinking of global value chain overdependence, have already begun to occur. However, I argue here that these shifts will be marginal rather than fundamental, and that the basic efficiency, comparative advantage, and rationalization arguments for global investment and trade will remain irresistible, even in a post-Covid-19 world.

HOW THIS PAPER IS ORGANIZED

It would first be useful to outline how globalization has multiple dimensions measured by scholars and consultancies, in order to frame the argument. Next, the paper will review the fundamental rationales or justification for international business, while recognizing its occasional negative externalities.[1] The following sections will argue that changes in the organization and configuration of multinational operations, in response to external factors such as rising nationalism and risk-aversion, will be marginal rather than fundamental. The concluding section will highlight why the world will need even more globalization and cross-border collaboration in the future.

MEASUREMENTS FOR GLOBALIZATION

International Business scholarship is about tracking cross-border movements. The most common measures include traded goods and services, and foreign direct investment (FDI) flows in and out of nations. Data on these are easily found in sources such as the World Investment Report (2020), the World Bank, and OECD. Critics decry the stagnation of the value of FDI and trade measured in current dollars in the post-2008 period, but this belies the fact that the 2008–2019 numbers averaged as much as ten times their 1990 levels.[2] Some scholars, from a short-term perspective focusing only on the post-2008 period, have taken an excessively pessimistic view, ignoring the fact that most FDI and trade indicators, taken over a long-term trend line, i.e., the 1990s–2020 period, show a five- to ten-fold growth (Witt, 2019).

To these as globalization indicators, Verbeke, Coeurderoy and Matt (2018) add cross-border movements of ideas, people, technology, portfolio capital, and "effective institutional practices" by which they imply that multinational companies are the catalysts and conduits of higher standards and practices in the nations in which they invest. Using different data points, the DHL Global Connectedness Index (Altman & Bastian, 2019) paints a rosier picture over the 2001–2018 period, with information flows (bandwidth, telephone, and printed publications) shown as growing by 76percent, people flows (migrants, tourists and foreign students) growing at 20percent, and the FDI Stock/GDP ratio showing an increase of 16 percentage points (or 71percent in terms of percentage growth) from 2001 to 2018). The DHL index shows no growth after 2001 in the *geographical breadth* coverage of multinational enterprises, echoing Rugman and Verbeke's (2004) assertion that most MNEs limit themselves to a regional coverage. However, Rosa, Gugler and Verbeke (2004) calculated an increased global coverage from the Fortune Global 500 list for 2017[3], stating that "…many large firms are still home-region oriented, but to a lesser extent than before."

Another significant globalization indicator, almost totally ignored by international business scholars, is the cross-border payments (mainly royalties) for the licensing of intellectual property, which increased from US$26.74 billion (current dollars) in 1990 to $397.23 billion in 2019.[4] Apart from their dramatic growth, international licensing is far less affected by recessions and pandemics,[5] and is likely to continue its fast growth in the knowledge economy of the future. The royalty numbers seem small in absolute terms, until one probes their strategic significance to global commerce and economics. Foreign sales by licensees at least partially substitute for exports or FDI affiliate sales. How do the sales of these three international business strategies compare? Royalty rates range from 2percent or less for some music and publications to over 8percent for valuable technologies and medicines, so that dividing $397.23 by the 0.08 or 0.02 royalty rates yields estimates of licensee sales (achieved by international licensing of intellectual assets) of $4965 billion to $19,862 billion, respectively.[6] (Notice that the latter number is comparable to the 2019 world merchandise export sales total).

That MNEs are instruments or channels for the upgrading of institutional standards by foreign host governments is documented in studies such as Jude and Levieuge (2015). The Contractor, Dangol, Nuruzzaman, and Raghunath (2020) study covering 189 nations shows that better institutional quality attracts larger FDI inflows. The "demonstration effect" of MNEs, in upgrading productivity, sustainability, and environmental and labor standards has been well documented for 45 years (e.g., Caves, 1974 or Moran, Graham & Blomstron, 2005).[7] Also, in recent years, the knowledge spillover effects (intended as well as inadvert) diffusing into the host nation in which the MNE operates have drawn increased attention (Contractor, 2019; Prud'homme, 2019).

Starting in February 2020, unsurprisingly, most measures of globalization declined. However, the fundamental rationales for international business remain unassailable and even more valid in the post-pandemic period.

THE CONTINUING RATIONALES OF INTERNATIONAL BUSINESS

The inescapable fact is that, into the long future, the world will remain fragmented (into nation states) and unequal (in terms of income, culture, laws, institutions, and business practices). Therein lies the fundamental rationale for international business, which will persist in the post-pandemic period, since inequalities and fragmentation will continue to create aggregation and arbitrage opportunities for MNEs, and for traders and alliances (Ghemawat, 2007). This cross-border "bridging" function performed by international firms will continue to benefit not only them, but also the citizens and companies in host nations to which better managerial, productivity, technological and institutional practices are "demonstrated" (Caves, 1974; Swenson & Chen, 2014). Consumers in both home and host nations benefit from improved methods and organization, and from heightened competition that results in better quality and design, at lower prices.[8] Such fundamental justifications for international business will not diminish but may even increase in the future (as discussed in a later section).

Global Production Scale Economies: Combining demand from several markets to achieve economies of production scale is a core argument of International Business theory (Chandler & Hikino, 2009; Dunning, 2015; Cantwell, 2015). This is especially pertinent when one considers that the vast majority of national markets are small. Among the 20 biggest markets, going downward we quickly have, at ranks 18 and 20, respectively, Saudi Arabia and Turkey, whose GDP is a mere 0.8percent each of global total GDP. Below rank 50, we have not only tiny but also politically risky nations. The bottom 174 countries put together comprise only 19.3percent of the world economy – a highly skewed distribution indeed. Of course, aggregating standardized demand across nations to achieve scale economies is not always easy. For one thing, there is the contrary pull of local adaptation as a marketing strategy. Katsikeas, Samiee and Theodosiou (2006) identify inhibiting factors, such as varying customs and traditions, customer characteristics, stage of product life cycle, regulations, technology, and intensity of competition. Their study shows, however, that, when these barriers are overcome and standardization enables scale economies, this does result in superior performance. The skewed distribution of national economic size and inequality will continue to justify the existence of MNEs.

Global Amortization Scale: Most of the costs of a multinational company are not at the factory but in central organizational and R&D overheads. Generally, MNEs exhibit a greater technology intensity and spend more on R&D than comparable domestic firms. Innovations initially have a local root, and most R&D is still carried out in the home nation of the firm. However, the technological and other overheads incurred in the MNE's home country, if spread over many foreign affiliates and markets, reduce the overhead burden (and hence cost) per unit of final production – a luxury that domestic competitors cannot replicate.[9] As economies become more technology-intensive in the future, this attribute of multinational companies will become even more strategically relevant.[10]

Specialization and Global Value Chain (GVC) Orchestration: Since February 2020, when the pandemic began, much attention has been focused on the coming need to deepen cross-border integration of global value chains, i.e., to make them more resilient (e.g., Verbeke, 2020).The reasoning is that unexpected shocks, such as pandemics, rising nationalism, geo-political frictions, and protectionism, can adversely affect GVCs, which can delay vital supplies, and in the worst case create "stock-outs" and shortages (Ivanov & Dolgui, 2020; Sherman, 2020). In brief, the hypothesis is that the design or orchestration of GVCs in the future will exhibit greater risk-aversion (Aylor et al., 2020), although, undoubtedly, this will vary depending on the sector in question.

This coming "resilience" of supply chains will be manifested in four ways, (1) an increase in the number of suppliers for the same component or item (or lower likelihood of reliance on one sole-source foreign supplier), (2) geographical diversification of supply sources to more than one country, (3) propinquity of supply sources, in terms of both geographical and political "distance", and (4) Increase in inventory levels at the point of use – all of which represent an increase in cost per unit.

However, I argue that this future shift will only be marginal and not fundamental. For one thing, as Miroudot (2020) argues, past experiences show how quickly supply chains recover from disruptions, in some cases more than making up for the business lost during the supply interruption. However, in a longer-term sense, the overarching fact remains that much of international business relies on price-based competitiveness. The strategic imperatives of efficiency or cost-reduction, through the "fine-slicing" of a company's value chain, the dis-internalization (outsourcing) of many of the "slices," and their dispersion internationally (offshoring), will remain a powerful, inescapable competitive mandate (Contractor et al., 2010). This will limit the coming reconfiguration of GVCs to only a marginal or slight shift. As illustrated in Figure 1, the vertical axis tracks "Cost Per Unit of Procured Item" as well as the company's "Risk", while the horizontal axis tracks increasing "Resilience" of a GVC (a composite index constructed from four sub-indicators.

Figure 1 is a representation of the trade-offs calculated by an MNC before and after the pandemic period. That is to say, the Figure 1 framework enables a company to assess whether it should reconfigure its GVC to make it more risk-resistant and resilient (or not). "Resilience" of the GVC increases along the horizontal axis based on four strategic components to be decided by the firm:

(i) Number of suppliers worldwide for the item,

(ii) Geographical diversification (number of distinct source countries),

(iii) Propinquity: weighted average of the political and geographic distance from supply sources to the point of assembly or demand, and

(iii) Overall inventory levels.

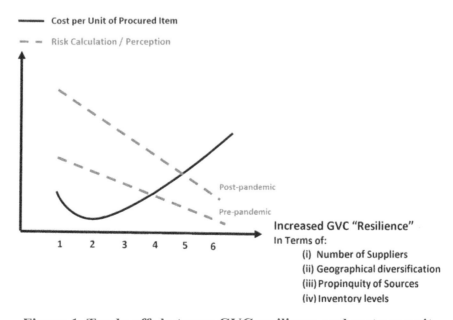

Figure 1. Trade-offs between GVC resilience and cost per unit.

The cost per unit procured is a J-curve, I hypothesize.[11] Often, a sole-supplier (being a quasi-monopoly) charges a higher cost per unit than a situation where competitive pressures between two or more suppliers reduces the cost. However, beyond two or three suppliers, the cost per unit is likely to increase simply because the multiplicity of supply sources increases (1) global logistics cost and (2) transaction costs (Berghuis, & den Butter, 2017).

Risk reduces from left to right in the graph. Resilience of the GVC increases towards the right of the x-axis, which reduces supply chain risk – as sources are diversified to more countries, as the weighted average distance from sources to demand points reduces, and as inventory/sales ratios carried for the item in question increase.[12] The optimum position is neither close to the extreme left of the x-axis nor far to the right, but somewhere in the middle.

Optimizing the supply chain is a balance between it being too lean on the above four indicators (in the interest of efficiency and low cost) and being too resilient or risk averse. For instance, being too risk averse and increasing inventory by more than a slight extent can put a firm at a competitive disadvantage. There is an echo of one of the variables in the J-curve hypothesis, found in Chen, Frank and Wu (2005) who showed that the stock market performance was best for US firms that held an intermediate level of inventory, as compared to rival firms that held too low, or too high, an inventory-to-sales ratio. This suggests that firms that are overly cautious in the future and carry too much inventory compared to rivals, or increase the number of worldwide suppliers by more than a marginal extent, will suffer a worse performance. (The exact shape of the J-curve will vary from one subsector to another.)

"Risk" can be a strategic perception, but can also be estimated by the MNE's Supply Chain Department using probabilistic models that include the likelihood of "stock-outs" and their consequences for each GVC configuration, in terms of lost sales or profits, as well as reputation.[13] This will of course vary firm by firm. Figure 1 is a schematic representation.

Prior to February 2020, when perceived risks were lower, a MNE could be content to have two or three suppliers worldwide. With higher nationalism and protectionism, the post-pandemic risk curve lifts upwards (the higher dashed line in Figure 1), which calls for, or allows, increased resilience (e.g., more suppliers worldwide) – but only to a limited extent – because costs per unit also rise to the right of the x-axis. Sensitivity to risk has increased. However, that will be offset by risk-reducing organizational and technical developments in GVCs, described below.

Hence the argument that the reconfiguration of GVCs will be small or marginal rather than radical.[14] There are two reasons. First, much of globalization is driven by competition between companies based on price and cost. Efficiency and competitiveness require cost-cutting. Only a marginal increase in GVC costs can be tolerated. Second, supply chain risks can (and will) be mitigated by three digital technologies still in their infancy, (1) Blockchain, (2) Integration of Vendor–Buyer Computer Systems and (3) Artificial Intelligence (AI) which produces predictive analytics (Lund et al., 2020; Kano & Oh, 2020). In general, over the past 30 years, information technology and closer communication between buyers and suppliers has led to the growth of GVCs (Gunasekaran et al., 2017). However, even in 2020, to a surprising extent, the computer systems of MNEs are only loosely integrated with those of their foreign suppliers, so that a MNE procurement manager often does not exactly know the status of an order in the foreign factory or service provider.

Blockchain-based contracts lead to greater assurance, lower information asymmetry, and real-time information which reduces uncertainties, risks, and transaction costs (Schmidt & Wagner, 2019; Kamilaris, Fonts & Prenafeta-Boldu, 2019). Integration of computer systems, or the ability of the MNE to monitor, at any time, the status of the vendor's production by accessing their servers, reduces uncertainty and helps schedule the MNE's own sales, inventories, and other processes (Frazzon et al., 2018). Systems integrated via 5G will further reduce GVC risks by providing real-time information in transportation pathways (Rundle, 2020). Finally, the use of AI that incorporates data from weather, volcanoes, politics, economic cycles, competitor moves, commodity and other price levels, etc., should lead to more accurate forecasting of demand and hence lower risk in the management of GVCs (Lund et al., 2020).

In summary, while sensitivity to risk will increase in the post-pandemic era, at the same time there will be countervailing risk-reducing effects from new technologies which will reduce risks by improving the management and coordination of foreign supplier systems. (A fuller discussion of new technologies that reduce risks is taken up in a later section of this paper.) Most pertinently, as noted above, in competition with other global firms, price and cost cutting are of paramount importance. Hence, I argue that the numerical and geographical diversification of suppliers will occur only to a limited or marginal extent.

The imperatives of globalization will continue.

THE OTHER IMPERATIVES OF GLOBALIZATION: MNEs AS INTERNATIONAL BRIDGING AGENTS, TRANSFERORS, AND ARBITRAGEURS

Why do multinational firms exist? In an atomistic, autarkic world, companies would remain domestic or national, and would deal across borders with other firms through contracts. International trade (sales of approximately $23 trillion in goods and services in 2019), as well as an unnoticed but huge set of substitute transactions in the form of international licensing of intellectual assets (also resulting in foreign sales by licensees of $5 trillion upwards[15] in 2019), is legally covered by contracts although some significant portion is between related parties.[16] Sales by MNE affiliates (not counting sales in the MNE's home nation) trump both at approximately $30 trillion. Whatever the foreign market entry strategy, the multinational firm plays a dominant bridging role.

The MNE as the carrier or transmitter of internalized proprietary capabilities to affiliates in foreign locations, or Internalization Theory (Buckley & Casson, 1976), has long lain at the heart of international business scholarship, and this core argument will not disappear in the future, even in a multi-polar, protectionist, or politics-driven world. The proprietary, internalized advantages or capabilities of successful international firms are alternatively described by Verbeke et al. (2018) as "firm-specific assets," which similarly result in the transfer of technologies (Monteiro, Arvidsson & Birkinshaw, 2008), including the occasional reverse flow of ideas and knowledge from affiliates back to headquarters (e.g., Kumar, 2013).

MNEs also result in the spread of best practices in management (e.g., Kostova & Roth, 2002), human resource management (HRM) (e.g., Ahlvik, Smale & Sumelius, 2016), gender equality (e.g., Abe, Javorcik & Kodama, 2016), sustainability (e.g., Marcon, de Medeiros & Ribeiro, 2017), and ethics (e.g., Johnson, 2017).[17] These contributions of MNEs will not disappear but will remain valid, even in a future world that may possibly be more nationalistic or fragmented (Petricevic & Teece, 2019).

MNEs are diffusers of knowledge, both unconsciously (like birds or insects that propagate flora), as well as consciously. Even while attempting to keep their core proprietary technologies internalized, there is inevitably a leakage or "spillover" of some knowledge and best practices to local firms through employee mobility or simple imitation. This may be a negative for the international firm, reducing its competitive advantage vis-à-vis local competitors, but for the latter there is a beneficial learning process. For example, Swenson & Chen (2014) found that the presence of international companies in locations in China resulted in improvement in the productivity, quality, frequency, and revenue capture of exports by local Chinese competitors in those regions.

Similarly, local firms learn as licensees of foreign companies. The World Bank (2020) reported that cross-border royalty payments for intellectual property crossed $400 billion in 2018. These transactions are covered under a contractual alliance agreement where the licensor, or intellectual asset provider, has a self-interested incentive to teach their foreign partner the auxiliary production techniques beyond just the patent, design, brand, or licensed intellectual asset – for the simple reason that royalties are typically linked to licensee sales, and therefore the licensor has an incentive to help the licensee succeed. Even imports of physical products and services have a learning value to the importer (Grosse & Fonseca, 2012).

International investment, trade, and licensing occur because of an arbitrageable gap, or "distance," between nations in terms of knowledge, capital, know-how, and corporate capabilities – a gap that is unlikely to disappear after 2021.

WHY, POST-PANDEMIC, THE WORLD ECONOMY WILL SEE EVEN MORE GLOBALIZATION

The indispensable role played by the multinational enterprise (MNE) as a bridging agent that aggregates demand and arbitrages differences across nations, as well as orchestrates and conduits the cross-border flows of capital (FDI), goods and services (trade), and intellectual assets (in affiliates and in contractual sharing of knowledge and capabilities with licensing and alliance partners[18]), will not diminish, but remain even more needed in a post-pandemic world. In a world remaining fragmented and unequal, the MNE also plays a salutary role as a catalyst of higher institutional, governance, sustainability, HRM, environmental and ethics standards, both through its own affiliate network (Foss & Pedersen, 2019) and by its external influence in countries that still have to catch up with "best practices."

The pandemic is more an accelerator of changes that were already under way rather than an event that enforces radically new patterns globally. Moreover, the impact of Covid-19 will affect a few nations and sectors more strongly than others. We have indeed seen, in the past three years and only in some nations, marginally more protectionism, nationalism,[19] and calls for greater self-sufficiency. Mimicking trends espoused by the Trump Administration, India's Modi declared his hope to "… transform India into a more self-reliant country, making the goods and providing the services consumed in the country largely at home" (Roy, 2020). However, these trends are not entirely orthogonal to globalization. Waldman and Javidan (2020) describe this as a "false dichotomy."

Protectionism and nationalism can even increase the geographical "footprint" of the MNE if trade barriers lead to increased tariff-jumping FDI (Buckley, 2020). For example, China's long tradition of protecting its automobile sector has resulted in substantial FDI investments by western companies from Volkswagen to General Motors to Tesla. Not only do the foreign companies dominate but, for some of them, China is their largest and most profitable market; moreover, Chinese industry has benefited greatly from the transfer of technology, designs, productivity, and best practices to China (Buckley, Clegg, Zheng, Siler, & Giorgioni, 2010).

Nationalist policies can sometimes increase globalization, a seemingly paradoxical effect. Glennon's (2020) study concludes that the more stringent enforcement of H1-B visas by the Trump Administration has already seen an increase in the offshoring of technological jobs. As a global orchestrator or network organizer, the international firm has more than one conduit of opportunity to enable cross-border transfers. If migration of talent is constrained, it can be replaced by remote virtual work. Observers suggest that, post-pandemic, more service functions will be carried out remotely (Tilley, 2020). However, by the same logic (i.e., the "Zoom Effect"), that job can be done even more remotely from Sofia or New Delhi. True, geographical and cultural distances impose higher organizational and transaction costs on the firm (Larson, Vroman, & Makarius, 2020), but these can be more than offset by the labor cost saving. Since there is no proposal to restrict the hiring of remote foreign employees, the "Zoom effect" and the growing worldwide familiarity with the "gig economy" can lead to even more offshored work. For example, while cross-border telemedicine faces significant regulatory barriers in advanced nations (Ferreira & Rosales, 2020), this is not the case everywhere. Instead of the patient crossing borders to visit the hospital abroad, some diagnoses and treatments will increasingly occur remotely.

Petricevic and Teece (2019) correctly identify the rekindling of the idea of government intervention in the foreign direct investment process. While most of the rest of the world has been lifting restrictions – liberalizing incoming FDI and eliminating lists of sectors requiring prior governmental approval (UNCTAD, 2019) and under the general rubric of "Ease of Doing Business" (World Bank, 2019) – the two biggest investors, China and the US, have been tightening scrutiny and vetoing a few proposed investments. The CFIUS (Committee on Foreign Investment in the United States) scrutinizes large FDI proposals for national security[20] concerns and is comprised of nine cabinet members, with the Treasury Secretary as Chair, and aided by senior intelligence officials. Ostensibly, China proclaims itself as a "champion of globalization" (Wang &

Quan, 2019). China's new "Foreign Investment Law" promulgated in January 2020 has slightly relaxed inward FDI regulations, reduced its "negative list," and promises "national treatment" (Dresden & Xia, 2020). However, the interventionist hand of the state remains just below the surface.

The few vetoes of FDI proposals in the US, and even rarer such occurrences in Europe, constitute an insignificant fraction of one percent of overall global flows. Anxieties elevated by the pandemic having abated, most countries may become more vigilant, but will resume their welcome towards FDI simply because it adds net value to the host nation. Petricevic and Teece (2019) go too far in characterizing the future of globalization as a "structural reshaping." They are correct in highlighting the rising techno-political rivalry between the US and China. Almost their entire paper (except for the first two pages) refers to – and is colored by – this bilateral relationship.[21] While China and the US remain the two biggest economies and direct investors, and they may partially decouple from each other, it is too much of a stretch to extrapolate this possible rivalry to the rest of the 191 nations on the planet. Only a handful of other nations will add some sectors to their list of "strategic industries." The fact remains that the vast bulk of FDI is in "…non-strategic sectors, such as agriculture, fashion, consumer goods, and even insurance." (Petricevic & Teece, 2019, p. 1502). Even in the US, an examination of Chinese FDI investments between January 2007 and June 2020 shows only a small percentage in technology-related sectors (American Enterprise Institute, 2020).[22] For all countries' MNEs seeking to invest in the US, CFIUS conducted 561 reviews for the entire 9-year period, 2009–2017, of which 145 FDI proposals were withdrawn during the investigation, and only 3 or 5 were vetoed by presidential order (Jackson, 2020).[23]

Buckley (2020) takes a balanced view, stating that "the fracture (between the US and China) may not be complete, nor be the only global policy change of significance in the post-virus world" (parentheses added). As noted in this piece above, I propose that, after the post-pandemic hiatus, globalization will resume and that changes will be marginal or incremental rather than structural.

REDUCING RISKS IN A POST-PANDEMIC WORLD

We are likely to see a world where perception of risks will be marginally increased. However, these risks will be ameliorated or counteracted by changes that were already underway, which augur an even more coordinated global economy:

1. *More sophisticated information systems amongst MNEs and Traders*: Volatility, Uncertainty, Complexity and Ambiguity (VUCA) are reduced "…by the increased collection of information …with greater transmission and coordination of informational resources…" (Buckley, 2020). Liesch and Welch (2019) make a similar argument. In practical terms, this means linking and integrating the computer systems of GVC buyers and vendors in real-time, so that the exact status of an order under production, as well as a vendor's schedules, are instantly available and transparent to the MNE or importer. Second, in transit across borders, 5G and satellite technology will further pinpoint the tracking of shipments (Rundle, 2020). Third, Bughin et al. (2017) show the huge – as yet unutilized – potential for the increased use of AI in global scanning and strategic planning, including demand forecasting in various national markets, forecasting and managing political or weather-related risks, input costs and selling prices, and optimization of transport and logistics, as well as culturally-adaptive marketing. These coming information technology advances are poised to reduce risk.

2. *Closer relationships between suppliers and buyers*: Verbeke (2020) and Kano (2018) suggest that even stronger joint "relational governance", accompanied by a willingness to be flexible when disruptions threaten GVCs, can further handle risk by substituting for, or augmenting, the digitized information flows discussed above. This echoes somewhat with the rather venerable concept of "keiretsu" in Japanese supply chains, where interfirm cooperation, homophily, and a familial relationship were aided by symbolically small cross-shareholdings between the focal firm and its constellation of suppliers (e.g., Lincoln, Gerlach, & Takahashi, 1992).

3. *Marginal increase in the diversification of input and assembly-point sources*: As a reaction to perceived risks, diversification is likely to be manifested in a slight *increase* in the numbers of vendors, alliance partners and source nations, per MNE. Buckley (2020) alludes to the greater flexibility this diversification provides by increasing the size of the "portfolio" of partners, especially if each partner has versatile and flexibly deployable assets, and the entire partner network is willing to share information for mutual efficiency. As proposed above in the J-curve paradigm (see Figure 1), the marginal increase in sources can increase costs per unit procured – *ceteris paribus*. However, even that unit cost increase is conditional upon minimum economies of production scale compared with the various sizes of the national markets the MNE serves. Moreover, if the incremental vendor added is closer to the

customer, the increase in the average unit production labor cost can be offset by the shorter logistical distance – for example, the partial substitution of a Mexican assembly operation (average distance 1629 km) instead of Chinese production (average distance 11,671 km).

Risk can also decrease with the use of alliance partners in R&D. The increased complexity of development and finished product design means that even large MNEs do not possess internally sufficient knowledge or efficiency for all aspects of research. The R&D portion of the value chain is increasingly "dis-internalized" and slices of the development process shared with partners. This results in speedier and lower-cost results; moreover, developmental risks are shared and reduced for the focal MNE (Contractor et al., 2010). Occasionally, valuable novel or idiosyncratic ideas can be accessed by including innovation partners in emerging nations (Ramamurti, 2016).

4. *A weighted-average decrease in "distance"*: This can be measured multidimensionally as per Berry, Guillén and Zhou (2010) in terms of cultural, political, and geographical distances between the MNE and its network partners). In addition, the GVC network will see (only a partial) locational shift or decoupling between US MNEs and Chinese sources. For example, Ha & Phuc (2019) show the benefit derived by Vietnam from the relocation of sourcing from China as a result of the Trump tariffs. However, that geographical shift had begun years earlier in reaction to rising Chinese labor rates.[24]

5. *Common standards – The hidden plumbing of globalization*: Imagine a world where each town maintained its own local time, where dimensions, voltages, current, nomenclature, and symbols varied not just from one country to another but from one firm to another. International trade, coordination, and competition were severely limited. Such a world prevailed until the International Meridian Conference of 1884 divided the world into 24 time zones, and in the year 1901 when the Engineering Standards (International) Committee met in London to begin to formulate common technical standards.

Internationally adopted standards lower risk by reducing information asymmetries, providing transparency, comparability, interoperability, scale advantages, and accountability, and supplying a common technical language that facilitates global commerce. Technology standards "…directly affect at least 80percent of international trade," according to Purcell, Kushnier and Law (2016).

I do not aver that common standards cause or trigger globalization. Rather, common technical standards are a necessary precondition and concomitant of globalization – its hidden plumbing. A technological civilization cannot exist without the world, or at least large enough coalitions of firms, adopting common standards. In a quiet, unheralded way under the aegis of organizations such as the ISO (International Organization for Standardization) and the World Bank, cross-border industry conferences and multinational committees have quietly hammered out jointly acceptable protocols on almost the entire range of products and services, from clinical trials[25] (Idänpään-Heikkilä, 1994), to air traffic (International Civil Aviation Guidelines), to financial transactions and remittances, to satellite and GPS receivers, to mobile telephony, to phytosanitary standards in food, horticulture, and medicine (Ramakrishnan, 2016), to insurance, to cybersecurity (Wilkins, 2020), to piping and instrumentation, to smart buildings, to corporate social responsibility (CSR), and to ethics (Nadvi, 2008), etc. A complete list of products and services under international standards would require thousands of pages.

A huge boost to the global expansion of trade occurred in 1965 when, after a three-year negotiation, ISO delegates from a dozen nations finalized the design of standardized shipping containers, resulting in an at least three-quarters reduction in freight and insurance costs, compared with the old system of "breakbulk freight", or the loading of individual cargo of miscellaneous shapes and sizes into the belly of a ship (Levinson, 2020).

The standardization process is not only incomplete, but, with new developments and accelerating technical growth, international standardization will be even more needed in the future.

CONCLUSIONS

After the pandemic, the "new normal" may be marginally different, but globalization in its various manifestations will continue, and global coordination will be even more important for collective intergovernmental action to meet future pandemics, climate change, emerging technologies, and international tax-avoidance, to set common product and technical standards, and to address the growing sensitivity of customers worldwide to sustainability, ethics, and CSR issues.

A greater degree of nationalism and protectionism need not impede FDI and in some cases may even increase it by inducing more tariff-jumping investments. Alliances such as international joint ventures and contractual alliances such as licensing of intellectual property, circumvent protectionism, and substitute for exports or FDI as a means of reaching foreign customers. In fact, over 1990–2019, licensing royalties (and the foreign sales resulting from the transfer of intellectual assets) have been the fastest-growing method of international business (10.13percent compound annual growth rate or CAGR) versus world exports (6.62percent CAGR) versus FDI flows (6.37percent CAGR).[26] In comparing the global strategic importance of FDI, trade, and licensing (loose contractual alliances), scholars have to be careful with the raw numbers. All three foreign market entry alternatives are biased by international tax avoidance, double-counting, and under-reporting biases. Nevertheless, it is clear that all three international business indicators have grown at a faster rate than the average growth rate of GDP (4.9percent CAGR). This illustrates the value and continued rationale for cross-border commerce, and the unique role played by the MNE as an agent that aggregates demand and arbitrages differences across nations, as well as orchestrates and conduits the cross-border flows of capital (FDI), goods and services (trade), and intellectual assets (in affiliates and in contractual sharing of knowledge and capabilities with licensing and alliance partners).

The art of global management has always been to seek the optimum middle ground between integration and fragmentation, between standardization and adaptation, and between resilience or assurance on the one hand and efficiency/cost reduction on the other. The global manager knows how to manage risk. In MNEs and governments, there will be a greater awareness of political and GVC risks. However, at the same time, this article has highlighted several risk-reducing methods and emerging technologies whereby global risks can be ameliorated. A small or marginal increase in surge or spare capacity (for "strategic" items), a small increase in inventories at point-of-demand, and the number of suppliers can slightly increase procurement costs per unit.

On the other hand, these incremental costs can be reduced or avoided altogether by implementing better information-gathering systems, 5G surveillance and monitoring, blockchain and other integration of vendor–buyer computer systems, AI-based demand and inventory prediction, relationship-based alliances (Kano & Oh, 2020), and the continuing evolution and consensus on common technical and governance standards.

One should not overstate the current rift between the US and China as a portent of the business environment to come. In certain technologies, such as 5G, there may indeed be an unfortunate bifurcation of technical standards. However, overall, the "Brussels Effect"[27] is likely to play a more powerful, albeit quiet role in shaping global commerce (Bradford, 2020). EU rules and standards, adopted around the world, on issues ranging from green technology, data protection

(GDPR), antitrust and competition rules, ethics, international law, arbitration, and technical standards ranging from AI to zucchini[28] (and to a lesser extent California standards) exert a disproportionate extraterritorial influence leading to "harmonization" and a lower-risk strategic planning environment.

We are building a global technological civilization, undergirded by common understandings, consensus, and cooperation. History has had examples of U-turns. The glories of Rome, Chang An, and Pataliputra were followed by some darker periods. However, today, the cross-border flow of information, spread of education, literacy, knowledge, and technology have progressed to a global scope and developed a nascent global consciousness, which makes it more difficult (although not impossible) for regression. The post-pandemic world is likely to need, and witness, even more globalization.

NOTES

[1]Individual examples can easily be found where the direct and indirect costs of an international investment project, or a particular kind of trade, are higher than the benefits it produces. However, that does not obviate the unequivocal overall net benefits produced by globalization. Admittedly also, the net benefits produced by globalization are not shared equally across nations, some of which may have had their industrialization stage in economic development prematurely aborted by the shift of manufacturing to more dynamic producers like China (Rodrik, 2016; Larson et al., 2016), as well as the general shift to a services-based global economy (Levinson, 2020). However, these are not issues pursued in this Point article.

[2]From World Bank data: https://data.worldbank.org/indicator/BX.KLT.DINV.CD.WD. And, of course, the numbers for 2020, and a year or two following, are likely to represent a significant drop.

[3]The number of MNEs from the Fortune Global 500 list, deemed by the authors to be "global," increased from a count of 9 in 2004 to 36 firms in 2017, using their perhaps overly stringent criterion that a global firm must have "at least 20percent of their sales in all three regions of the triad, but less than 50percent in any one region." This does not measure sales of a company's products worldwide through trade, contractual alliances, and minority equity joint ventures, all of which are not separately counted in UNCTAD or World Bank data. Nevertheless, Rugman & Verbeke's (2004) overall conclusion is correct, that most MNEs principally serve their home and contiguous regions.

[4]https://data.worldbank.org/indicator/BX.GSR.ROYL.CD.

[5]Most royalties are linked by a formula as a percentage of sales achieved by the licensee/alliance partner. Compared to the profit of a FDI affiliate, licensee sales are axiomatically far less volatile, for two reasons/ First, sales of any firm are far less volatile than profits. Secondly, royalties are steady because the

agreement remains in force for the number of years of the alliance agreement. Returns from licensing out intellectual assets are hence intrinsically steadier and more assured compared with foreign affiliate dividends. FDI flows are also more volatile and sensitive to business cycles, because a FDI involves a conscious initial investment decision, made in return for the expected discounted cash flow of future affiliate profits. Hence FDI falls off in recessionary periods.

[6]The latter figure is an overestimate. However, unfortunately we have no comprehensive information on international royalty rates, this being a gaping data hole in international business and economics studies. We only have some sketchy figures from consultants (e.g., Podlogar, 2018). Using the typical "reasonable" average royalty rate of 5percent, touted by licensing negotiators, by dividing the royalty remittances by a factor of 0.05, we get an estimate for foreign licensee sales stemming from licensed intellectual property at $7945 billion. This is smaller than "World Exports (i.e., Sales)" or "Sales by MNEs Outside Their Home Country". Nevertheless, licensing of intellectual assets constitutes an inescapably important, albeit neglected, component of global strategy.

[7]Undoubtedly, a tiny minority of FDI cases produce negative effects on the host country. However, that does not obviate the overall conclusion of the beneficial impact of FDI.

[8]Of course, there are some net costs of international business and globalization. However, these are, on average, more than offset by the benefits.

[9]This argument sounds similar to the advantage of larger firm size, except that the MNE, by expanding abroad, transcends or escapes the operational size limitation that constrains domestic competitors. Also, this paragraph addresses the benefits of size or global scale but with a specific focus on the amortization of R&D and central overheads in the MNE as opposed to scale economies in production, where factory-level fixed costs, spread over more units of output, reduce average cost per production unit.

[10]Easy scalability, accompanied by network effects, can also occasionally lead to oligopolies and monopolies, as we see in digital services such as Google or Facebook (e.g., Smyrnaios, 2018). However, this is not a widespread phenomenon and is not the focus of this article.

[11]The author, despite many searches, has been unable to find a Supply Chain Management paper where the cost per unit of procurement has been theorized or mapped as a function of the number of supply sources. This is likely a research opportunity.

[12]For US-based firms, the inventory-to-sales ratio had been declining since 1981 but then increased from a low of 1.25 in 2010 to 1.39 in June 2020 according to the US Census Bureau. https://www.census.gov/mtis/www/data/pdf/mtis_current.pdf.

[13]Again, the author has been unable to find papers that go in this direction, in which case this is a research opportunity for Supply Chain Management or IB scholars.

[14]With rising geo-political tensions, perhaps the most noticeable changes in global GVCs will be for supply sources from China, where the plateauing labor force has also seen labor costs escalate at well above China's inflation rate between 2010 and 2020.

[15]Estimates can range up to an unlikely $19 trillion, depending on our assumption of the global average royalty rate, which is unknown.

[16]The data have to be interpreted with great circumspection, however, because of double-counting and interrelatedness. UNCTAD (2013) estimated that a multinational firm functioning as either exporter or importer was involved in three-quarters of world trade. Some reports suggest that intrafirm trade is 40percent of the world total. In the licensing or contractual alliance category, an unknown fraction of deals, for tax-avoidance reasons, are between a MNE and its own foreign affiliate as licensee. All said, the MNE plays a dominant role in all three modes of foreign entry.

[17]The upgrading of standards may be weaker, but only in some cases, when FDI is between emerging nations. For example, the literature on Chinese FDI in Africa admits that there is an overall economic benefit, but takes a more circumspect view of managerial and HRM practices used by Chinese managers within their affiliates and projects in Africa (e.g., Jackson, 2014).

[18]Many IB scholars still seem to be not fully aware that IJVs are today covered by as detailed and long an agreement as in contractual or "non-equity" alliances, both of which are based on the letter of the agreement, as well as the relationship, although the relationship is, on average, stronger and deeper in IJVs than in contractual alliances (Velez-Calle, 2018; Contractor & Reuer, 2019). Both lie along a spectrum that can be described as "quasi-internalization."

[19]The various aspects and nuances of nationalism are a complex subject which deserves a more richly textured analysis than can possibly be covered in this article.

[20]What comprises "national security" is of course open to question and to political considerations.

[21]The word "China" is not seen in the first 771 words of the introduction to Petricevic and Teece's (2019) paper. However, "China" then occurs as many as 224 times throughout the rest of their article.

[22]In the largest 20 Chinese investments between 2009 and 2017 which exceeded $2 billion, aircraft leasing and food (pork) companies were the two biggest American targets, others including innocuous sectors such as entertainment, textiles, tourism, real estate, and consumer white goods. In the top-20 list, there were four technology companies, but these included peripherals such as printers (Lexmark) and personal computers (IBM personal computer division purchased by Lenovo).

[23]Of course, the numbers do not include prospective Chinese investments that may not have been initiated in the first place, because of fear of refusal.

[24]For the foreseeable post-pandemic future, the shift away from Chinese sources is likely to be small, partial and manageable because (1) other nations like Vietnam do not have as large a labor pool, (2) to some extent, rising Chinese labor costs have already been offset by the greater use of automation in Chinese factories, (3) it is not easy to replicate the sub-contractor and knowledge clusters in Chinese cities that have specialized in certain product types, and (4) the anti-China animus in the US and some other nations may not escalate further.

[25]Good clinical practice guidelines developed by the International Conference on Harmonization and first published in May 1996.

[26]World Bank Data: data.worldbank.org.

[27]While the US federal government has, at least temporarily, abdicated its role as an exemplar and standard setter, the European Union (EU) has quietly had a big impact in establishing standards of corporate conduct and trade, as well as technology.

[28]The EU name for zucchini is "courgette."

[29]https://data.worldbank.org/indicator/BX.GSR.ROYL.CD.

REFERENCES

Abdelal, R. 2020. Of learning and forgetting: Centrism, populism, and the legitimacy crisis of globalization. In *Harvard business school, working paper 21-008*, July.

Abe, Y., Javorcik, B., & Kodama, N. 2016. Multinationals and female employment: Japanese evidence. *Centre for Economic Policy Research*. https://voxeu.org/article/multinationals-and-female-employment-japanese-evidence.

Ahlvik, C., Smale, A., & Sumelius, J. 2016. Aligning corporate transfer intentions and subsidiary HRM practice implementation in multinational corporations. *Journal of World Business*, 51(3): 343–355. **Article Google Scholar**

Altman, S., & Bastian, P. 2019. *DHL Global Connectedness Index 2019 Update*, Bonn, DHL and NYU Stern School of Business

American Enterprise Institute. 2020. *China global investment tracker*. https://www.aei.org/wp-content/uploads/2020/07/US-China-Tracker_July-2020.xlsx.

Aylor, B., DeFauw, M., Gilbert, M., Knizek, C., Lang, N., Koch-Weser, J. & McAdoo, M. 2020. *Redrawing the map of global trade*. Boston Consulting Group, July 20, Boston https://www.bcg.com/publications/2020/redrawing-the-map-of-global-trade?utm_medium=Email&utm_source=esp&utm_campaign=none&utm_description=ealert&utm_topic=none&utm_geo=global&utm_content=202008&utm_usertoken=ea5d31c9eface5908574b9100817aff75d5a50a0.

Baldwin, R., & Tomiura, E. 2020. Thinking ahead about the trade impact of COVID-19. *Economics in the Time of COVID-19* (pp. 59–72).

Berghuis, E., & den Butter, F. A. 2017. The transaction costs perspective on international supply chain management; evidence from case studies in the manufacturing industry in the

Netherlands. *International Review of Applied Economics,* 31(6): 754–773. **Article Google Scholar**

Berry, H., Guillén, M. F., & Zhou, N. 2010. An institutional approach to cross-national distance. *Journal of International Business Studies,* 41(9): 1460–1480. **Article Google Scholar**

Bradford, A. 2020. *The Brussels effect: How the European Union rules the world.* Oxford: Oxford University Press. **Google Scholar**

Buckley, P. J. 2020. The theory and empirics of the structural reshaping of globalization. *Journal of International Business Studies,* 51: 1580–1592.

Buckley, P. J., & Casson, M. C. 1976. *The future of the multinational enterprise.* London: Macmillan. **Google Scholar**

Buckley, P.J., Clegg, J., Zheng, P., Siler, P.A., & Giorgioni, G. 2010. The impact of foreign direct investment on the productivity of China's automotive industry. In *Foreign direct investment, China and the world economy*: 284–304. London: Palgrave Macmillan.

Bughin, J., Hazan, E., Ramaswamy, S., Chu, M., Allas, T., Dahlström, P., Henke, N., & Trench, M. 2017. Artificial intelligence the next digital frontier? In *McKinsey Global Institute, discussion paper 47*. June.

Cantwell, J. 2015. *The eclectic paradigm: A framework for synthesizing and comparing theories of international business from different disciplines or perspectives.* London: Palgrave Macmillan. **Google Scholar**

Caves, R. E. 1974. Multinational firms, competition, and productivity in host-country markets. *Economica,* 41(162): 176–193. **Article Google Scholar**

Chandler, A. D., & Hikino, T. 2009. *Scale and scope: The dynamics of industrial capitalism.* Cambridge: Harvard University Press. **Google Scholar**

Chen, H., Frank, M. Z., & Wu, O. Q. 2005. What actually happened to the inventories of American companies between 1981 and 2000? *Management Science,* 51(7): 1015–1031. **Article Google Scholar**

Contractor, F. J. 2019. Can a firm find the balance between openness and secrecy? Towards a theory of an optimum level of disclosure. *Journal of International Business Studies,* 50(2): 261–274. **Article Google Scholar**

Contractor, F. J., Dangol, R., Nuruzzaman, N., & Raghunath, S. 2020. How do country regulations and business environment impact foreign direct investment (FDI) inflows? *International Business Review,* 29(2): 101640. **Article Google Scholar**

Contractor, F. J., Kumar, V., Kundu, S. K., & Pedersen, T. 2010. Reconceptualizing the firm in a world of outsourcing and offshoring: The organizational and geographical relocation of high-value company functions. *Journal of Management Studies,* 47(8): 1417–1433. **Article Google Scholar**

Contractor, F. J., & Reuer, J. J. 2019. *Frontiers of alliance research.* Cambridge: Cambridge University Press. **Google Scholar**

Dresden, M. & Xia, S. 2020. How China's new foreign investment law affects you (or not) China Law Blog, (February 24), https://www.chinalawblog.com/2020/02/how-chinas-new-foreign-investment-law-affects-you-or-not.html.

Dunning, J. H. 2015. The eclectic paradigm of international production: A restatement and some possible extensions. In *The eclectic paradigm*: 50–84. London: Palgrave Macmillan.

Ferreira, W. & Rosales, A. 2020. International telemedicine: A global regulatory challenge. In: *Hogan Lovells*, March 9. https://www.lexology.com/library/detail.aspx?g=f2d9946b-e5c3-43f5-b813-9528e23afbda.

Fontaine, R. 2020. Globalization will look very different after the coronavirus pandemic. In: *Foreign policy*, April 17. https://foreignpolicy.com/2020/04/17/globalization-trade-war-after-coronavirus-pandemic/.

Foss, N. J., & Pedersen, T. 2019. Microfoundations in international management research: The case of knowledge sharing in multinational corporations. *Journal of International Business Studies,* 50(9): 1594–1621. **Article Google Scholar**

Frazzon, E., Albrecht, A., Pires, M., Israel, E., Kück, M., & Freitag, M. 2018. Hybrid approach for the integrated scheduling of production and transport processes along supply chains. *International Journal of Production Research,* 56(5): 2019–2035. **Article Google Scholar**

Ghemawat, P. 2007. Managing differences: The central challenge of global strategy. *Harvard Business Review,* 85(3): 58–68. **Google Scholar**

Glennon, B. 2020. How do restrictions on high-skilled immigration affect offshoring? Evidence from the H-1B Program (Wharton School Working Paper, February 21, 2020). Available at SSRN: https://ssrn.com/abstract=3547655 or http://dx.doi.org/10.2139/ssrn.3547655.

Grosse, R., & Fonseca, A. 2012. Learning through imports in the internationalization process. *Journal of International Management,* 18(4): 366–378. **Article Google Scholar**

Gunasekaran, A., Subramanian, N., & Papadopoulos, T. 2017. Information technology for competitive advantage within logistics and supply chains: A review. *Transportation Research Part E: Logistics and Transportation Review*, 99: 14–33. **Article Google Scholar**

Ha, L.T., & Phuc, N.D. 2019. The US-China trade war: Impact on Vietnam. In *Asian Development Bank Yusof Ishak Institute working paper*. http://hdl.handle.net/11540/11697.

Idänpään-Heikkilä, J. E. 1994. WHO guidelines for good clinical practice (GCP) for trials on pharmaceutical products: Responsibilities of the investigator. *Annals of Medicine,* 26(2): 89–94. **Article Google Scholar**

Ivanov, D., & Dolgui, A. 2020. Viability of intertwined supply networks: extending the supply chain resilience angles towards survivability. A position paper motivated by COVID-19 outbreak. *International Journal of Production Research,* 58(10): 2904–2915. **Article Google Scholar**

Jackson, T. 2014. Employment in Chinese MNEs: Appraising the dragon's gift to sub-Saharan Africa. *Human Resource Management,* 53(6): 897–919. **Article Google Scholar**

Jackson, J. 2020. The committee on foreign investment in the United States (CFIUS). In *Congressional research service*, Washington, D.C. https://fas.org/sgp/crs/natsec/RL33388.pdf.

Johnson, T. (Ed.). 2017. *Globalization and the ethical responsibilities of multinational corporations: Emerging research and opportunities.* Hershey, PA: IGI Global. **Google Scholar**

Jude, C. & Levieuge, G. 2015. Growth effect of FDI in developing economies: The role of institutional quality. In *Banque de France working paper no. 559.* https://papers.ssrn.com/sol3/papers.cfm?abstract_id=2620698.

Kamilaris, A., Fonts, A., & Prenafeta-Boldú, F. X. 2019. The rise of blockchain technology in agriculture and food supply chains. *Trends in Food Science & Technology,* 91: 640–652. **Article Google Scholar**

Kano, L. 2018. Global value chain governance: A relational perspective. *Journal of International Business Studies,* 49(6): 684–705. **Article Google Scholar**

Kano, L., & Oh, C. H. 2020. Global value chains in the post-COVID world: Governance for reliability. *Journal of Management Studies,* 57: 1773–1777. https://doi.org/10.1111/joms.12626. **Article Google Scholar**

Katsikeas, C. S., Samiee, S., & Theodosiou, M. 2006. Strategy fit and performance consequences of international marketing standardization. *Strategic Management Journal,* 27(9): 867–890. **Article Google Scholar**

Kostova, T., & Roth, K. 2002. Adoption of organizational practice by subsidiaries of multinational corporations: Institutional and relational effects. *Academy of Management Journal,* 45(1): 215–233. **Google Scholar**

Kumar, N. 2013. Managing reverse knowledge flow in multinational corporations. *Journal of Knowledge Management,* 17(5): 695–708. **Article Google Scholar**

Larson, G.M., Loayza, N., & Woolcock, M. 2016. The middle-income trap: myth or reality? In *World bank research and policy briefs*, March 2016.

Larson, B., Vroman, S., & Makarius, E. 2020. *A guide to managing your (newly) remote workers.* Brighton: Harvard Business Review. **Google Scholar**

Levinson, M. 2020. *Outside the box: How globalization changed from moving stuff to spreading ideas*. Princeton: Princeton University Press. **Google Scholar**

Liesch, P. W., & Welch, L. S. 2019. The Firms of Our Times: Risk and Uncertainty. In *International business in a VUCA world: The changing role of states and firms (progress in international business research, vol. 14)*: 41–53. Emerald.

Lincoln, J. R., Gerlach, M. L., & Takahashi, P. 1992. Keiretsu networks in the Japanese economy: A dyad analysis of intercorporate ties. *American Sociological Review,* 57: 561–585. **Article Google Scholar**

Lund, S., Manyika, J., Woetzel, J., Barriball, E., Krishnan, M., Alicke, K., Birshan, M., George, K., Smit, S., Swan, D., & Hutzler, K. 2020. *Risk, resilience, and rebalancing in global value chains*. McKinsey Global Institute. https://www.mckinsey.com/business-functions/operations/our-insights/risk-resilience-and-rebalancing-in-global-value-chains#.

Marcon, A., de Medeiros, J. F., & Ribeiro, J. L. D. 2017. Innovation and environmentally sustainable economy: Identifying the best practices developed by multinationals in Brazil. *Journal of Cleaner Production,* 160: 83–97. **Article Google Scholar**

Miroudot, S. 2020. Resilience versus robustness in global value chains: Some policy implications. In *COVID-19 and trade policy: Why turning inward won't work*: 117–130. VoxEU/CEPR. https://voxeu.org/article/resilience-versus-robustness-global-value-chains.

Monteiro, L. F., Arvidsson, N., & Birkinshaw, J. 2008. Knowledge flows within multinational corporations: Explaining subsidiary isolation and its performance implications. *Organization Science,* 19(1): 90–107. **Article Google Scholar**

Moran, T., Graham, E., & Blomström, M. 2005. *Does foreign direct investment promote development?* New York: Columbia University Press. **Google Scholar**

Nadvi, K. 2008. Global standards, global governance and the organization of global value chains. *Journal of Economic Geography,* 8(3): 323–343. **Article Google Scholar**

Petricevic, O., & Teece, D. J. 2019. The structural reshaping of globalization: Implications for strategic sectors, profiting from innovation, and the multinational enterprise. *Journal of International Business Studies,* 50(9): 1487–1512. **Article Google Scholar**

Podlogar, E. 2018. Intellectual property trends: Average royalty rates, most active industries, and more. In *BVR/ktMINE royalty rate benchmarking guide* (Chapter 18). https://www.bvresources.com/blogs/intellectual-property-news/2018/04/18/intellectual-property-trends-average-royalty-rates-most-active-industries-and-more.

Prud'homme, D. 2019. Re-conceptualizing intellectual property regimes in international business research: Foreign-friendliness paradoxes facing MNCs in China. *Journal of World Business,* 54(4): 399–419. **Article Google Scholar**

Purcell, D., Kushnier, G. & Law, D. 2016. Globalization and standardization. *IEEE Standards University.* August. https://www.standardsuniversity.org/e-magazine/august-2016-volume-6/globalization-and-standardization/.

Ramakrishnan, K. 2016. From local to global ambitions: The benefits of standards compliance. In *World bank blog,* July 5. https://blogs.worldbank.org/trade/local-global-ambitions-benefits-standards-compliance.

Ramamurti, R. 2016. Internationalization and innovation in emerging markets. *Strategic Management Journal,* 37(13): 74–83. **Article Google Scholar**

Rodrik, D. 2016. Premature deindustrialization. *Journal of Economic Growth,* 21(1): 1–33. **Article Google Scholar**

Rosa, B., Gugler, P., & Verbeke, A. 2004. Regional and global strategies of MNEs: Revisiting Rugman and Verbeke. *Journal of International Business Studies,* 51: 1045–1053. **Article Google Scholar**

Roy, R. 2020. India's leader calls for economic self-sufficiency, promises relief. *Wall Street Journal,* May 12.

Rugman, A. M., & Verbeke, A. 2004. A perspective on regional and global strategies of multinational enterprises. *Journal of International Business Studies,* 35(1): 3–18. **Article Google Scholar**

Rundle, J. 2020. 5G promises radical overhaul for supply chains. *Wall Street Journal,* April 12, https://www.wsj.com/articles/5g-promises-radical-overhaul-for-supply-chains-11586556432.

Schmidt, C. G., & Wagner, S. M. 2019. Blockchain and supply chain relations: A transaction cost theory perspective. *Journal of Purchasing and Supply Management,* 25(4): 100552. **Article Google Scholar**

Sherman, E. 2020. 94percent of the Fortune 1000 are seeing coronavirus supply chain disruptions, *Fortune*, February 21.

Smyrnaios, N. 2018. *Internet oligopoly: The corporate takeover of our digital world*. Bingley: Emerald. **Google Scholar**

Swenson, D. L., & Chen, H. 2014. Multinational exposure and the quality of new Chinese exports. *Oxford Bulletin of Economics and Statistics,* 76(1): 41–66. **Article Google Scholar**

Tilley, A. 2020. Zoom targets prolonged remote-work era as coronavirus drags on. *Wall Street Journal*, July 15.

UNCTAD. 2013. *World investment report 2013: Global value chains: Investment and trade for development*. New York: United Nations. **Google Scholar**

UNCTAD 2019. Investment policy monitor no. 22. (December). https://unctad.org/en/PublicationsLibrary/diaepcbinf2019d8_en.pdf.

UNCTAD. 2020. *World investment report 2020: International production beyond the pandemic*. New York: United Nations. **Google Scholar**

Velez-Calle, A. 2018. *Joint venture governance: A dissection of agreements and their anatomy*. Doctoral dissertation, Rutgers University-Graduate School-Newark.

Verbeke, A. 2020. Will the COVID-19 pandemic really change the governance of global value chains? *British Journal of Management,* 31(3): 444–446. **Article Google Scholar**

Verbeke, A., Coeurderoy, R., & Matt, T. 2018. The future of international business research on corporate globalization that never was…". *Journal of International Business Studies* 49: 1101–1112. **Article Google Scholar**

Waldman, D., & Javidan, M. 2020. *The false dichotomy between globalism and nationalism*. Brighton: Harvard Business Review. **Google Scholar**

Wang, Z. & Quan, S. 2019. How China is drawing on its own history to champion globalisation, peace and prosperity. *South China Morning Post*. October 3. https://www.scmp.com/comment/opinion/article/3031131/how-china-drawing-its-own-history-champion-globalisation-peace-and.

Wilkins, M. 2020. What is the value of industry standards in Today's world? ARC advisory group, https://www.arcweb.com/blog/what-value-industry-standards-todays-world.

Witt, M. A. 2019. De-globalization: Theories, predictions, and opportunities for international business research. *Journal of International Business Studies,* 50(7): 1053–1077. **Article Google Scholar**

World Bank. 2019. *Doing business 2020*. Washington, DC: World Bank. **Google Scholar**

World Bank. 2020. Charges for the use of intellectual property, receipts (BoP, current US$). https://data.worldbank.org/indicator/BX.GSR.ROYL.CD.

Young, J. 2020. China, Covid-19 and the end of globalisation as we knew it. *MSN Newsroom*, April 10. https://www.msn.com/en-nz/news/other/china-covid-19-and-the-end-of-globalisation-as-we-knew-it/ar-BB12s5Vp.

Author information

Farok J. Contractor
Corresponding author

Management and Global Business Department, Rutgers Business School, Rutgers University, 1 Washington Park, Newark, NJ, 07102, USA
Correspondence to Farok J. Contractor.

Additional information

Accepted by Alain Verbeke, Editor-in-Chief, 27 October 2020.

APPENDIX

IDEAS FOR FURTHER RESEARCH STEMMING FROM THIS CHAPTER

(1) Seeking the Optimal Balance Between "Resilience" of Global Value Chains (GVC) and Overall Procurement Costs.

As Figure 1 indicates, GVC resilience can be operationalized using four variables: (1) the number of vendors for the same component or item, (2) geographical diversification of supply sources to several countries, (3) propinquity of supply sources, in terms of both geographical and political "distance", and (4) increase in inventory levels at the points of use. This lowers risk (from left to right in the dashed lines in Figure 1 exhibiting a negative slope) and increases resilience. However (1) through (4) also could represent an increase in procurement cost per unit.

- How do companies arrive at a balance between these contrary considerations?
- How are the four measures to be operationalized? What weightage should be given to each of the variables?

- Focusing only on two variables: is the nexus between Procurement Cost Per Unit and Number of Suppliers a J-curve? If so, how does the J-curve vary depending on product or sector?

   This represents a research opportunity to international business and supply chain scholars, as well as being a fundamental post-Covid-19 question for companies.

(2) Propinquity of GVCs.

It has been hypothesized that the shock of the pandemic will, to some extent, make GVCs more "regional", and that MNEs will trim excessively long-distance sources of supply. While it is unlikely that there will be large-scale reshoring (Miroudot, 2020) or substantial decoupling, as suggested by Petricevich & Teece (2019), nevertheless some reduction in geographic coverage could occur. If so, in which sectors, regions or products?

(3) A Microfoundational Approach to Increasing GVC Resilience.

Instead of restructuring value chains, as indicated above, Kano (2018) and Verbeke (2020) suggest a behavioral or micro-foundational approach. They propose a more "relational" interaction between buyer and supplier. That is to say, a stronger and more intimate linkage between the two, accompanied by a willingness to be flexible – with mutual accommodation – in the face of exogenous shocks, would be congruent with the "structural" adjustments suggested in (1) above, and would make the GVC even more resilient.

   Another aspect of strengthening this relationship is technological (Schmidt & Wagner, 2019; Kamilaris et al., 2019). Integration of buyer–seller computer systems, which would give the MNE access to the vendor's servers and help it more closely monitor, in real-time, the status of their orders, reduces uncertainty and helps the MNE's own scheduling of sales and inventories (Frazzon et al., 2018). However, here again, giving such access requires trust, which is a microfoundational or behavioral issue.

(4) Reexamining the Structures and Relationships in Cross-Border Partnerships.

Interfirm relationships (and GVCs are one example) cover a spectrum from purely contractual ordering, or basic patent licensing unaccompanied by any significant interaction between licensor and licensee, all the way to forming an international joint venture where the managers, engineers, and personnel of the partners "rub shoulders" on a daily basis

(Contractor & Reuer, 2019). Much of past alliance literature, unfortunately, has used bifurcated dependent variables such as "Equity" JV (EJV) versus "Non-equity" alliances. This a distortion of reality. Actually, the majority of alliances involve some degree of interaction or relationship. For example, even in a contractual alliance, the licensor, after transferring the intellectual property rights and accompanying "know-how" (or unregistered knowledge), will continue to support and help their licensee, out of self-interest. Even more pertinently, in recent years, EJVs are covered by as detailed, or even more detailed, an agreement as are contractual alliances (Velez-Calle, 2018; Contractor & Reuer, 2019). Research has only partially provided answers to questions such as how to construct or structure an agreement (i.e., with what clauses, depth, and length) depending on the strategic objectives (e.g., resilience, flexibility, irreversibility (Verbeke, 2020), and duration) – questions that occur in a world of increasing interorganizational relationships and supply chains.

(5) The Significance of International Royalty Payments: A Gaping Lacuna in IB Studies.
IB Scholars have long known that, instead of FDI or exporting as a means of achieving sales in foreign markets, the licensing of intellectual assets (registered property such as patents, brands, and copyrights, as well as unregistered trade secrets and tacit "know-how") results in sales by the licensee in the assigned country/territories. These licensee sales can act as a substitute strategy to FDI or trade—in terms of reaching the foreign customer. The licensee pays the licensor royalties, which are typically a percentage of the sales achieved for the licensed item. Even GVC and IJV agreements often have a licensing component because the supplier or partner first needs to receive the legal permission to produce the MNE's designs. Moreover, payment of royalties is most often a deductible expense, reducing the licensee's corporate tax liability.

We know from World Bank and other data that cross-border royalty payments in 2019 amounted to $397.23 billion, and that these have grown faster, over recent decades, than the growth rate of FDI or trade.[29] The $397.23 billion number is not a sales number, it is only royalties, which are a small percentage of the licensees' achieved sales.

Astonishingly, nobody knows the strategic significance of international licensing (in terms of foreign market sales, compared with exporting or FDI affiliate sales) because we have no basis, yet, for estimating the foreign sales that result from the international licensing of intellectual assets. If we assume that the global average royalty rate is 8percent of sales, by dividing 397.23 by 0.08, we obtain an estimate of foreign licensee sales (achieved by international licensing of intellectual assets) of $4965 billion. If, on the other hand we assume a global average royalty rate of 2percent, by dividing 397.23 by 0.02, we arrive at a foreign sales estimate of $19,862 billion (resulting from international licensing). The actual figure is likely somewhere in between. However, we just do not know, because there is no available datum about the global average royalty rate. Either estimate tells us that international licensing is a substantial *substitute* strategy to FDI or trade as a means of serving foreign markets.

However, there is another conundrum. Is licensing really a *substitute* strategy to FDI and trade? Only partially. In many cases, licensing is a *complement* to FDI and trade (as in GVC agreements) and not the main strategic driver. For parties related by ownership such as Parent–Subsidiary or IJV partner–JV company, the licensing portion of the agreement may only be an "add-on" clause for tax-avoidance and legal purposes. On the other hand, when the licensor and licensee are *unrelated* parties, then the royalty payment is based on an arms-length negotiation. Here again, astonishingly, we have no firm idea of the proportions of related party versus arms-length transactions in international business.

This investigation should be of great interest to MNEs, IB scholars, and tax authorities around the world.

CHAPTER 5

Tax Avoidance by Multinational Companies:
Methods, Policies, and Ethics[*]

In 2021–2022, a flood of articles have been published about increased government scrutiny of tax-avoidance tactics – which amount to many hundreds of billions each year. In 2022, more than 130 nations are negotiating a treaty that would narrow the differences in tax rates across nations and impose a minimum tax percentage. But there are no easily understood articles explaining the methods or actual tax-avoidance techniques used by multinational corporations and the government policies that enable them. This chapter provides simple illustrations as to how it is done.

These examples are followed by a discussion of ethics and corporate responsibility. The tax-avoidance phenomenon affects global operations, supply chains, and location decisions, placing this issue directly at the heart of global strategy.

There is no world government or supranational tax authority. Thus, a world fragmented into more than 190 nations (each seeking local optimization of revenues) is in tension with MNCs that look on the entire world as their blank canvas (global optimization) and fall prey to the temptation of using the tax-avoidance practices outlined here.

[*]Contractor, Farok J. Tax avoidance by multinational companies: methods, policies, and ethics. *Rutgers Business Review,* Vol. 1, No. 1, pp. 27–43 (2016): https://rbr.business.rutgers.edu/article/tax-avoidance-multinational-companies-methods-policies-and-ethics. A version was also published in *AIB Insights,* Vol. 16, No. 2 (2016): http://documents.aib.msu.edu/publications/insights/v16n2/v16n2_Article3.pdf. An amplified version of the original article also appeared on *GlobalBusiness.blog* in 2016, updated on August 29, 2018: https://globalbusiness.blog/2018/08/29/tax-avoidance-by-multinational-companies-methods-policies-and-ethics/. Also see related blog posts: "The [2016] G20 Summit in China: An Annual 'Talking Shop?' Or a Potential Bedrock of Global Civilization?" *and* "Tax 'Amnesty' for Multinationals—But Not for Illegal Immigrants."

Introduction: Why This Review of International Tax Issues Should Be Read by Business Executives

To most executives, scholars, and teachers, global taxation may appear to be an obscure topic. But actually, it is central to global decision-making because most foreign direct investment (FDI) and global operations these days are biased by tax considerations. The numbers are huge. For instance, with around $10 trillion worth of world trade being intrafirm

and a similar portion being intermediate (as opposed to finished products or services), it is the multinational firm that gets to decide internally what unit price it will type on its export invoice. No "arms-length" equivalent benchmarks are easily available.

Because of a US tax provision, between $2.1 and $3 trillion in accumulated profits of US multinationals' foreign affiliates have not been repatriated back to the home country. I conservatively estimate that out of the million-odd subsidiaries or foreign **affiliates[1]** of all multinationals listed in the United Nations Conference on Trade and Development (UNCTAD) 2015 database, between 300,000 and 400,000 are shell or dummy companies (firms that have no economic activity except a part-time accountant or a lawyer behind a shining brass nameplate). The entire FDI inflow statistics of major nations such as China or India are biased by the "round-tripping" of local investment masquerading as foreign investment.

Global strategists and international business (IB) scholars grapple with a key dilemma—the tension between a world divided into 190-odd territorial and tax jurisdictions versus the desire of multinational corporation (MNC) executives to look upon the planet as a single economic space within which to optimize by shifting taxable profits, operations, and finance from one country to another. Awareness and sensitivity about international tax avoidance are growing, exemplified by the EU's introduction of a "Tax Avoidance Package" in 2016,[2] and by strident voices on the American right—Trump labeling corporate inversions as "disgusting")[3]—and left—Sanders describing tax avoidance as a "scam." Executives, however, argue that it is their fiduciary duty to maximize shareholder value by taking every advantage of provisions and loopholes available under various countries' laws.

An Overview of Tax-Avoidance Methods and Their Relative Importance

"Inversions" have been much in the news, at least in the US, such as the planned $150 billion merger between New York-based Pfizer and Dublin-based Allergan, torpedoed by the

Obama Administration's new rules in April 2016.[4] In simple terms, an inversion involves a company shifting its corporate headquarters from a higher-tax nation by merging with a firm in a lower-tax jurisdiction, such as Ireland (whose tax rate is 10–12.5 percent). But despite eliciting pseudo-patriotic opprobrium, the number of large inversions has actually been very few, less than 50 since 2000.

The tax-avoidance methods summarized in the examples below, starting with the ones that have the biggest impact, are mostly legal because they use provisions and loopholes granted by the countries involved.

1. Exemption of Foreign Affiliate Income from Additional Home Country Tax

Most advanced nations typically tax multinational home-country operations, but do not additionally tax profits of the company's foreign affiliates (Markle, 2015). This is the biggest tax benefit for multinational companies—being able to pay corporate tax only in each nation where the profits are earned. Some other countries treat the multinationals' worldwide income (home nation as well as foreign) as taxable.

The US used to be an example of this policy, in theory making US companies' foreign affiliate profits *additionally* taxable in the US.[5] No longer. The US now does not additionally tax foreign affiliate profits.

2. Transfer Pricing (Invoice Values)

In international supply chains, multinationals ship goods and services whose unit value, decided by the MNC itself, is often biased by tax considerations. Consider two firms, A and B, both owned by the same MNC. Firm A has been exporting 1,000 items per year to Firm B, invoiced at $1.30 each. But if they are invoiced at $1.80 each, B would then pay A $500 more annually. Firm A's profit would increase, and B's would decrease; but the MNC *as a whole* would increase its after-tax income from $2,250 to $2,325. The idea is simple: pay higher amounts to affiliates where taxes are lower, and show lower values where taxes and/or tariffs are higher. (See Table 1.)

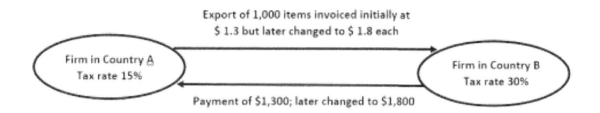

Table 1. Export of 1,000 Items — Payment of $1,300 Changed to $1,800

	Before Change in Transfer Price (Export Shipment Invoiced at $1.30 Each)		After Change in Transfer Price (Export Shipment Invoiced at $1.80 Each)	
	Firm A	Firm B	Firm A	Firm B
	Tax Rate 15%	Tax Rate 30%	Tax Rate 15%	Tax Rate 30%
Pretax Profit	1,000	2,000	1,500	1,500
Tax	150	600	225	450
After-tax Profit	850	1,400	1,275	1,050
Total MNC Profit	$850 + $1,400 = $2,250		$1,275 + $1,050 = $2,325	

No real change has occurred, except for just one keystroke—when typing the invoice, "8" is entered instead of "3" (1.8 instead of 1.3).

The above is only one example. Millions of shipments are made annually—a great many where the exporter and importer are the very same MNC, which can internally decide on the invoice value depending on the tax differential between the import and export nations. Intrafirm trade is huge, estimated to range between 42 and 55 percent of world trade (around $23 trillion). Moreover, much of international trade is not in finished, but in intermediate, products—some with unique designs and embedded proprietary technology—so that no comparative arms-length valuations are possible, and the MNC itself declares the shipment's value (Lanz & Miroudot, 2011).

In the above example, if Firm A's country's tax rate were higher than Firm B's, or if A's country levied an import tariff, then the situation would be reversed: the MNC would be tempted to under-value the shipment to reduce its total worldwide tax and tariff liability.

3. Royalty Payments: Based on Transferring Intellectual Property (Patents or Brands) to Subsidiaries in Low-Tax or Tax-Haven Countries

Tax avoidance through interfirm royalty payments occurs because of three salient facts:

1. Typically, MNCs are technology-intensive, and most value resides in their proprietary technologies or intangible assets.

2. Even if research and development (R&D) costs have been incurred by Firm A (say the home country of the MNC), current rules allow the transfer of the patents or brands to a holding company or subsidiary (in a low-tax country, such as Ireland) or a shell company (in a zero-tax country, such as Bermuda), which then charges royalties to headquarters and other affiliates (Dischinger & Riedel, 2008).

3. Most governments allow deductions for royalty payments, which reduces tax liability to the licensee—even if the licensee is part of the same MNC, and even if no R&D had been performed in the licensee's nation.

First, we will review a simple example of how interfirm royalties reduce tax liability. A Japanese company, having done its R&D in Japan, establishes a subsidiary in the US. In Scenario 1, the US subsidiary pays no royalty for the Japanese technology. In Scenario 2, nothing has changed except that the Japanese parent has signed an additional side agreement with its US subsidiary, which will then pay a 5 percent royalty to its parent. Under US rules, despite the US operation's being the fully owned "child" of its Japanese "parent," the royalty payments are a deductible expense. US tax liability is legally reduced from $90 to $75. And the total remittance (after-taxes) to Japan increases from $210 to $225. (See Table 2.)

94

Less re-investible profits are left in the US operation, and more goes to Japan. The side royalty agreement makes sense if the effective tax rate in Japan (say 20 percent) is less than the US tax rate of 30 percent.

Table 2. Japanese MNC's US Subsidiary Royalties — Scenario 1–No Royalty vs. Scenario 2–5% Royalty

Scenario 1: Japanese MNC's US Subsidiary Pays No Royalty		Scenario 2: Japanese MNC's US Subsidiary Pays 5% Royalty	
Sales by Japanese subsidiary in US	1,000	Sales by Japanese subsidiary in US	1,000
Total costs (no royalties involved)	700	Royalty (at 5% on sales)	50
Profit before tax	300	Total costs (excluding royalties)	700
US tax (at 30%)	90	Profit before tax	250
Profit after US tax	$210	US tax (at 30%)	75
		Profit after US tax	175
		Royalty remittance to Japanese parent	50
		Total remittance to Japanese parent	$225

Even more aggressive moves: transferring patents to low- or zero-corporate-tax nations: What makes even more sense (from an aggressive tax-avoidance point of view) is for the Japanese MNC to transfer the patent rights to its subsidiary in a lower-tax nation, such as Ireland. By making the Irish operation the licensor and collecting the royalties there, they would be taxed at an even lower corporate tax rate − perhaps as low as 10 percent instead of the Japanese tax rate of, say, 20 percent (Mutti & Grubert, 2009).

Even more aggressively, despite the R&D's having been done in Japan or the US, the patent and brands could be transferred to a Bermuda or Cayman Islands affiliate (shell company), as Google, Apple, and many pharmaceutical firms have done. We use the term "shell company" because the MNC's affiliate in those nations do not do any real business (other than collect royalties), and they face no or minimal corporate tax. Making the shell affiliate a (i) Patent Holder and (b) Licensor to other affiliates of the MNC means the other affiliates pay royalties to the shell affiliate – with royalties collected there at near-zero tax liability – while other affiliates that are paying the royalties deduct them as expenses, thus lowering tax liability in the higher-tax nations. (See an example in Figure 1.)

Favorite Money Routing for Large Multinational Companies

1. An advertiser pays money for an ad in Germany.
2. The ad agency sends money to its subsidiary in Ireland, which holds the intellectual property (IP).
3. Tax payable in Ireland is 10 - 12.5 percent, but the Irish company pays a royalty to a Dutch subsidiary, for which it gets an Irish tax deduction.
4. The Dutch company pays the money to yet another subsidiary in Ireland, with no withholding tax on inter-EU transactions.
5. The last subsidiary, although it is in Ireland, pays no tax because it is controlled from outside Ireland, in Bermuda or another tax haven.
6. Money is parked in the tax haven from where it can be used for other global investments.

Source: **Wikipedia, Double Irish arrangement**

Graphic Image by Maxxl2 – Own workNews.com.au, GFDL

Figure 1. Favorite Money Routing for Large MNCs

4. Intracorporate Loans

Another provision governments offer companies is deducting interest payments on loans as an expense item. Indeed, paying interest is an expense for the borrower/payer. But if the lender (source of funds) and borrower are companies within the same MNC, albeit in different nations, then the MNC has a clear path to paying less tax in high-tax jurisdictions—it can make its lower-taxed affiliates extend loans to its affiliates in higher-tax nations and can then enjoy a juicier tax deduction on the interest payment.

FDI flows consist of three components: FDI Flow = New Equity + Retained Earnings + Net Intracorporate Loans. Although we lack comprehensive data on the magnitude of the stock of worldwide intracorporate loans, they would very conservatively exceed three quarters of a trillion dollars (UNCTAD, 2015). We have no comprehensive idea of how many loans are motivated by tax avoidance, and even less about the extent to which the intracorporate interest rate deviates from the actual cost of capital to the lending affiliate or parent. Clearly, if the intracorporate interest rate set by the MNC internally is higher than, or lower than, the actual cost of capital, the MNC has another tax-liability-transference device. In recent years, "…a number of countries have imposed restrictions on the tax deductibility of interest…" (DeMooij, 2011); but the enforcement of rules is lacking, especially in developing nations (Faccio, Lang & Young, 2010).

5. Other Central MNC/Parent Overheads and Costs

An inescapable fact of modern multinational business is that significant costs, especially having to do with R&D, are incurred by the parent firm, which then logically has to charge some fraction of its central overheads to each of its foreign subsidiaries and affiliates (Sikka & Willmott, 2010). For reasons scholars have not fully understood, the R&D expenditures of MNCs remain highly clustered in the parent firm nation, or at least in far fewer countries than the number of territories in which the fruits of the R&D are derived (Belderbos, Leten & Suzuki, 2013).

As we saw in Technique 3 above, charging royalties to each affiliate for centrally developed technology is one technique. But other categories of overheads, such as the costs of maintaining brand equity, and other central administrative costs at headquarters, such as global information technology, supply-chain management, human resources, etc., should not be borne entirely by the parent firm. Rather, they should be spread over the various subsidiaries and foreign operations that enjoy the benefits of the MNC's central administration overheads.

In principle, this sounds fair. But in practice, how does the MNC carve up slices of its central overheads pie and proportionally allocate (charge) a slice to each foreign affiliate? Even trying to be globally equitable (and tax *un*biased) is difficult because the allocation or proportion will vary depending on the weight of each foreign operation (in the planetary total). The calculation depends on whether the weighting for each country is based on numbers of employees, versus value added in the nation, versus assets, and so on.

An obvious further complication is that exchange rates fluctuate, affecting the share of each affiliate in the worldwide total pie from year to year.

But, of course, MNCs are not unbiased. They face a clear temptation, *ceteris paribus*, to allocate a larger slice of the overheads pie to operations in higher-tax nations and *vice versa*. There is no standard methodology. The EU has been attempting, since 2000, to formulate relevant rules for a unitary (pan-European) system for the future. But each formula has its problems and detractors (Picciotto, 2012; Altshuler, Shay & Toder, 2015).

6. Other Uses of Tax Havens: "Round-Tripping" and Evading Currency Convertibility Restrictions

We saw above how tax havens in zero- or low-tax countries such as Bermuda, the British Virgin Islands, or the Cayman Islands can be used to incorporate shell companies. Such companies serve two functions: (1) They can hold the MNC's patent and brand rights. (2) And they can serve as the licensor to collect royalties charged to other affiliates globally—this reduces their taxes because each affiliate claims a deduction in their nation for the royalties paid, while the royalties collect tax-free in the tax haven.

Some tax havens and low-tax nations are used for "round-tripping." According to the Organization of Economic Cooperation and Development (OECD, 2013), as much as 57.4 percent of China's outbound FDI capital in 2011 went to Hong Kong affiliates or subsidiaries, and another 12.7 percent went to Caribbean entities. That means that as much as 70.1 percent of Chinese outbound FDI capital flows, exceeding $100 billion per year since 2011, have gone to two tiny economies—the Caribbean and Hong Kong. (By contrast, Chinese companies' direct FDI outflow to European or US affiliates was a mere 8.2 percent of the Chinese total.)

So, what happened to the 70.1 percent of Chinese outward FDI that went to Hong Kong and the Caribbean? Much of this Chinese money made a round trip, returning to mainland China under the guise of "foreign investment" in order to take advantage of the still slightly better terms (e.g., tax breaks, cheaper land, loans) offered by the Chinese central and provincial governments to "foreign" as opposed to purely "domestic" investors. (See Figure 2.)

Figure 2. China's Outward FDI

China's Outward FDI

How Many Multinationals Are There?

	Parent Firms in That Country	Foreign Affiliates in That Country
Developed Nations	73,144	373,612
Developing Nations	30,209	512,513
-- Of Which China	12,000	434,248
TOTALS	103,786	892,114

Sources: OECD Science, Technology and Industry Scoreboard 2013 and UNCTAD World Investment Report, 2011

Another driver for the Chinese FDI outflow is the desire by Chinese companies and rich individuals to evade currency convertibility restrictions (Contractor, 2015). One cannot convert the Chinese renminbi (RMB) into dollars or euros without a written justification. Creating a dummy subsidiary in Hong Kong or the Caribbean provides that justification, on the grounds that capital has to be sent out to support the Chinese parent's foreign operations.

Note: More recent data at this level of detail are not available. However, the same situation and incentives still exist so that many Hong Kong and Caribbean subsidiaries continue to serve the dual purposes of (1) tax avoidance and (2) overcoming currency convertibility limits.

As a result, UNCTAD (2011) reported an implausible number of Chinese foreign affiliates: as many as 434,248 out of a worldwide total of 892,114 affiliates for all MNCs. One has to conclude that a large majority are shell companies, with no economic activity or purpose other than round-tripping and evasion of capital controls.

It is not just China. For Europe, OECD (2015) reports that such "special purpose entities" (SPEs, or shell companies) account for more than 80 percent of FDI into Luxembourg and the Netherlands, more than 50 percent in Hungary, and more than 30 percent in Austria and Iceland. Around a third of FDI into India used to emanate from Mauritius because the two countries had a tax treaty. (See Figure 3.)

Figure 3. The Prime Ministers of Mauritius and India Seal a Deal

Sources: Simply Decoded and The Economic Times, India

Considering these facts, I conservatively estimate that 30–40 percent of all FDI affiliates worldwide in the UNCTAD World Development Reports or World Bank databases are shell companies—a sobering thought for analysts and scholars using these data. And my estimate may, in fact, be low.

7. Inversions

In simple terms, an inversion involves a company shifting its corporate headquarters to a lower-tax jurisdiction by acquiring/merging with a foreign firm in a lower-tax country. For large multinational companies, the annual savings can be in the billions, as illustrated by the aborted Pfizer (US)-Allergan (Ireland) merger in April 2016.[6] In Ireland, corporate taxes max out at 12.5 percent, which is lower than many advanced nations. Other examples since 2012 include Mylan moving to the Netherlands, Burger King to Canada, and Medtronic to Ireland—all of which had lower tax rates than the US.

Politicians of all stripes labeled inversions as unpatriotic. Announcing rules in April 2016 that make such foreign takeovers much tougher,[7] President Obama described inversions as "insidious" and added that "…fleeing the country just to get out of paying their taxes… [American MNCs] benefit from our research and our development and our patents. They benefit from American workers, who are the best in the world. But they effectively renounce their citizenship."[8]

For all the political bluster and opprobrium, the numbers of inversions have been very few, and now after 2018 with reduced tax rates in the US, they are likely to be very rare. For the US, six were completed in 2015, up from four in each of the previous two years. (See Figure 4.) As long as MNCs have the perception that home nation taxes are higher than in other nations, inversions will continue in the future.

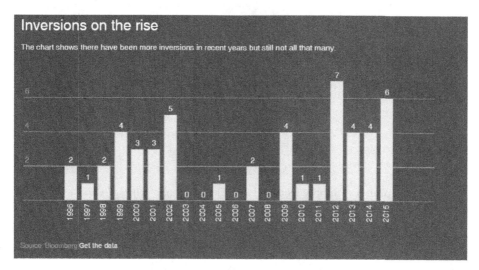

Figure 4. US Corporate Inversions

Source: **Bloomberg** *via* **The Conversation:**
Crackdown on corporate inversions highlights monstrosity of U.S. tax code, April 20, 2016

How Good Are Government Enforcement and Audits?

There is an awakening realization (at present confined to the EU and OECD Secretariats) that a considerable disconnect exists between the desire of governments to collect reasonable revenues from companies in each territory or region (local optimization) and the desire of MNCs to ensure shareholder interests by "arranging" investments, supply chains, and invoices to minimize global tax payments (global optimization).

What about audits? Despite nascent intergovernmental cooperation and exchange of information, for the most part governments can audit tax filings only within their own territories. Even in terms of "audits," governments face a stark practical reality. Each year, for the world as a whole, multinational companies and their affiliates file around one million tax returns. In all the governments on the planet—including rich countries such as the US, Japan, and Europe—there cannot be more than a couple of thousand auditors or inspectors that view or scrutinize MNC returns.

Only a very tiny percentage of tax filings are read by a human (although some advanced nation governments use special artificial intelligence software programs, or algorithms, that flag anomalies or egregious outliers). There is no "world tax authority," and even the exchange of information between governments is only just a trickle. This means that MNCs can, and do, push the envelope to minimize global tax payments, their proclivities limited only by ethical self-restraint.

Ethical Pros and Cons: The Corporate and Governmental Perspectives

Many executives believe that corporate taxes are already too high and that taking advantage of loopholes to reduce payments is legitimate. And many would also argue that the company's fiduciary duty to maximize shareholder interests is paramount, and that taking advantage of provisions and loopholes is legal and ethically defensible.

The corporate viewpoint generally is that:

- MNCs paying high taxes suffer a competitive disadvantage *vis-a-vis* firms located in lower-tax nations. Paying higher taxes means less money is left over, and this in turn means:
- Shareholders get smaller dividends, and
- Less is put back into R&D—which ultimately determines the competitiveness of the firm in global competition.
- Paying taxes only encourages profligate governments to spend more money on other programs.
- If government rules allow certain loopholes, it is the company's fiduciary duty toward shareholders to use such loopholes to (legally) avoid tax payments.

During mergers/acquisitions for "inversions," the change of domicile is only for tax purposes—necessary operations and jobs would remain in the original nations.

Critics of MNC behavior argue that:

- Tax avoidance may be legal, but is not ethically defensible because many of the loopholes and tax provisions have been written to favor corporate interests by lobbying and political influence on the part of the companies. Critics assert that, even prior to 2018, the much-trumpeted US corporate tax rate actually was not 35 percent—that was only the *marginal* rate on the last slab of income, with average effective rates variously estimated to be not more than 19.4 percent (according to Citizens for Tax Justice[9]) or 27 percent (according to Price Waterhouse[10]). This put the US tax burden in the middle of the OECD advanced-nation group. Since 2018, under the new tax law, US corporations effectively enjoy a well-below OECD nation tax burden.
- Multinationals enjoy several other tax-avoidance schemes, outlined in this article, such as international licensing (royalty payments) between affiliated entities, charging central fixed costs and overheads to various foreign affiliates, creating intracorporate loans or export shipment "transfer-pricing," and tax-haven subsidiaries.
- It is true that if a MNC pays less tax, more money is left over for shareholder dividends or to put toward replenishing the R&D budget. But critics argue that higher after-tax profits from tax avoidance may be diverted instead into fatter bonuses and stock options for top executives.

- Inversions may maintain necessary jobs and operations in the original countries. However, shifting the headquarters of the company increases the chances of additional job creation in the other nation or elsewhere.

"I deal with tax avoidance - **he** *deals with tax evasion."*

Corporate Social Responsibility (CSR) for Multinationals?

The dilemma multinational company executives face is how to reconcile the ethical desire for the corporation to contribute something to each country in which it operates with the need to maximize global total earnings, after taxes, for shareholders. Large firms operate in dozens of nations (and recall that there are more than 190 nations in all). But shareholders of each company are still concentrated in one or few countries.

From a CSR perspective, a company should contribute something of value to each nation in which it conducts business. Paying reasonable taxes to each government is one type of contribution, which would enable the nation's government to build roads, support education, and so on. But a multinational firm can make other types of contributions to a country, such as helping to upgrade local technology and skills, building up ancillary or supplier firms to multiply the local economic impact of the foreign investment, and transferring best practices in a range of areas from effluent standards to logistics to human resource management and training. All contributions the MNC makes to a nation need not be monetary. But in focusing on global after-tax profit maximization, the net welfare of each individual nation is often forgotten by the company.

Solution? My recommendation would be that each company appoint a Global CSR Officer (CSRO), whose staff would annually calculate—*for each nation*—the net benefit (monetary and non-monetary) contributed by the MNC. The CSRO would be senior enough and have sufficient clout to "push back" against the tendencies of the CFO (Chief Financial Officer) or the company's Treasury Department to engage in global after-tax profit maximization, heedless of individual countries' interests.

This dilemma between the interests of shareholders, typically concentrated in one or a few headquarter nations, versus the interests of each country or market the MNC operates in is only going to get more acute with greater awareness and publicity through social media.

Conclusion

No decision in large MNCs is made these days without assessing tax implications. The magnitude of the international tax-avoidance phenomenon—the extent to which global operations, supply chains, and location decisions are affected by tax considerations—places this issue at the heart of global strategy. In large companies, executives consider tax angles concurrently with strategy, rather than as an afterthought. Consequently, an acquaintance with this topic is absolutely essential to students of business and to all executives.

There is no world government or supranational tax authority.[11] A world fragmented into more than 190 jurisdictions (nations) is at odds or is in tension with MNCs that look on the entire world as their blank canvas (Contractor, 2014), are willing to relocate operations wherever it suits them and may fall prey to the temptation of using the tax-avoidance techniques outlined in this chapter.

Notes

[1] A firm is classified as an FDI "affiliate" if at least 10 percent of its shares are held by a foreign owner. The term "subsidiary" generally—although not always—denotes majority or full control of the shareholding by a foreign entity or owner.

[2] *European Commission, Taxation and Customs Union*: Anti Tax Avoidance Package, January 2016.

[3] *Fortune*: Why Washington Is Tackling the Tax Inversion Problem All Wrong. Chris Matthews, November 25, 2015.

[4] *Reuters.* Obama's inversion curbs kill Pfizer's $160 billion Allergan deal. Caroline Humer and Ransdell Pierson, April 6, 2016.

[5] However incidentally, the US used to offer a gigantic loophole: after paying each country's taxes, the additional US tax on US multinationals' foreign affiliate profits used to be legally deferred indefinitely by the simple expedient of not remitting those profits back to the US. Instead, the funds were parked in tax havens, such as Bermuda, or reinvested in other foreign operations. The accumulated, but non-repatriated, profits of American multinationals' foreign subsidiaries—which legally escaped US taxation—were estimated at between $2.1 and $3 trillion at the start of 2018. The new US tax law now allows these past accumulated, non-repatriated foreign profits to be brought home to the US at concessionary tax rates of 15.5 percent for cash and other liquid assets and 8 percent for non-cash assets.

[6] *Bloomberg.* Pfizer Seen Avoiding $35 Billion in Tax Via Allergan Merger. Lynnley Browning, February 25, 2016.

[7] *US Department of the Treasury Press Center*: Fact Sheet: Treasury Issues Inversion Regulations and Proposed Earnings Stripping Regulations, April 4, 2016.

[8] *The White House Office of the Press Secretary:* Remarks by the President on the Economy, April 05, 2016.

[9] *Citizens for Tax Justice*, February 2014: The Sorry State of Corporate Taxes: What Fortune 500 Firms Pay (or Don't Pay) in the USA And What they Pay Abroad — 2008 to 2012.

[10] *PWC Price Waterhouse*: Paying Taxes 2014: The global picture—A comparison of tax systems in 189 economies worldwide.

[11] And some would say that is a good thing.

REFERENCES

Altshuler, R., Shay, S. E., & Toder, E. J. (2015). Lessons the United States Can Learn from Other Countries' Territorial Systems for Taxing Income of Multinational Corporations, *Available at SSRN 2557190.*

Belderbos, R., Leten, B., & Suzuki, S. (2013). How global is R&D [quest] firm-level determinants of home-country bias in R&D, *Journal of International Business Studies*, *44*(8), 765–786.

Contractor, F. (2015). Seeking Safety Abroad: The Hidden Story in China's FDI Statistics, *Yale Global*. September 10.

Contractor, F. (2014). Global Management in a Still-Fragmented World, *GlobalBusiness.me*, October 7.

DeMooij, R. (2011). Tax Biases to Debt Finance: Assessing the Problem, Finding Solutions, *IMF Staff Discussion Note*, May 3rd.

Dischinger, M., Riedel, N. (2008). Corporate taxes, profit shifting and the location of intangibles within multinational firms, *Munich Discussion Paper*, No. 2008–11.

Faccio, M., Lang, L., Young, L. (2010). Pyramiding vs leverage in corporate groups: International evidence, *Journal of International Business Studies*, 88–104.

Lanz, R., Miroudot, S. (2011). Intra-firm Trade: Patterns, Determinants and Policy Implications, *OECD Trade Policy Working Paper* No. 114.

Markle, K. (2015). A Comparison of the Tax-Motivated Income Shifting of Multinationals in Territorial and Worldwide Countries, *Contemporary Accounting Research*.

Mutti, J., Grubert, H. (2009). The effect of taxes on royalties and the migration of intangible assets abroad, in *International trade in services and intangibles in the era of globalization* by Reinsdorf, M. & Slaughter, M., University of Chicago Press. 111–137.

OECD (2013). OECD Science, Technology and Industry Scoreboard 2013, OECD iLibrary 2013.

OECD (2015). How Multinational Enterprises Channel Investments Through Multiple Countries, *OECD Statistics*. February.

Picciotto, S. (2012). Towards Unitary Taxation of Transnational Corporations, Tax Justice Network. December.

Sikka, P., Willmott, H. (2010). The dark side of transfer pricing: Its role in tax avoidance and wealth retentiveness, *Critical Perspectives on Accounting*, **21**(4), 342–356.

UNCTAD (2011). *World Investment Report 2011* (United Nations publication, Sales No. Sales No.: E.11.II.D.2).

UNCTAD (2015). *World Investment Report 2014* (United Nations publication, Sales No. E.14.II.D.1).

CASE 1 PRESENTATION

Odysseus, Inc.:
The Decision to Expand Internationally
in a Medium-Sized Company

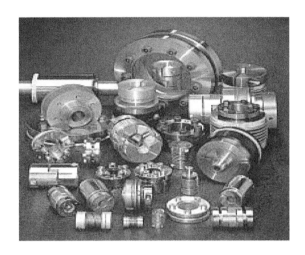

This is a case about the international expansion opportunities faced by a medium-sized company in the US, called Odysseus, Inc.[1] Europe is their principal foreign market. Exports to Europe have been consistent but have never amounted to more than a small share of total turnover. Odysseus has two licensing agreements in place, in the UK and France. These have yielded good royalties, which seem akin to pure profits. However, Mr. Odysseus has sometimes wondered if these royalties are "peanuts" compared with the profits that could have been earned had they established their own operations via a Foreign Direct Investment subsidiary in Europe. In fact, there is a company in Germany that is available for acquisition.

This case should be analyzed retrospectively as well as prospectively. First, how would you assess Odysseus' foreign strategy so far? Second, what should they do next, to expand their business in Europe? (See also the Guidelines and questions supplied with this case).

---

[1] This case was written by Prof. Warren Keegan and modified and used with permission of the author.

Background

Mr. Donald R. Odysseus, president of the Odysseus Manufacturing Company of Kansas City, Kansas, was actively considering the possibilities of major expansion of the firm's currently limited international activities and the form and scale such expansion might take.

Odysseus was founded in 1926 by Edward Odysseus as a small machine shop. The head office and production facilities of the company were located in a 500,000square-foot modern factory on a 30-acre site near the original location. In 2014, net sales were $169,400,000 while after-tax profits were about $9,670,000. Odysseus employed just over 300 people, and its stock was held by 1,000 shareholders. (The company's 2014 income statement and balance sheet are given in Exhibits 1 and 2.)

However, the management of the firm remained small and already over-stretched in just the very competitive US market. Mr. Odysseus realized that sending any of his key managers or engineers to Europe incurred an opportunity cost on US operations. Second, he was not sure about the negotiations or cultural skills of his staff, or indeed his own.

Product Line

Odysseus produced several lines of coupling and clutches -- mechanical components that connect the source of mechanical power (e.g., and engine) to the place where the power is needed (e.g., the wheels of a car or a forklift truck). A coupling is a device that permanently connects the source of power to the place of its application. A clutch, on the other hand, can be disengaged.

The various types produced by the company include flange, compression, gear type, flex pin, and flexible disc couplings, and overrunning and multiple disc clutches.

In all, Odysseus manufactured about 600 different sizes and types of its eight standard items. Demand was in small batches of a few hundred pieces of each clutch or coupling. Hence the operation was not mass-production, but rather batch production of a few hundred pieces at a time. With 600 different sizes and types, production scheduling was not easy, as each new type required re-setting the machine tools. The company's single most important product was the Odysseus Flexible Coupling, which its research department had developed and which, produced in about 70 different sizes and combinations, now accounted for one third of Odysseus's sales. Odysseus held patents throughout the world on its flexible coupling as well as several other devices. Odysseus had carved itself a secure niche in the clutch and couplings market, despite the competition in this market of larger firms with widely diversified product lines.

Exhibit 1:
Income Statement, 2014

Income

Net sales	$169,400	
Royalties, interest, other income	348	
		$169,748

Costs and expenses

Cost of goods sold	$108,038	
Depreciation	3,546	
Selling, administrative, and general expense	37,690	
Interest on long-term debt	438	
		$149,712
Income before income taxes		20,036
Federal taxes on income (estimated)		10,314
Net income		$9,722

Exhibit 2: Balance Sheet, 2014

Assets

Cash	11,334	
Marketable securities	7,376	
Accounts receivable	12,798	
Inventories	51,156	
Total current assets		82,664
Investments and other assets		2,704
Property, plant, and equipment (net)		46,290
Total assets		131,658

Liabilities

Accounts payable	4,030	
Dividends payable	1,490	
Accruals	6,788	
Federal income tax liability (estimated)	7,504	
Installment on long-term debt	554	
Total current liabilities		20,336
Long term debt (20-year notes, final maturity 2014)		10,070
Preferred stock		12,740
Common stock and retained earnings		88,512
Total liabilities		131,658

Customers

Odysseus was not dependent on any single customer or industry. Sales were made to original equipment manufacturers (OEM) for use in motor drives for a wide range of products including machine tools, test gear, conveyors, farm implements, mining equipment, hoisting equipment, cranes, shovels, and so on. No more than 10 percent of its output went to any single industry; its largest single customer took less than 4 percent of production. In brief, Odysseus supplied a great many different industries and catered to their disparate demand with over 600 different product types.

Odysseus couplings and clutches were mostly used by producers of general-purpose equipment than by large manufacturers of highly automated machines. Odysseus's sales manager believed that demand for the company's couplings and clutches would benefit from continuation of a long-term trend toward increased installation of labor-saving equipment in medium and large enterprises. This trend and the breadth of its market had provided some protection against cyclical fluctuations in business activities. During the period 2004 to 2014, sales had increased from $64 million to over $169 million; the largest annual decline during the period had been 8 percent, while in the most recent recession year sales had actually increased by 5 percent.

The company's commercial objective was to operate as a specialist and creative designer in a product field in which its distinctive skills would give it a strong competitive position. In the past, the company had experimented with various products outside its coupling and clutch line; it had tried to make components for egg-candling machinery, among other things. The investment in these products was initially considered a means of more efficiently utilizing the company's forging and machining capacity, but the firm had not been particularly successful. The Odysseus management had come to the conclusion that it should concentrate its efforts on its line of couplings and clutches; and Mr. Odysseus stated the company's corporate objectives explicitly as being a coupling and clutch manufacturer. New investments were made to develop better products within this field, and to open new markets for Odysseus products.

Odysseus's production and assembly facilities were located in its modern factory near Kansas City, Kansas. The site offered ample room for expansion and was well located for both rail and highway transportation. The company maintained warehousing facilities in Boston, Jersey City, Atlanta, Columbus, Ohio, and Oakland, California. The economies stemming from concentrating production in one factory (by occasionally combining batches from different customers) can be seen from the following examples. One of the company's largest selling items, product K-2A (a flexible coupling component) produced in lots of 750, cost $10.38 each; in lots of 1,200, $8.44 each. The incremental 450 units produced after the initial 750, therefore, cost only $5.21 each. Put differently, on this particular product, a 50 percent cost saving could be realized on the marginal production from the 750-unit level to the 1,200-unit level. In Exhibit 3, the saving from a larger batch is earned in the Machine Shop operation. In the first of three major steps in the manufacture of couplings or clutches, steel bars or tubing were cut and forged. Apart from the unit cost reductions stemming from more complete utilization of the existing forging facilities, economies in this department were limited. Second, the forged steel pieces were machined to close tolerances in the machine shop. Here costs varied significantly with lot sizes. For most products, the choice among two or three alternative methods of production depended on the lot size. If a large lot size were indicated, special-purpose automatic machines with large setup costs and lower variable unit costs were used. Smaller lot sizes were produced on general-purpose turret and engine lathes where setup time was less but unit costs were higher. Hence the economies of producing a larger batch derived principally from the ability to switch to automatic machines.

The benefits of combining orders for the same model – if achievable – was that marginal cost typically was significantly less than average cost and that important economies could be had by achieving larger lot sizes. However, with so many different models, over so many different customers, this did not happen very often as orders from two different companies were unlikely to be received for just-in-time (JIT) delivery on the same schedule. This would be especially true if the company tried to combine orders from one domestic and one overseas buyer. This would occasionally prove to be possible, and would reduce costs. However, the fragmented nature of Odysseus' customer base, covering many different industries and many different types of finished machines (into which their clutches and coupling were assembled) meant that their production scheduling normally could not expect to combine orders from two different buyers.

Exhibit 3: Variation of Production Costs Depending on Lot Size for Model N-15C1

Operation	Lots of 150	Lots of 400
I. Foundry	$51.67	$51.67
II. Machine Shop		
1. Boring	55.67	32.69
2. Turning	14.17	11.43
3. Facing	19.79	16.25
4. Drilling	32.23	26.30
5. Turning	18.95	15.41
6. Facing	19.95	14.76
7. Finishing	18.76	18.76
8. Finishing	17.95	18.24
III. Assembly	7.96	7.96
	$ 257.10	$ 213.49

Mr. Odysseus regarded Odysseus's U.S. and Canadian market position as a strong one. The patented Odysseus Flexible Coupling possessed unique characteristics that no other coupling device duplicated, and many other Odysseus products served special functions not performed by competitive devices. While the patent, *per se*, might not be very defensible – because patents in mechanical devices can easily be worked around by competitors -- the real strength of Odysseus was in its unique design, which was highly appreciated by customers. Of course, other coupling and clutch systems competed with Odysseus, but no single company could be said to compete directly by introducing an identical product line. Mr. Odysseus estimated that there was ample room for Odysseus to expand its sales in this domestic market as the total market grew and through an increase in its share of industry sales.

Distribution Channels

For the most part, Odysseus clutches and couplings are critical components that go into *other companies'* cranes, forklift trucks, hoists, conveyors, farm implements, mining equipment, shovels, etc. and are sold to OEMs directly. Critical to marketing success is cultivating and maintaining good relations with Purchasing or Supply Chain Departments in the client companies. The Purchasing Manager is a key target audience. "The Purchasing Manager is a god," said Donald Odysseus. They make or break orders. Another critical factor is just-in-time delivery where the supplier, like Odysseus, is expected to deliver batches on a precise schedule to customers' assembly lines. For spare parts however, there was not the same time pressure, and sales were made through distributors who generally carried Odysseus couplings and clutches and sold them off-the-shelf. The main task of a 45-person Odysseus sales force was to call on Purchasing Departments in client companies.

Key Company Policies and Strategy Assumptions

In the US Odysseus sold products on flat price basis (FOB warehouse). In competing with other suppliers of similar products, Odysseus stressed delivery time, quality, service, and merchandising, but not price. Delivery time is a crucial issue as clutches and couplings, being critical components, have to be delivered "Just-In-Time" to the customer's assembly-line operation. Quality is obviously crucial because the final forklift truck, crane, shovel, or mining equipment should not fail because a key component was deficient. In management's view, improvements in its products or in delivery or service promised more than temporary competitive advantage. Price-cutting moves, in contrast, would likely be matched by competitors the same day. No added sales would be gained, and total revenues would be cut.

Exports

In 2014, export sales were $2,707,724, on which the company made a $400,000 operating profit. Although export sales had never been actively solicited, a small but steady stream of export orders trickled into the Kansas City sales office, and these were always filled expeditiously. But the active exploitation of export markets was considered too difficult in view of the barriers of international delivery time, cultivating relationships with foreign purchasing departments, cost, transport, tariff, language, and currency risk.

Although he recognized that foreign wages were increasing more rapidly than those in the United States, Mr. Odysseus had always believed that Odysseus could not compete in export markets because its costs in Kansas City were too high. Also, tariffs imposed on Odysseus products by foreign governments were typically 10 percent *ad valorem* or higher. Apart from costs, a main obstacle to serving Europe through exports was the just-in-time delivery required by

OEM customers for their assembly operations in Europe. Perhaps exporting could serve the replacement or spare part demand in Europe, because spares are stocked by distributors who sell "off the shelf" unlike OEMs who demand just-in-time delivery. The company's export pricing policy was identical to its domestic policy. This meant that the foreign importer paid the U.S. free-on-board (FOB) price plus freight and import duties.

Combining demand for a particular model or size to make a bigger production batch obviously leads to lower costs. But could this be an argument in favor of serving Europe via export orders that were combined with domestic US demand? "This could work for European spare parts orders," noted Donald Odysseus. But, given the very large variety of his products, he did not think it would be possible to meet the just-in-time delivery needs of OEM clients, because at a particular point in time, US demand for particular models would not coincide with demand for the exact *same* models from Europe. Hence US and European batches could not be combined unless, coincidentally, two orders for the *same model* were received at the same time -- or unless a *huge* order on a continuous basis was received from a European customer.

Licensing Agreement in the UK

Along with filling orders, Odysseus's activities outside the United States and Canada consisted of a licensing agreement with an English coupling manufacturer. In 2009, while on a vacation trip in England, where Odysseus's vice president in charge of engineering had spent his youth, Donald Odysseus made a side trip to meet the chairperson of Siren Ltd. of Manchester -- a manufacturer of related equipment. Siren was anxious to diversify by adding other power transmission products. Consequently, Siren became interested in several Odysseus products, particularly those on the Odysseus Flexible Coupling. In 2009, Odysseus granted the English concern an exclusive 15-year license to manufacture and sell all present and future Odysseus products in the United Kingdom.

The licensing arrangement specifically defined the United Kingdom to include England, Scotland, Wales, and Northern Ireland. Siren was granted also a non-exclusive license to sell products produced from Odysseus patents in all other countries except the United States, Canada, Mexico, and France. The terms of the license agreement stipulated a 1.5 percent royalty on the ex-factory sales price of all products in which devices manufactured from Odysseus patents were incorporated. The 2012 royalty income from Siren amounted to $257,878 and was expected to rise to $322,348 in 2013.

Mr. Odysseus had noted Siren's success with considerable interest. The royalty payments were a welcome addition to Odysseus income, especially since they had not necessitated any additional investment. "It is just a very good addition of nearly a million dollars to our bottom line, in the past five years," said Mr. Odysseus.

But the licensee was also receiving very generous profits from this deal, as Siren had almost tripled its sales (which by 2013 were equivalent to $131million) during its five-year association with Odysseus and its equity had appreciated many times the total royalties of about $967,044 that Odysseus had received. Sometimes Mr. Odysseus wondered if he had struck a very one-sided deal, with royalties in this agreement a meager 1.5 percent. In his heart he wondered if he was a poor negotiator.

UK Licensee Claims "Eastern Hemisphere": During the five years Odysseus and Siren had worked together, however, the English firm had made it understood that in general it considered its territory to be the Eastern Hemisphere, while Odysseus's was supposed to be in the Western Hemisphere, according to Siren. Siren was especially interested in the German market (the biggest in the EU by far) for couplings and clutches, and was a licensee of a German brake shoe manufacturer.

Licensing Agreement in France

In addition, Odysseus had a licensing agreement on the same terms (1.5 percent royalty) with Scylla, S.A. Scylla was a family-owned, medium-sized French manufacturer of clutches and complementary lines located near Paris. The company was financially sound and well headed by a young and aggressive management team. Scylla had been granted an exclusive license in France and a nonexclusive license in Belgium to sell products incorporating Odysseus-patented devices. Odysseus had entered the agreement starting January 1, 2013 for an initial period of 10 years. Royalty income in 2013, the first full year of operation in France, had totaled roughly $64,400. Odysseus expected a doubling of this figure in 2014. What was the potential of the French market, Mr. Odysseus asked himself? A colleague pointed out that the French economy was roughly the same size as the UK.

Proposed Joint Venture in France: In 2014, M. Scylla, the president of the French firm, had proposed to Mr. Odysseus a closer association of their two companies. M. Scylla was anxious to expand his operations and needed capital to do this. He, therefore, proposed that Odysseus form a joint venture with Scylla. According to the terms of the proposal, Odysseus would bring $1,290,000 into the joint venture, paid in cash, while Scylla would provide a 40,000-square-foot plant, equipment, a national distribution system, and managerial personnel. Scylla S.A. would cease to exist as a corporate entity; its expanded organization and plant would become Scylla Odysseus, S.A. (SOSA).

The original owners of Scylla, S.A. (the Scylla family) would own 60 percent of SOSA, and their return would be in the form of dividends plus salaries of members of the Scylla family employed by SOSA. Odysseus would own 40 percent of SOSA. However, for tax reasons, Odysseus would receive fees and royalties rather than dividends totaling 5 percent of the ex-factory price of all products incorporating Odysseus patents. This was the French proposal.

Initially Donald Odysseus was quite happy with the proposal. But his deputy pointed out that, on closer examination, this was nothing more than a glorified licensing agreement. True, the royalty rate would jump by 3.5 percent. But the French family would be in the driver's seat, and simply contribute what they already had – whereas Odysseus Inc. was supposed to contribute an incremental $1,290,000 in hard cash. Mr. Odysseus nevertheless thought that he should give this proposal serious attention. He asked his finance manager to calculate the incremental costs of the French proposal versus the incremental benefits to Odysseus. The finance manager noted that the first full year's operation by the French licensee had only been an exploratory first step.

Everything depended on the potential size of the French market. In order to calculate [Total Royalty Revenue = Royalty Rate x Sales] one had to estimate Sales in France for each year in the future.

The French Market Size: Mr. Odysseus had no ready means of precisely quantifying the market potential for clutches and couplings in France. The French market for couplings looked very attractive, and France was at least as big an economy as the UK, in GDP or population. So perhaps, one approach could be to expect sales growth in France to follow the same trajectory as sales growth seen in the UK.

Alternatively, the total market for Odysseus's "type L" couplings in the United States was $145 million, or 14 percent of the U.S. market. Odysseus assumed that the coupling market in France was correlated with sales of durable equipment in France, which were 12 percent of the U.S. total. The French type-L coupling market, therefore, would be $17.4 million a year, of which SOSA should expect to capture 14 percent, or $2,436,000. But this was only for type-L couplings.

Additionally, the geographical location of France within the European Community would make it possible to supply the even larger German market from the SOSA plant in France. M. Scylla had indicated that he considered Germany a primary target for future expansion.

German Acquisition Possibility

So far, Odysseus had not actively pursued business leads in Germany in spite of several inquiries about licensing from German companies. Odysseus even had the possibility of acquiring an existing German manufacturer of couplings, Charybdis Metallfabrik GmbH (CMF) of Kassel. Mr. Odysseus had learned that CMF's aging owner managers were anxious to sell their equity interest in the company but would stay on in managerial capacity. Odysseus's British licensee, Siren, had made it clear, however, that although it had no sizable business in Germany, it considered this market to be in Siren's sales territory and a move into Germany by Odysseus without Siren an "unfriendly act." In the light of Odysseus's growing royalty income from Siren, Mr. Odysseus did not want to antagonize the British licensee.

Similarly in Germany, durable equipment sales were 20 percent of those in the United States. The type-L coupling market could, therefore, be expected to be about $29 million, of which a company using Odysseus patents and know-how should obtain between 10 percent and 15 percent. Sales of comparable lines by both Scylla, S.A. and CMF appeared to justify these estimates; Scylla had sold $1,740,000 of a device closely comparable to the type-L coupling, or 10 percent of the assumed French market, and CMF had sold $2,320,000 of virtually the same device, or 8 percent of the assumed German market.

Whichever way one looked at it, the German market was by far the biggest in Europe and represented tremendous potential, especially if one added the contiguous East European territories. But a direct investment in a German subsidiary also presented high risks for a small company. The purchase price was not presently known. But, reasoned Mr. Odysseus, if it took $1,290,000 to acquire 40 percent of the shares of a French company, it may take many millions of dollars to acquire 100 percent of a German firm. If things went wrong in Germany, this money would all go down the drain.

Who would run the German subsidiary? If he sent managers from the US, American operations may suffer. If the aging owners of CMF simply retired, the key to success – namely personal contacts with German Purchasing Managers – could be undermined. German companies consider their engineering quality to be superior, and key out-sourced components like clutches or couplings are purchased very carefully based on long dealings, and delivery and quality assurance. Mr. Odysseus was advised that whereas in the US even large purchasing decisions may occur over the internet, European culture placed greater importance on long-time cultivated relationships.

On the other hand, the German market potential was so attractive that if success were achieved, the dividend and equity growth returns from a subsidiary would be far greater than from any licensing agreement. "Our net returns would not be capped at a lousy 1.5 percent or 5 percent," noted Donald Odysseus.

Why Expand into Europe?

In 2014, the European market with its pace of technical development and automation appeared to offer great opportunities for Odysseus. Mr. Odysseus was therefore most anxious to capitalize on these opportunities, presumably by manufacturing in Europe in cooperation with a European firm.

He saw three reasons why Odysseus should expand its foreign operations. First, the corporate objectives of focusing on a single line of products sold in as large a market as possible-the policy of area instead of products diversification-dictated expansion into markets outside the United States and Canada. The nature of the demand for Odysseus's products appeared to limit near-term sales potential in less developed areas but especially in Europe the potential was good. Odysseus couplings and clutches appeared to find ready acceptance. Proof of this seemed to be contained in Siren's success in the United Kingdom.

Second, an important improvement on the Odysseus multiple disc clutch had been the result of European research. Mr. Odysseus felt that by becoming an active participant in the European market, the company could obtain valuable recent innovations that would be important to its competitive position in the United States. There was considerable activity in the clutch and coupling field in Europe, and Mr. Odysseus wanted to be in touch with the latest developments in the industry.

Third, Mr. Odysseus was seriously worried about the trend of costs in his Kansas City plant. He had heard that a French firm was planning to invest in a manufacturing plant in Mexico where wages were 16 percent of those in the United States. How could Odysseus compete against this kind of cost advantage? Ultimately, Odysseus might have to follow the lead of U.S. watch and bicycle firms and perform much of its manufacturing abroad and import parts, or even finished products, into the United States. At the present time, Mr. Odysseus felt that there was some reluctance on the part of American manufacturers to buy foreign couplings and clutches, and foreign competition was low in this market. But Mr. Odysseus was worried about the future and wanted to preserve Odysseus's competitive position by assuring a foreign source of supply. Also, the company would be in a better position to withstand exorbitant demands from the local labor union if it possessed alternative manufacturing facilities. The problem with overseas sourcing remained delivery time from foreign locations, although the southern US was an overnight truck delivery from the *maquiladora* zone (border).

Before definitely deciding whether Odysseus should become more deeply involved in foreign operations, Mr. Odysseus wanted to review the ways this might be done. First, Odysseus could, in theory, expand export sales. Mr. Odysseus believed, however, that Odysseus's costs (labor, transport, tariff) might be too high for it to compete successfully on this basis, and the just-in-time delivery issue, for OEM business, seemed insurmountable. Perhaps exporting could mainly serve the replacement or spare part demand in Europe because spares were stocked by distributors who would sell "off the shelf" unlike OEMs who demanded just-in-time delivery. Second, the company could enter into additional licensing agreements. This it had done with Siren in England and Scylla in France, but there was a definite ceiling on the possible profit potential from use of this method. Third, the company could enter joint ventures with a firm already established in foreign markets Presumably, Odysseus would supply capital and know-how and the foreign firms would supply personnel (both local managerial skill and a labor force), market outlets, and familiarity with the local business climate. This approach appeared particularly promising to Mr. Odysseus.

Foreign Direct Investment Obstacles for a Small Company

Finally, the company could establish wholly owned foreign subsidiaries. However, Mr. Odysseus saw formidable barriers to such action since Odysseus lacked managerial skill in foreign operations. More critically, being a small or medium-sized firm, they were critically short of good engineering and managerial personnel. To depute anybody to run European operations would mean losing a valuable manager or technician – something a smaller firm cannot afford easily. They did not have executives to spare from the Kansas City operations who might learn the intricacies of foreign business, and the development of wholly owned operations from scratch would require significant investment of time and money. Finally, they were unfamiliar with foreign markets and business practices.

As he reflected on these issues, he looked at a set of tables on global income and population, productivity, wages, exports/imports, and trade and investment (Exhibit 4) and decided to attempt to comprehend what, if any, significance the data in these tables had for Odysseus. Mr. Odysseus recognized that certain deep-seated ideas of his tended to make him predisposed toward active development of overseas business. These included a view that his

business should not shrink from difficult tasks. Organizations, he believed, couldn't stand still --
the choice was one of moving forward or falling backward. He considered "taking the plunge" into
less familiar areas and learning from the experience was generally preferable to long-extended and
expensive inquiry before taking action. Nonetheless, he wanted to be sure that the most basic
issues related to expansion overseas by Odysseus were thought through before firm decisions were
made.

Exhibit 4

GDP Rank	Country/Region	GDP (Millions of US$) 2013	Average Cost of a Manufacturing Worker in US Dollars Per Hour 2012
--	*World*	**73,982,138**	--
--	*European Union*	17,371,618	--
1	United States	16,799,700	35.67
2	China	9,181,377	2.06
3	Japan	4,901,532	35.34
4	Germany	3,635,959	45.79
5	France	2,737,361	39.81
6	United Kingdom	2,535,761	31.23
7	Brazil	2,242,854	11.20
8	Russia	2,118,006	n.a.
9	Italy	2,071,955	34.18
10	India	1,892,651	1.98
11	Canada	1,825,096	36.59
12	Australia	1,505,277	47.68
13	Spain	1,358,687	26.83
14	Mexico	1,258,544	6.36
15	South Korea	1,221,801	20.72

Sources: World Bank Data; Bureau of Labor Statistics

CASE 1 GUIDELINES AND DISCUSSION QUESTIONS

Odysseus, Inc.

The Odysseus case exemplifies the situation faced by small or medium-sized US firms, new to international business, and preoccupied by their domestic market, but seeking to expand their foreign operations. So far, they have two alliance (licensing) agreements in the UK and France, and some sporadic reflexive exports. Now they wish to expand further in the European market. This case casts light on the different international expansion methods including doing business at a distance (exporting), forming an alliance (arms-length licensing, or equity Joint Venture) or full control in the form of direct investment in a foreign subsidiary.

As you should do for any case analysis, begin by reviewing some very generic questions:

- What is the nature of their operations?
  Concentrated into a few items, or do they have a broad product line?
- Is this a mass-production operation?
- What does sales success depend on? That is to say, what is most crucial to customers? Who are the principal purchase decision makers?
- Is high technology an issue? Are there patents? How critical are these?

Next, while reading the Odysseus case, write down, in bullet points, how the story illustrates the *pros* and *cons* of the following strategies:

1) **Exports from the US as a means of serving the European market: pros and cons.** (Refer to the discussion of Exporting in the associated readings or text. Not all the concepts will apply. Write in your notes only the ones that do apply to Odysseus.)

2) **Licensing: advantages and drawbacks.** (Has the UK license been good or bad for Odysseus? Refer to the discussion of Licensing in the associated readings or text. Not all the concepts will apply. Write in your notes only the ones that do apply to Odysseus.)

3) **Proposed joint venture with French partner.** Looking at it from Odysseus' perspective, what are the **negative and positive aspects** of the French proposal?

4) **Fully owned subsidiary in Germany: dangers and opportunities.**

5) **What strategy do you recommend for the firm**?

Best Strategy for Odysseus?	
• German Subsidiary?	
• French JV Proposal?	
• Do Nothing Different?	
• Some Combination of Above?	

BRING YOUR NOTES TO CLASS FOR THE SCHEDULED CASE DISCUSSION

STUDY QUESTIONS

Chapters 1 – 5 (Part I)

1. Why have FDI and licensing, as methods of International Business, been expanding faster than international trade?

2. In an alliance with another international company, describe ways (obvious or subtle) by which one partner can exercise control over the other or keep them in line.

3. Mention a few of the prominent factors that go into the decision as to locating a factory within a foreign market, as opposed to locating the plant outside that nation and exporting the output to the country.

4. Describe conditions which favor the use of exporting as a strategy to serve foreign markets and those which are necessary for exporting to be possible.

5. What are the principal impediments to exporting in 21st-century international trade?

6. Detail the several advantages and drawbacks to licensing as a mode of foreign business. The primary focus of your answer should be on licensing between separate international companies in two different nations. However, also indicate when some of the points you make also apply to licensing between parties that are related by equity investment.

7. Why is licensing an often quicker mode of entering a market compared to alternatives?

8. Why does licensing income generally become more steady over time, compared with the returns on say FDI?

9. Why does foreign direct investment (FDI) take place? That is, what are the strategy motivations that impel firms to engage in FDI?

10. What kinds of risk affect the three classic international expansion alternatives? State each type of risk and then briefly state how each risk affects trade, licensing and FDI differently.

11. Briefly describe the different tax implications of FDI, licensing and trade.

The next 5 questions relate to the Odysseus Case:

12. How does the structure of an industry, and the character of a company, affect the international strategy that it uses? Outline the characteristics (strategy, marketing, nature of competition, etc.) (i) of the industry or business that Odysseus, Inc. operated in and (ii) of the company *itself*. Then for each of your points, indicate how that characteristic would either favor or deter the use of exporting, licensing, or foreign direct investment, as the case may be.

13. By citing examples from the case, show how the Odysseus case illustrates the uses and drawbacks of exporting as an international business strategy.

14. Describe by citing examples how the Odysseus case illustrates the uses and drawbacks of licensing as an international business strategy.

15. In negotiating partnerships and alliances, including licensing, are short agreements better than long agreements? Debate both sides of this specific question, bringing in a few examples from the Odysseus story.

16. When contemplating the offer from Scylla of France for a proposed joint venture, first describe aspects of the French proposal that appeared negative to Odysseus, and then describe aspects or factors that appeared positive. In both cases, take Odysseus, Inc.'s point of view. If this were a "take it or leave it" proposal, would you recommend to Odysseus that they should accept the French offer as stated?

---

17. Discuss what *criteria* the strategist would use in *comparing* FDI, exporting, and licensing, assuming that a foreign market can be served by either of these methods. For each criterion, describe what considerations favor or disfavor each method.

18. Describe why many global companies appear to use exporting/importing, licensing and direct investment simultaneously with the same foreign country operation. That is, the relationship with a foreign operation may at once involve a trading, equity investment, as well as a contractual relationship. Discuss why.

19. What exactly is "political risk" these days? Illustrate with a couple of real or hypothetical examples.

20. Should companies charge the same price for the same or similar product in different international markets? Discuss the principles and considerations that tend to suggest that there should be price discrimination. Then describe contrary pressures on companies that point to the opposite, namely lower price differentials across nations.

21. Describe four different types of "tax-avoidance" methods and their motivations.

22. The effective corporate income tax rate for affiliate A of a global firm is 20 percent, whereas the effective corporate income tax rate for affiliate B in country B is 30 percent. A exports a certain good to B, where the import tariff is 20 percent. Since A has a lower income tax rate compared to B, does it make sense to increase the intrafirm unit transfer price? Discuss this question, not just in words, but also by creating your own numerical example along the lines of "transfer pricing" in Chapter 5.

23. What four methods or technologies can multinational companies use to make their international supply chains more resilient or less prone to risks?

Part II. The Economics Basis

for International Business

NOTE TO READERS:

For Relevant Materials Not Included in This Textbook,
Refer to the Appendix: Additional Suggested Readings

CHAPTER 6

Comparative Advantage Theory Overview

This chapter is intended as a quick introduction to the basic concepts of Comparative Advantage Theory, and is merely an overview, to acquaint managers with its core ideas. More importantly, it is to illustrate what is behind the argument for "free trade" espoused by most economists as conferring net benefits on most nations – something that drove the 45-year effort under the WTO (World Trade Organization) to get countries to mutually, and reciprocally, reduce tariffs on each other's products and lower other non-tariff barriers to imports). The idea of "free trade" and less protectionism is still a powerful argument that, even in more turbulent times, has been driving nations to negotiate trade treaties, customs unions, or free-trade zones.

At the same time, policy makers and managers need to understand how opening up a country to more international trade also has some negative effects. Generally, the benefits outweigh the costs, which is why until 2016, and even today, most nations remain guardedly in favor of bilateral or multilateral trade treaties. But entering into an international trade treaty, or reducing import barriers, creates "winners" as well as "losers" within the country. Moreover, the benefits and costs, are not equally distributed by region or population group. This frequently unequal distribution of "gain" and "pain" creates domestic policy dilemmas and affects voting patterns, as seen in many elections in North America , Europe, and Asia after 2016.

The following sections present the theory in as simplified fashion as possible, with only two countries, two products, and two factors of production. Of course, in real life there are 193 nations and hundreds of thousands of products and services. Nevertheless, the discussion in this chapter, simplified as it may be, reflects real-life truths.

FOLLOW THE DISCUSSION ALONG WITH THE DIAGRAMS

<u>Section I</u>: Dissimilar Factor Endowments as the Basis for International Trade

The idea of comparative advantage goes back more than 150 years, a time when economists could only think of (1) The primary sector (e.g., agriculture or food, extractive industries, and raw materials, and (2) Manufacturing (e.g., Machines). At that time, the services sector was not thought of. Even though this is a more-than-a-century old idea, the comparative advantage theory continues to have immense policy relevance in the 21st century – as witnessed by countries continuing to sign up for trade treaties. (e.g., RCEP – 15 countries, 2020; United States-Mexico-Canada Agreement (USMCA) – 3 countries, 2020; TPP – 11 countries, 2016; and many more recent examples).

To keep this simple, in this world we have only two products (**Food** – symbolizing the primary sector; and **Machines** – symbolizing the manufacturing sector) and only two factors of production, Land and Capital. The world is divided into two (hypothetical) nations, Argentina and Japan.

The key takeaway is that **international trade occurs because the trading nations are *dissimilarly* endowed**. Our hypothetical Argentina has a lot or land in relation to capital. Japan is the opposite. It has a lot of capital and is relatively short on land.

That is all you need to remember. (The rest of the curves and graphs are only of interest in an International Economics class, which this is not).

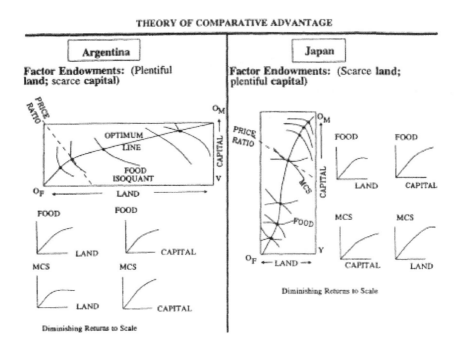

Section I Takeaway: International trade occurs because nations are *dissimilarly* endowed.

Before we go on to Section II, please read below the brief reviews of "Indifference Curves" and "Production Possibility Frontiers."

A Brief Review of "Indifference Curves"

Once upon a time, I happened to visit Death Valley National Park. At 2 PM on a hot August afternoon, the thermometer read 118 degrees Fahrenheit. I had not had lunch, nor did I carry any water. But, impulsively, I went off on a hike in a side canyon. Rather soon, I felt light-headed and partially dizzy. In my economics delirium, I saw a man approaching me with a silver tray on which there was a jug of water and some bread, which he offered me if I would first answer two questions.

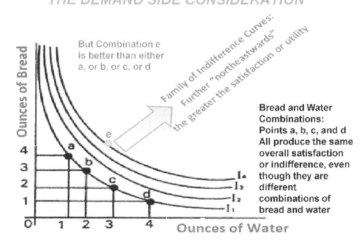

Family of Indifference Curves
THE DEMAND SIDE CONSIDERATION

Question 1: "How do you compare Point a (4 ounces bread + 1 ounce of water) with Point b (3 ounces bread + 2 ounces water) and Point c (2 ounces bread + 3 ounces water)?" By now I was really hungry and thirsty. "More bread vs. less water, or less bread vs. more water?" I asked myself. Try as I might, I could not decide. Finally, my answer to him was "I am indifferent. All three combinations, a or b or c, will produce for me equal satisfaction, or equal indifference." Hence the concept of an "Indifference Curve" where all points on the same curve produce equal satisfaction or utility or indifference – even though the mixes of bread and water are different in each.

Question 2: "Compare **Point b** with **Point e**." 'that's easy," I cried. "Point e is unquestionably superior to Point b because Point e has *both* more bread *and* more water!" The man gave me the much-desired bread and water I craved.

Takeaway: On *each* indifference curve, different combinations of bread and water (or food and machines) nevertheless produce the same overall consumer satisfaction or indifference. But there is

Farok J. Contractor, Ph.D.

a *family* of indifference curves going in the "northeasterly" direction (see arrow) where the farther "northeast" the curve the higher the level of overall satisfaction.

A Brief Review of "Production Possibility Frontiers"

Discussing Indifference Curves, we focused on consumer desires or demand. Now we look at the supply side. Each nation only has so many resources to produce anything – only so much land and capital. There is a limit, therefore, as to how much the nation can produce.

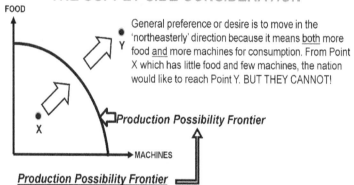

How Do They Know What Combination of Food and Machines to Produce?
THE SUPPLY SIDE CONSIDERATION

General preference or desire is to move in the 'northeasterly' direction because it means <u>both</u> more food <u>and</u> more machines for consumption. From Point X which has little food and few machines, the nation would like to reach Point Y. BUT THEY CANNOT!

Production Possibility Frontier
BUT THEY CANNOT GO BEYOND THE FRONTIER! Given only so much Capital and only so much land, there is a "*Production Possibility Frontier*" or limit of possible production combinations of Food and Machines, so that the nation cannot (from a supply side consideration) reach Point Y and has to <u>limit itself to points on or within</u> the *Production Possibility Frontier, such as Point X*

A limited amount of Food and Machines at Point X can be produced by the country. But, of course, they wish to have not only more, but if possible, more of both Food and Machines, such as Point Y. But Point Y would require factors of production, such as land and capital, that are simply not available. So, Point Y, while desirable, is not attainable because of the supply-side constraint.

By allocating more land and capital to production, the nation can produce more of both food and machines, but only up to certain points, or a certain outer limit. This limit is called the "Production Possibility Frontier (PPF)," which is the curve shown in the figure at left. Going beyond that "frontier" or limit is not possible.

The conclusion is that the nation will try to do better than Point X and move "northeastwards" to reach a point on the Production Possibility Frontier – neither below it, nor can they go beyond the frontier.

<u>**Takeaway:**</u> A nation, or group of consumers, will go as far "northeast" as possible to reach a point where the highest attainable Indifference Curve just touches the Production Possibility Frontier. (See Section II).

130

Section II: In the Beginning There Is No International Trade – Each Nation Is Self-Sufficient

As yet, no trade has occurred between our hypothetical Japan and Argentina. Each nation therefore produces internally all that it consumes internally. Each nation chooses that mix of food and machines which maximizes its utility function (highest "indifference curve going "northeastward") within the constraints of its PPF. For Argentina, this is where its highest attainable indifference curve just touches its Production Possibility Frontier (PPF) at Point A on the diagram, with 100 food units and 20 machines. (For simplicity take these numbers as given for this illustration). For Japan similarly, their chosen mix of internal production and consumption is at point X.

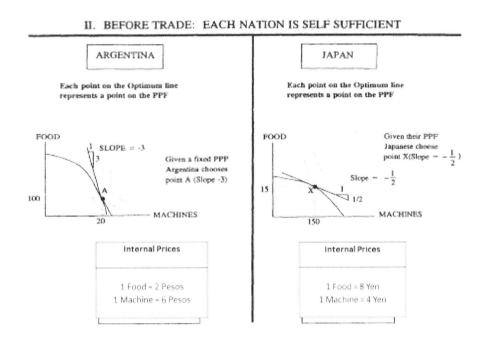

For each nation, at their optimal consumption/production point, there is a common tangent to the PPF and the indifference curve. The slope of the tangent represents "relative prices." For example, at point A, Argentines value machines three times as highly as food units. If the price of one food unit is 2 Pesos, then one machine will be valued at 6 Pesos. Similarly, in Japan, with the slope of the price tangent being "- ½" if one machine is. Say, 4 yen, then one food unit is valued at 8 yen.

Money in the form of Pesos and Yen are introduced only as a convenience to facilitate commerce, and as a medium for exchange. Money itself has no value, except what you can do with it – what you can "purchase" with it.

Comparative Advantages of Argentina and Japan: We see that prior to international trade, in Argentina food is relatively cheap and machines are expensive. In Japan it is the opposite: food is relatively expensive, and machines are abundant and cheap. Argentina has a comparative advantage in agriculture. Japan, by comparison, has a relative advantage in manufacturing machines. This sets the stage for mutually beneficial international trade in Section III.

Section III: The Gains from International Trade

This section illustrates the fundamental argument for international trade – that both nations tend to gain. A simple "Before/After Table" below shows both Argentina and Japan being better off by an experimental trade of "3 food for 3 machines," as an illustration of a 1Food = 1Machine Ratio. (By the way, both nations benefit even if we use many different ratios of international trade). Now that money (pesos and yen) has been introduced, this enables us to see how *both* countries are better off. Argentina exports (gives up) 3 food units, but imports (gets) 3 machines, ending up with a new consumption mix of 97 food and 23 machines with an overall higher peso value of 332 pesos[1] (which is superior to the old combination of 100 food units and 20 machines, which resulted in a peso value of 320 pesos). Japan is also better off with their new consumption mix: 732 yen instead of 720 yen.

III. EXPERIMENTAL TRADE AT A RATIO OF 3 FOOD = 3 MACHINES (1 : 1 Ratio as an example)							
NOTE: International Trade could actually happen at any ratio between 1 Food = ½ Machine and 1 Food = 3 Machines. So the 1 Food = 1 Machine ratio is somewhere in the middle and is used as an example							
ARGENTINA				**JAPAN**			
Trade at 1 : 1 Ratio				Trade at 1 : 1 Ratio			
	Machines	Food	Value		Machines	Food	Value
BEFORE	20	100	320 Pesos	BEFORE	150	15	720 Yen
AFTER	23	97	332 Pesos	AFTER	147	18	732 Yen

So both countries feel better off AFTER than BEFORE. Both benefit, although not necessarily equally, from participating in international trade

So far, the 1 Food = 1 Machine ratio (or 3 Food = 3 Machines) for international trade was only an illustration of the gains from trade. Many alternative ratios of international trade would also leave each nation better off trading, rather than not trading. In fact, at many ratios in between

---

[1] Food is at 2 pesos each unit, and machines are valued at 6 pesos each.

"1 Food = ½ Machine" and "1 Food = 3 Machines" each nation is likely to gain something from international trading, in terms of being better off compared to not trading.

Section III Takeaways: The theory does not promise that both nations will *always* be better off – but that *usually* or typically both nations will be better off. This is the main argument of the WTO and the IMF (International Monetary Fund).

Nor does the theory say that the gains from international trade will be *equally* shared – just that each nation will typically be better off compared with it not participating in international trade.

Since the two nations now realize that they are both better off participating in international trade, they not only wish to continue the same for next year, but also lift the restriction or trading only 3 Food for 3 Machines. "Let trade be unlimited," both nations proclaim. "Let any party buy any amount of food from Argentina and trade it for machines in Japan."

Section IV: Specialization by Comparative Advantage

ASSUMPTIONS: International Trade Is No Longer Restricted to 3 Food = 3 Machines. Any Amount of Food and Machines Can Be Imported/Exported. (However, for illustration purposes, Import/Export Is Shown at a Ratio of 1 Food = 1 Machine.) For simplicity, assume No Transportation Costs and No Tariffs.

International trade is now unrestricted, except for our use of 1 Food = 1 Machine Ratio for illustration purposes. Since there is no transport cost and no tariffs, any person can export one food unit from Argentina to Japan, exchange it for one machine, bring the machine back (import) to Argentina, sell it at a higher Peso price, and make a profit. There is a natural desire to make such arbitrage[2] profits. Hence, many Argentine and Japanese traders will do so, exporting machines out of Japan and importing back food from Argentina. See Figure IV.

---

[2] Arbitrage is buying something for a low price and simultaneously or soon selling it for a higher price to make a risk-free profit.

IV. TRADE BETWEEN ARGENTINA & JAPAN UNLIMITED EXCEPT FOR 1:1 RATIO

With unlimited trade internal prices will change and the price ratios of the two countries will approach one another until they are the same:

	MCS	FOOD
Produce	17	103
Consume	23	97

(Trade 6 units each along Slope -1)

Internal Prices
1 Food = 3 Pesos
1 Machine = 3 Pesos

1 PESO = 2 YEN*

	MCS	FOOD
Produce	153	12
Consume	147	18

(Trade 6 units each along Slope -1)

Internal Prices
1 Food = 6 Yen
1 Machine = 6 Yen

(Balanced trade of 6 FOOD for 6 Machines occurs when Exchange Rate at PPP of 1 Peso = 2 Yen)

As more and more machines enter Argentina (via imports), adding to the stock of locally made machines, the total supply of machines in Argentina will grow. Hence machine prices in Argentina will start to fall (below the old level of 6 pesos, to some new level such as 3.0 pesos). Similarly, Japan is giving away (exporting) its machines. Fewer machines will be left inside Japan. Hence machine prices in Japan will rise (above their old level of 4 yen, to say 6.0 yen).

A similar, but opposite phenomenon will occur for food. As Argentina exports (gives away) its food, less food supply is left inside Argentina, and food prices in Argentina will rise (from their old level of 2 Pesos, to say 3.0 Pesos). Japan will import (receive) food. The supply of food in Japan will increase. Hence food prices in Japan will drop (from their old level of 8 yen, to say 6.0 Yen). (These numbers are made up for illustration purposes, but the overall trend reflects reality.)

The Effect of International Trade on Internal Prices: How long will this import/export arbitrage[3] continue? Answer: Until such time as food prices in Argentina have risen, and machine prices have dropped sufficiently, so that there is no further incentive for arbitrage profits. In our (simplified) world of no transport cost and no tariff, this will happen when food and machinery prices are equal in both Argentina and Japan (at the levels shown as an illustration in the diagrams for Section IV, where the equal prices for food and machines are shown as a negative 45-degree

---

[3] Much of trade ultimately is arbitrage: buying and selling to make a profit.

slope of tangents in both nations). Once prices for Food and Machines are equalized in Argentina and Japan, there is no further arbitrage profit to be made. No additional international trade will occur, beyond that level.

But even if we introduce the real-world concepts of transport costs and tariffs, the same overall effects will happen – that international trade will affect prices within a nation. Trade may not completely equalize prices in the real world. But typically the price of exported items increases while the price of imported items decreases until further trade (or arbitrage) is no longer profitable for traders.

The Effect of International Trade on Consumers Within a Country: The Table in Section IV, as an illustration, shows a 6 Food for 6 Machine international trade as being sufficient to bring about price equalization and equilibrium. Both nations end up with a new mix of food and machines – but the new mix is considered better than the old. Both countries reach a higher indifference curve (satisfaction or utility) as a result. In fact, international trade has enabled both nations to reach a consumption satisfaction point higher than the best they could do before and escape the limitations of their Production Possibility Frontier.

Trade almost always makes consumers in a nation better off, because they achieve a new consumption mix (e.g., point C for Argentina) that is superior to what they had before (e.g., the old point A for Argentina). Notice that international trade has enabled Argentina to escape the confines of its Production Possibility Frontier and reach a higher indifference curve at point C. Similarly, the new Japanese consumption mix (point Z) is better for them than the old consumption mix (point X). International trade has enabled Japan also to escape the confines of its Production Possibility Frontier and reach a higher indifference curve at point Z.

On the consumption (or demand) side, international trade theory is usually optimistic – that both nations are usually better off. This is the main argument of trade theory and the WTO. But the benefits and costs are not spread uniformly.

The Not-Always-So-Happy Effects of International Trade on Production Within a Country:

Trade will increase exports. Hence food exporters (and farmers) in Argentina, as well as machinery manufacturers in Japan, will be happy to produce and sell more. Japanese food importers and Argentine machinery importers will also be happy.

But the theory of comparative advantage has a mixed message on the production (or supply) side – that some entities will be happy, while *some others will be unhappy as they can go bankrupt.*

Who will go bankrupt? Some Japanese farmers, seeing lower food prices will suffer. *Some* Japanese farms – the ones that are less efficient – will go bankrupt. But not all of them. The more efficient farms will survive. Production will shift from the old point X in Figure IV (15 food units produced) to the new production point Y (12 food units produced). Argentine machinery makers will also be unhappy, as machinery prices inside Argentina drop. Some of them will also go bankrupt in the face of import competition. Production in Argentina will shift from the old point A (20 machines) to the new production point B (17 machines).

Section IV Takeaways: Pains versus gains and policy implications. As in all economic policy changes, there are some winners and some losers. For a society, the overall question is whether the concentrated pain suffered by some losers (e.g., some machinery manufacturers in Argentina, or some farms in Japan that go out of business) is *more than offset* by the gain of other producers (e.g., farmers in Argentina or machinery producers in Japan) – and most importantly the increased *overall consumer benefit* enjoyed by millions of customers in the nation.

The message of Comparative Advantage Theory (and indeed the experience of the last fifty years of tariff and non-tariff barrier reductions achieved under WTO) is that the overall benefit to a society usually greatly outweighs the concentrated pain suffered by some segments of a country's society, once international trade increases. Hence more trade, lower trade barriers, and more International Business, are usually good for a nation. That is why more than 150 countries, including for example China in 2001, signed on with WTO.

WTO, over the past decade, is now more than just a "trade" organization. It encompasses not just Trade, but also Foreign Direct Investment (FDI),[4] Intellectual Property, Licensing, etc. The basic motivation is the same – that the more International Business there is, the better for all nations – be it under trade, licensing, or FDI. The 21st century hopes to continue evolving a global rules-based framework. This inevitably means, to a lesser or greater extent, that if a nation signs a

---

[4] For example, the TRIMs Protocol that deals with an individual nation's ability to put requirements and restrictions on foreign companies' subsidiaries operating within its borders.

treaty, the individual nation needs to voluntarily give up some of its sovereign rights over economic policy, over to a world body or a supranational organization like the European Union.[5]

Section IV Onward: Transitioning from Comparative Advantage to Purchasing Power Parity (PPP Theory)

Money (pesos, yen, dollars, etc.) being paper, plastic, metal, or electronic entries, has no intrinsic value, except what you can do with it – what you can purchase with it. It logically follows that, in a free and efficient foreign exchange market, the exchange rate will be set so as to equalize (i.e., put on "parity") the purchasing powers of the currencies exchanged. As seen at the bottom of the figure above, 1 Food or 1 machine = 3 pesos or 6 yen, that means that the "purchasing power" of 3 pesos is equal to the "purchasing power" of 6 yen. Hence in the foreign currency exchange market there should be 3 pesos = 6 yen, or **1 peso = 2 yen,** as the exchange rate predicted by PPP Theory.

Otherwise, rational people will not exchange currencies, unless they feel they are exchanging equal purchasing power.[6] This simple, but very profound, idea is explored in the PPP Theory chapter. The Purchasing Power Parity (PPP) theory, and exchange rates, may appear to have little to do with Comparative Advantage Theory, but they are a fundamental part of a country's overall trade policy.

SUMMARY OF CONCEPTS

- Comparative Advantage: Differences in Nations" Factor Endowments Constitute the Basis for Trade
- International Trade Usually Benefits All Trading Nations: A Country is Typically Better Off Participating in World Trade. Much of the growth in the world economy in the last 50 years has been the result of a huge expansion in world trade. Most nations are better off.
- The Benefits of Trade Are Not Necessarily Equally Spread Over Participating Countries
- Within a Country, Trade Will Mean Internal Adjustments. Production Mix Will Shift to Reflect the Country's Comparative Advantage

---

[5] This is exactly what has caused the reaction against globalization after 2016 from governments that do not wish to give up their sovereign rights to decide things within their own country.

[6] This applies only in the context of a free foreign exchange market, not one controlled by a government.

- More International Trade Will Benefit Export Sectors and Traders, But Some Producers in Import-Competing Sectors (e.g., Machinery in Argentina or Farmers in Japan) will suffer. Consumers Will Gain Much.

- Some Firms in Import-Competing Sectors Will Go Bankrupt. But the More Efficient Will Survive, Despite Import Competition.

- Internally, There Will Be (An Often Painful) Readjustment as Factors of Production Such as Land, Capital and Labor are Re-Allocated Away from the Shrinking Import-Competing Sector to the Growing Export Sector.

- **Overall Picture:** The Gains of Consumers, Traders and Exporters Typically Is Greater Than the Suffering or Cost Borne by Import-Competing Companies (and their Workers and Shareholders).

WHY IS COMPARATIVE ADVANTAGE THEORY REVIEWED IN THIS TEXT?

Because all of the above predictions of the theory have been proved correct. The idea of mutual gains from trade, accruing to all nations, is the fundamental belief that led (under GATT and WTO) to a massive dismantling of trade barriers over the last 50 years until the year 2016. This policy assumption is now accepted by virtually every government (with the exception of a handful of highly nationalistic nations). Much of humanity has benefited, and standard of living worldwide is higher because of the expansion of International Business.

The basic argument for freer world trade remains a powerful idea today in the 21st century.

On the other hand, some of the assumptions of the classic theory, and the overall predictions of the theory as to the composition of world trade, are incorrect in the context of modern commerce. We summarize these deficiencies in the theory below.

PREDICTIONS OF THE CLASSIC THEORY

The classic theory led some to believe that the composition of world trade should be roughly balanced between the primary and secondary sectors, and between developed and developing nations. This used to be true more than fifty years ago. Actual patterns of world trade today are very different, with most trade in manufactures and services, and with most trade occurring between advanced nations.

THE ASSUMPTIONS OF CLASSIC THEORY

The assumptions of the classic Comparative Advantage Theory are simple-minded, partially outdated and do not reflect modern commerce. They include the following:

- That countries have fixed factor endowments that do not change
- That factors are homogeneous
- That knowledge and technology are a public good
- That products are homogeneous
- That consumers and producers are atomistic, and each has no power to affect market prices
- That there is no such thing as a multinational corporation that can carry factors or advantages (e.g., knowledge or technology) from one country to another.

These assumptions are not all borne out in the real world of international business. Nevertheless, the idea of comparative advantage as constituting the basis for international trade, remains a valid and powerful idea in the 21st century.

CHAPTER 7

Purchasing Power Parity Theory:
Overvalued and Undervalued Currencies

The basic idea of purchasing power parity (PPP) is that in the long run, absent distortions, the exchange rate between two currencies will reflect the purchasing power of each currency. Picking up from our discussion in the previous chapter, let us suppose that in Argentina one unit of food or machines costs 3 pesos. And that one unit of food or machines in Japan costs 6 yen. Sensible persons in the foreign exchange market will see that the purchasing power of the peso is twice that of the yen. Hence, logically, if someone wants to exchange pesos for yen, they will want to exchange at 3 pesos = 6 yen, or 1 peso = 2 yen. Why? Because the 1 peso = 2 yen exchange rate equalizes the purchasing power of the currencies exchanged.

Argentina	Japan
1 Machine = 3.0 Pesos	1 Machine = 6 Yen
1 unit of Food (e.g. 1 tonne) = 3.0 Pesos	1 unit of Food (e.g. 1 tonne) = 6Yen
Purchasing Power Parity Theory What Can Money Purchase?	
What Can 1 Peso Purchase?	What Can 1 Yen Purchase?
1 Peso = 1/3.0 = 1/3 = 0.3333 Food or Machine	1 Yen = 1/6 = 0.1666 Food or Machine
Hence the Peso is more powerful in "purchasing power." 1 Peso can buy two times as much as 1 Yen. Hence in the foreign exchange market (to exchange equivalent "purchasing power") someone offering 1 Peso will demand 0.3333/0.1666 = 2 Yen. Hence the exchange rate 1 Peso = 2 Yen	

Recall, that money (as only a piece of metal, plastic, paper, or an electronic entry) has no intrinsic value, except what one can do with it – what one can purchase with it. Parties in the foreign exchange market will compare what 1 peso can purchase (i.e., 0.3333 food or machine) with what 1 yen can purchase (i.e., 0.1666 food or machine. Since the purchasing power of the peso is twice that of the yen, someone offering 1 peso will expect 2 yen in return. After all, in a foreign exchange market, why would anybody agree to receive less "purchasing power" than they are giving the other party? The 1 peso = 2 yen exchange rate, for now, equalizes the purchasing powers of the currencies exchanged between the two parties.

Inflation

While the basic concept is simple, money presents one complication. It so happens that almost all currencies lose purchasing power over time in a (still mysterious) process known as inflation. Inflation is nothing more than an erosion of the purchasing power of a money over time. For example, in the US, if in 2022 it takes $106.50 to purchase what took only $100 in 2021, we would say that the US suffered an annual inflation rate of 6.5percent between 2021 – 2022. Or we can say that the US dollar lost some purchasing power between 2021 and 2022.

To complicate matters, different currencies lose purchasing power at different rates over time. In our hypothetical Argentina and Japan example, assume that Argentina suffers a 33.33percent inflation. This means that food and machines in Argentina which used to cost 3.0 pesos each, will next year cost 4.0 pesos. Since 4.0/3.0 = 1.3333, economists will say that Argentina has suffered a 33.33percent inflation from one year to the next. To keep the example simple, let us assume that in our hypothetical Japan there is 0percent inflation – meaning that prices in Japan do not change, so that food or machines continue to cost 6 yen, the same as in the previous year.

Next Year	
Now suppose that, over the course of a year, **all prices in Argentina rise by one-third**. If so, <ul><li>There has been 33.33 % inflation in Argentina</li><li>In Japan zero inflation. Prices do not change</li></ul> One Year Later the New Price Levels Will Be	
Argentina	**Japan**
1 Machine = 3.0 (1.3333) = 4.0 Pesos 1 unit of Food (e.g. 1 tonne) = 3.0 (1.3333) = 4.0 Pesos	1 Machine = 6 Yen 1 unit of Food (e.g. 1 tonne) = 6 Yen (no change)
What Can 1 Peso Purchase? 1 Peso can now buy 1/4.0 = 0.25 Food or Machine	What Can 1 Yen Purchase? 1 Yen can still buy 1/6 = 0.1666 Food or Machine.
The Peso is *still* more powerful in "purchasing power." However the Peso has lost some purchasing power due to inflation, even if it remains more powerful than the Yen. Hence in the foreign exchange market (to exchange equivalent "purchasing power") someone offering 1 Peso will demand 0.25/0.1666 = 1.50 Yen. Hence the **new exchange rate** <u>SHOULD BE</u> **1 Peso = 1.50 Yen** The Peso should devalue from 1 Peso = 2.0 Yen last year, to 1 Peso = 1.50 Yen this year	

According to PPP Theory, however, the peso should devalue in the foreign exchange market. Sensible parties in the exchange markets will ask again, "What Can 1 Peso Purchase?" and "What Can 1 Yen Purchase?" One year later, the answer is different. Because now the purchasing power of 1 peso is only ¼ or 0.25 food or machine, and the purchasing power of 1 yen is still

0.1666 food or machine (i.e., no change). In order to equalize the purchasing power of the currencies in an exchange market, the new exchange rate should be 0.25/0.1666 or 1 peso = 1.50 yen.

Hence the corollary to the PPP theory is that the currency that has suffered higher inflation (peso) than its trading partner currency (yen) should devalue. The peso, according to the theory, should devalue because it has lost (more) purchasing power than the yen. In our calculation the exchange rate which a year ago was 1 peso = 2 yen, should change to 1 peso = 1.5 yen, a year later.

In Real-Life, How Do Economists Measure the (Theoretical) PPP Exchange Rate?

In our real lives, individuals and households consume hundreds of items, from toothpaste, to vegetables, to cars, to streaming services, to software subscriptions – all of which add up to a cost to each person per year.

Economists, assuming the consumption pattern for an average consumer in a country, enter into a spreadsheet hundreds of items and their cost. This adds up to a "cost of living" for a "consumption basket" or Consumer Price Index. They then compare the cost of the basket of goods and services in two countries, and from that deduce the theoretical PPP exchange rate. If, for example a basket of several hundred goods and services in the USA costs $40,000, and the same basket costs 4,800, 000 Argentine pesos, the economist would say that the theoretical PPP exchange rate for the Argentine peso should be 120 pesos per 1 dollar.

(Incidentally, as of April 2021, the actual exchange rate of the Argentine peso crossed 90 per dollar. Even though the peso was weakening (devaluing over time) an economist would say that peso is "overvalued" in comparison with its theoretical PPP rate of 120. Overvaluation of a currency is equivalent to saying that the actual exchange rate is not sufficiently devalued to bring the actual rate in line with the theoretical PPP rate. Such deviations between the actual and PPP rate are a common occurrence in the short run.)

What Distortions Prevent PPP Theory from Working in the Short to Medium Run

The PPP theory works well in the long run, but not so in the short or medium run, because of distortions which temporarily overvalue or undervalue a currency.

(1) Interest rates that are 'set" by the central banks of each country.

Short term interest rates are 'set" or influenced by the decision of each country's central bank. In simple terms, higher interest rates attract capital into a currency. If, for example interest on a short-term money market deposit in Country A is 0.50 percent per annum compared with say 1.60 percent in Country B, the preference of money managers will be to park their funds in Country B. But in order to do that, Currency A will have to be sold (supplied) in the foreign exchange (FX) market and Currency B bought (demanded) in the FX market. The higher demand for Currency B (or equivalently, the greater supply of Currency A, to the tune of millions or more) will boost the exchange rate for Currency B – over and above what PPP theory would say it should be, temporarily. That is what economists characterize as an overvalued currency.

(2) Investor psychology affecting cross-border capital movements.

Investing in foreign assets – portfolio investments in a country's equity or bond markets, or foreign direct investment (FDI), or investing in a foreign nation's real estate – sometimes seems very attractive. That is to say, there is a collective bandwagon desire to invest in that country because it appears to be an attractive destination for parking money, at least temporarily. But investing in a country's assets requires that nation's currency. In order to invest there, the rest of the world has to first demand that country's currency in the FX market, and in exchange, supply their own. The higher demand for the foreign currency can artificially boost its value or exchange rate, for a while, beyond what the PPP theory prescribes – i.e., the currency becomes "overvalued."

The opposite can also happen. For political or other reasons, global investors may lose confidence in a country and pull out their investments – selling the local assets for local cash and then supplying the local currency cash to the FX , i.e., an extra supply of millions or billions of that currency, which means the FX value of the currency drops and it devalues. If the devaluation of the currency is severe, its actual exchange rate may drop below what PPP theory prescribes. Then the currency is described as "undervalued."

(3) Governments intervening in FX markets or "fixing" their exchange rates.

Governments of major currencies such as the US dollar, the euro, the UK pound, or the yen do not often intervene to change or directly influence the value of their currencies in the FX market. For the most part, such governments take a "hands off" position, preferring to leave exchange rate to market influences. This is truest for a few advanced economies.

However, most governments do intervene to "manage" the value of their currency, to at least a mild extent. In extreme cases, some emerging country governments may even "fix" the value of their currency, by official fiat, for a short or extended period of years, by ordering their banks and financial institutions to exchange their currency only at the prescribed rate. If the government-prescribed (or government influenced) rate for the currency is too weak, or overly devalued, then we would call that currency "undervalued" or over-devalued. More common is a situation where the government-prescribed or government influenced rate is left unchanged for a long time – notwithstanding inflation in the country, then the currency can become "overvalued" – meaning stronger than it should be according to PPP theory.

> For more details, see the chapter entitled "What Do We Mean by Undervalued or Overvalued Currencies?" reprinted from my article in *Rutgers Business Review*, Spring 2019, Volume 4, No 1: https://rbr.business.rutgers.edu/article/what-do-we-mean-undervalued-or-overvalued-currencies

The Effects of Overvalued and Undervalued Currencies

Overvaluation of a currency – that is to say, a currency that is not allowed to devalue, or not devalued enough – compared with its PPP theory value – is a phenomenon particularly seen in emerging nations such as Argentina. At the moment, we will not detail the political or economic reasons *why* overvaluation occurs in anywhere from 40 – 60 emerging countries. (This is summarized at the end of this chapter). Rather, below we will first see the effects (mostly deleterious) of overvaluation.

To summarize, an overvalued currency hurts or dampens the exports of country, while at the same time, it makes imports look artificially cheap in the country's currency. In many situations, this creates a trade deficit (i.e., imports exceed exports) which can only be temporarily financed by a net outflow of hard currency reserves from the nation. Eventually, the situation is not sustainable, and the long-deferred devaluation of the currency takes place.

Exports Hurt by Currency Overvaluation

This will be clearer going back to our hypothetical Argentina and Japan example.

Earlier, we saw that, following rising prices for food and machines, i.e., a 33 percent inflation in Argentina, PPP theory prescribed a devaluation of the peso from the previous 1 peso = 2 yen, to the new level of 1 peso = 1.5 yen. But what if, for political or other reasons, the government of Argentina does not allow (or retards) the devaluation? The peso then would be considered "overvalued."

Below we see the effects of overvaluation, or insufficient devaluation. Exports of a country can only happen if foreigners demand the country's products. In this example, Japanese wish to import Argentine food. But we see in the table below that following Argentine inflation but with the exchange rate unchanged, Argentine food which used to cost the Japanese importer 6 yen, one year later costs 8 yen. Being more expensive – in the importer's currency – the Japanese will buy less Argentine food, and the *volume* or quantity of Argentina's food exports (pounds, kilos, tonnes, etc.) will reduce. Critically, as a result, Argentina will earn less yen from the country's exports than one year ago.

Why is this critical? Because yen are needed by Argentine companies to import Japanese machines. The Japanese would love to ship machine exports to Argentina. But the Japanese will be unwilling to accept pesos in payment. They will insist on being paid in yen (a "hard" currency). After all, if you were a Japanese exporter, would you be willing to accept pesos (a 'soft' currency), or an overvalued currency prone to losing purchasing power and eventually devaluing? (A "hard" currency is one that has low inflation and does not lose purchasing power quickly. A 'soft' currency is one that more quickly loses purchasing power).

EFFECTS OF OVERVALUED FIXED EXCHANGE RATES ON THE COUNTRY'S EXPORTS AND IMPORTS

Example: Argentina Prevents Devaluation and Fixes its Exchange rate at 1 Peso = 2 Yen

Despite Inflation in the Preceding Year of 33 %; Theoretical PPP Rate 1 Peso = 1.5 Yen)

EFFECT ON ARGENTINE EXPORTS WITH OVERVALUED RATE

Yen Cost of 1 Argentine Food Unit to Japanese Importer With Fixed Exchange Rate of 2 Yen per Peso	
LAST YEAR (3.0 Pesos) (2 Yen per Peso) = 6 Yen	THIS YEAR (4.0 Pesos) (2 Yen per Peso) = 8 Yen

Conclusions:

- Argentine Food Looks More Expensive to Japanese Buyers.
- They Will Buy Less Quantity This Year.
- The Volume (quantity) of Argentine Food Exports Will Decline.
- Argentina Will Earn Less Yen (Hard Currency)

OVERVALUED EXCHANGE RATE HURTS EXPORTS

Import Demand Exaggerated Because of an Overvalued Currency

On the import side, an overvalued peso does exaggerate or inflame the demand for the import of Japanese machines. In the calculation below we see that, with an unchanged or fixed (or overvalued) peso exchange rate, the imports of Japanese machines the previous year cost 3.0 pesos and one year later also cost 3.0 pesos – no change. However, let us not forget that in the meanwhile, domestically, Argentina suffers a 33 % inflation, which means that the price of domestically produced machines has jumped to 4.0 pesos. *Imports look artificially cheaper compared with domestically produced equivalent items.* Hence there is often a surge in import demand. This import demand can be met as long as the country has earned enough yen from its exports, to pay for its imports. But that may not be possible, in the medium or long run.

EFFECTS OF OVERVALUED FIXED EXCHANGE RATES
ON THE COUNTRY'S EXPORTS AND IMPORTS
Example: Argentina Prevents Devaluation and
Fixes its Exchange rate at 1 Peso = 2 Yen
(Despite Inflation in the Preceding Year of 33 %
making the theoretical PPP Rate 1 Peso = 1.5 Yen)

EFFECT ON ARGENTINE IMPORTS WITH OVERVALUED RATE

Peso Cost of 1 Japanese Machine Unit to Argentine Importer	
LAST YEAR (6 Yen)/(2 Yen per Peso) = 3.0 Pesos	THIS YEAR (6 Yen)/(2 Yen per Peso) = 3.0 Pesos
Price of Argentine-Made Machine = 3.0 Pesos	Price of Argentine-Made Machine = 4.0 Pesos

Conclusions:
No Change in Peso Cost of Imports Because of Fixed Exchange Rate.

But in the Meanwhile, This Year, Argentine-Made Machines Are Priced at 4.0 Pesos Because of Inflation.

Imported Japanese Machines Look (Artificially) Cheaper.

Every Argentine Importer Prefers to Import Machines Rather Than Buy Argentine-Made Machines.

There is a Surge in Import Demand Volume (Quantity) into Argentina

RESULT: EXTRA HIGH IMPORT VOLUME

A Trade Deficit as a Result of Overvaluation of a Currency

Recall that Japanese exporters would love to sell their machines to the Argentines, provided they are paid in yen (a hard currency). A Japanese exporter is understandably unwilling to accept payment in pesos. The peso being a "soft" currency, it loses value more quickly over time. Moreover, outside of Argentina's currency regime and controls, in say the Japanese foreign exchange market, the peso may have devalued already. Hence, Japanese exporters insist on being paid in yen, and not pesos. This means that in the longer run – notwithstanding the exaggerated demand for imports – the ability of such an emerging nation as Argentina to import is going to be constrained.

However, for a while, imports can exceed exports, if and only if the government of Argentina's central bank can release past reserves of yen to prospective importers of machines – from past built-up reserves of yen, or by borrowing more hard currency (e.g., yen) from the International Monetary Fund (IMF) or from the international bond market.

EFFECTS OF OVERVALUED FIXED EXCHANGE RATES ON THE COUNTRY'S EXPORTS AND IMPORTS

Example: Argentina Prevents Devaluation and Fixes its Exchange rate at 1 Peso = 2 Yen

(Despite Inflation in the Preceding Year of 33 % making the theoretical PPP Rate 1 Peso = 1.5 Yen)

OVERALL EFFECT ON ARGENTINA'S TRADE BALANCE

- **Export Side:** Declining Exports and Less Foreign (Hard) Currency Earned

- **Import Side:** Surge in Imports (Requiring Hard Currency)

RESULT: Trade Deficit

The trade deficit cannot go on indefinitely. Many such emerging countries draw down their reserves of hard currency, until the reserves are almost gone. Even the IMF or the international bond market refuses to loan the country any more hard currency. Some emerging nations then may take up draconian measures to limit imports by rationing the now scarce hard currency to only priority importers (e.g., critically important industries, hospitals, or politically connected individuals and companies). In some cases, as a result, a semi-illegal "parallel market" in hard currencies emerges. Such measures can delay the devaluation (that PPP Theory prescribed should have occurred long ago).

But this delaying of the PPP theory prescribed devaluation also cannot go on forever. Recall that with continued domestic inflation (but no devaluation or insufficient devaluation occurring) exports of the country are hurt even more – because Japanese buyers of Argentine food find the cost in yen increasing each year, and buy less. The Argentine economy earns fewer and fewer yen each year.

The "day of reckoning" then arrives if hard currency (yen) reserves are depleted, and very few yen are earned by Argentine exporters, so that even necessary imports of medicines, components and other critical items cannot be imported.

At that stage, reluctantly, the government allows a significant devaluation of its currency, commensurate with PPP theory.

Following a Devaluation

Once a devaluation does occur, there is a natural new equilibrium or balancing out. Following a devaluation of a currency:

(1) Export volume rebounds because exporters either,

    a. Earn more local currency from their hard currency export revenues (i.e., more pesos per yen converted in the foreign exchange market, following the devaluation) and/or

    b. With fatter margins for the exporters (i.e., more pesos per yen converted in the foreign exchange market, following the devaluation) lower the price per unit charged to foreign buyers, which in turn boosts exports.

(2) Import volume shrinks because in the local currency (pesos) imports cost more following the devaluation.

As a result, the trade deficit narrows or disappears, in a new hoped-for equilibrium.

Why Do 40 – 60 Emerging Countries Overvalue Their Currencies or Delay Devaluation (for as Long as They Can)?

Because many negative effects of overvaluation occur, why do so many dozens of emerging nations (and also several advanced nations) continue this policy? The reasons are at least partially political. In some nations, if the import lobby is stronger than the exporters' lobby, there is a tendency to stop or delay a devaluation. The reason is obvious. An overvalued currency makes the local currency cost of imports artificially cheap (e.g., in the above example, imported Japanese machines cost 3.0 pesos instead of 4.0 pesos).

In other cases, the country may have become dependent on the import of medicines, food, energy, and other basic items for a volatile population that may 'take to the streets and protest if a devaluation increases the local currency (peso) cost of the needed imports following a devaluation.

In yet other countries, the government is reluctant to devalue because it feels the net outcome will be even worse. According to pure economics theory, following a devaluation, exports are supposed to get a boost (or rebound) – for reasons we saw in the above section. But in many emerging nations that theory may not work. It is true that (other things being equal) a devaluation should boost the country's exports because exporters who convert their hard currency earnings (yen) at the bank will receive more local currency (pesos) after devaluation. But that is a *necessary but not sufficient condition*. Boosting a country's exports also requires (i) mobilization of capital to increase export capacity in factories and offices, (ii) entrepreneurship and talent, and (iii) skilled labor. If a country lacks sources of investment capital, talent or entrepreneurship, and adequate skilled labor, then the devaluation may only (painfully) increase the local currency cost of necessary imports, without seeing an increase on the export side. In such situations, the government sees no benefit from a devaluation, and seeing only the danger of higher prices for imports, tries to prevent a devaluation of the currency.

Finally, some countries get caught in an inflationary psychology. A devaluation that increases the local currency costs of food, medicines, energy and other necessities can make the public demand higher wages and salaries from the companies they work in. Granting wage increases means the costs for all companies goes up. The companies are, in turn, forced to raise the unit prices for the products they sell. That makes inflation even worse, which in turn leads to even more wage demands – called a "Wage-Price Spiral." The cycle of Higher Wages > Higher Prices > More Wage Increases > Yet Higher Prices, can lead to a "hyper-inflationary" runaway cycle in the country. The fear that a devaluation could trigger a runaway cycle of hyperinflation, forces some nations to take desperate measures to avoid, or delay, any devaluation of their currency, for as long as possible.

Some Nations Allegedly Undervalue Their Currency (The Opposite Case)

For decades, US administrations, based on PPP calculations for the Chinese Yuan or Renminbi's (RMB's) theoretical exchange rate, have alleged that the Chinese government has deliberately undervalued its currency. Historically, and to a diminishing extent in 2021/22, the reason offered is job creation and job maintenance in China. This simple logic is illustrated below.

An allegedly undervalued RMB artificially boosts China's exports (since Chinese exporters get at their bank 6.5 RMB for each export dollar earned – as opposed to getting only 5.0 RMB/$at the bank if the RMB were allowed to appreciate to its PPP level). That creates and maintains millions of export jobs in China, it is said.

At the same time, if 1 dollar's worth of an import coming into China costs 6.5 RMB – instead of the theoretical PPP cost of only 5.0 RMB – then imports into China look artificially expensive. This reduces the volume of China's imports, which protects import-competing Chinese firms, and is said to artificially maintain higher employment inside China (for companies that produce local substitutes for imports).

Thus, an allegedly undervalued currency, both on the export side, and on the import side, creates and maintains jobs.

EFFECTS OF UNDERVALUED EXCHANGE RATES
(e.g., CHINA at ~ 6.5 RMB/$ Summer 2021;
8.27 RMB/$ June 2005)
(PPP Rate According to IMF or OECD) in 2021
Around 5.00 or less RMB/$)

The "Undervaluation" Allegation

CHINESE EXPORTS
Since exporters earn as many as 6.5 RMB/$
Chinese Exporters Can Price Exports Low (in $, and especially in Euros, Yen)

- Hence Export Boom
- More Jobs/Economic Activity in China
- Fewer Jobs/Economic Activity in US, EU, and Japan

CHINESE IMPORTS
Having to pay as many as 6.5 RMB/$
Chinese Importers Find RMB Price of Imports High (or Higher than Local Production)

- Hence Imports from (US, Europe, Japan) into China Less Than Otherwise
- Local Suppliers Safer from Foreign Competition
- More Jobs/Economic Activity in China

Chinese Yuan or RMB's Historical Record

In the historical graph below, showing the exchange rate of the RMB (entirely controlled by the People's Bank of China) it is clear that in the early days of China's internationalization (1985 – 1995), a massive five-fold devaluation – from less than 2.0 RMB/$to 8.8 RMB/$– was deliberately engineered in order to spark China's export "engine" and make China the "factory of the world." It was a strategy that succeeded brilliantly. Literally hundreds of millions of unemployed or underemployed villagers from the interior of China migrated to its east coast to become factory workers for exporters, as well as for the beginning domestic market producers. These internal migrants earned higher wages than they could earn in their original homes in the rural countryside.

The Chinese then held the RMB at 8.27/$ for ten years, from around 1995 until June 2005, followed by some appreciation for the RMB, holding it in a range between 6.0 and 7.0 RMB/$ (between 2008 and 2019).

(Sources: Federal Reserve; www.Globalbusiness.blog)

In the Year 2021/22, the situation is a bit different. In early summer 2021, the RMB exchange rate set by the Chinese government was around 6.5 RMB/$. Many economists continue to argue that the RMB remains undervalued at 6.5 since their PPP calculation shows it should theoretically be 5.0 or less. That is to say, they continue to allege deliberate undervaluation. But the gap between the theoretical PPP exchange rate and the actual is narrowing. Because of the effects of the "one child policy," labor supply is much tighter. Chinese wages over the 2000–2020 period rose considerably faster than general inflation. Labor costs in China having risen the gap between PPP and the actual exchange rate has narrowed. Also, the Chinese economy is not as dependent on exports as before and now depends more on domestic market demand. Third, China is gradually making the transition from making basics like toasters and air-conditioners to making high tech items where the labor content is a lower fraction of value. The Chinese population size has plateaued. Hence the underlying pressure to undervalue the RMB is far less intense than in years past. Nevertheless, a majority of economists maintain that to a lesser degree, the RMB remains somewhat undervalued.

Farok J. Contractor, Ph.D.

Conclusion: Despite Limitations, the Purchasing Power Parity PPP Theory Has Several Uses

The PPP theory's main drawback is that it is seen to work with reasonable accuracy only in the long run, which could be a few or many years. In the short run, other stronger influences, such as interest rates set by central banks, investor psychology, reluctance to devalue by dozens of emerging nation governments, or deliberate undervaluation by some governments, can obscure the theory's prescriptions.

But the theory does have important practical uses, as summarized below:

(1) To **get some sense of the trajectory of a currency** and whether the exchange rate is due for a change. Is a devaluation or appreciation of the currency due in the future?

(2) For **multinational companies to do capital budgeting** for future investments in order to estimate the cash flow projections for the future (Year 1, Year 2....Year 10), some estimated exchange rates for each year into the future have to be plugged into the spreadsheet. The estimates for future exchange rates can be derived from PPP theory.

(3) For **some governments to "manage" their exchange rate** and not allow it to become overvalued or undervalued.

(4) For bodies like the IMF or World Bank to **compare the size of countries' economies** to give a more realistic comparison of economic size (corrected for purchasing power or cost of living).

CHAPTER 8

What Do We Mean by Undervalued or Overvalued Currencies?[*]

Abstract

This article explains currency overvaluation and undervaluation and reveals the means through which currency valuation can be measured. The benefits, costs, and consequences of currency overvaluation and undervaluation, including its implications for global trade are presented. Currencies such as the Chinese Renminbi and the Indian Rupee are discussed in detail.

For decades, going back to the Clinton administration, US presidents have complained that the Chinese government has kept its currency (the renminbi yuan [RMB]) undervalued,[1] thereby giving the Chinese economyan unfair advantage. Indeed, this is one of the sticking points in the ongoingnegotiation between the Trump administration and the Chinese government. Chinese negotiators have apparently agreed not to devalue theircurrency.[2] Contrariwise, for many years, other currencies ranging from the Nigerian naira, to the Norwegian krone, to the Indian rupee are said to be overvalued.

What exactly do we mean by currency undervaluation and overvaluation?How do we measure this? And what are the benefits, costs, and consequencesof overvaluation and undervaluation?

The Foreign Exchange Market

Every 24 hours, over $5.1 trillion in currencies change hands worldwide. The US dollar dominates, making up one side of the transaction in 85percent of alltrades.[3] The other side of the trades are taken up by the euro, yen – and increasingly, emerging market currencies such as the Indian rupee, Brazilian real, and Chinese yuan, which tend to exhibit greater overvaluation or undervaluation.

Many large, advanced country currencies "float" as depicted in Figure 1. Their value goes up or down depending on demand and supply in the foreignexchange markets – and there is little or only rare government intervention.Examples include the US dollar, the euro, the Japanese yen, and

---

[*] Reprinted from Farok J. Contractor (2019), What Do We Mean by Undervalued or Overvalued Currencies? *Rutgers Business Review*, 4(1), 1-9.

the British pound. But that does not mean that government actions, such as interest-rate setting by their central banks, cannot affect their currency value.

The majority of currencies on the planet, especially in emerging countries, are partially controlled, or pegged, by their governments.[4] The government's agent can directly buy or sell its own currency in order to influence its value. In extreme cases, there is a hard peg, or currency value dictated, by fiat from the government.

There are advantages and disadvantages to currency overvaluation or undervaluation, depending on a country's circumstances, as we discuss later.But first let us examine some of the other causes of undervaluation (low value, or too much devaluation against other currencies such as the dollar) and overvaluation (too strong a value, or not enough devaluation, againstother currencies such as the dollar).

Figure 1. Extent of Government Intervention

- [ ] Floating (floating and free-floating)
- [ ] Soft pegs (conventional peg, stabilized arrangement, crawling peg, crawl-likearrangement, pegged exchange rate with horizontal bands)
- [ ] Hard pegs (no separate legal tender, currency board)
- [ ] Residual (other managed arrangement)

Source: Exchange-Rate Regime, *Wikipedia.*

Causes of Undervaluation or Overvaluation

Government actions are often a root cause. For example, even in free-floating currencies, deliberate government actions such as interest rates (setby the nation's central bank), can affect the currency markets. When interestrates offered by banks in a nation are raised, greater demand by foreigners for that currency in the foreign exchange market can raise its price (or exchange rate) thereby strengthening or appreciating it – sometimes too much – which leads to overvaluation – or too much appreciation.[5] Correspondingly, when a nation's central bank lowers interest rates, parkingfunds in that currency becomes less attractive, and foreign holders liquidate their accounts, take the local cash, and dump/sell it in the foreign exchange market, thereby lowering its value. Too much capital flight out of the nationcan undervalue it (i.e., too much devaluation).

Governments often manipulate their currency value (up or down) also bydirect buying or selling of the currency in the foreign exchange market.[6] Other nations mandate that trading only occur within a small band or range – a range that can be kept in place for months and adjusted, as thegovernment decides. In the extreme case, the government simply dictates theexchange rate, by fiat, and can enforce that dictated rate for months or years.[7]External factors or influences from outside the nation, such as market sentiment, can also appreciate or devalue currencies, as foreigners buy or sellassets in a nation and move their money in or out, depending on their perception of the country's economy. Political crises can undervalue (i.e.,excessively devalue) a currency. As happened in Brazil and Turkey (from 2013to 2019), both foreigners and locals lose confidence in the economy, liquidateassets, and take their local cash to the foreign exchange market to try andconvert into hard currencies like the dollar or euro. This severely devaluedthe Brazilian real and the Turkish lira.[8] Sometimes, desperate governmentsthen try to stem the outflow by introducing restrictions or limits on currency conversions.

Currencies may become overvalued when foreigners desire that currencyin the exchange markets because they seek to hold portfolio or real assets in that nation. Or if the country's central bank raises internal interest rates, money fund managers wishing to earn higher interest then demand that currency in the spot market.

Especially in the emerging world, governments may deliberately keep their currency overvalued (prevent devaluation) – for political reasons. By contrast, in the case of China, US officials and others allege that the People's Bank of China (its central bank) has consistently undervalued the renminbi/yuan since the early 1990s, in order to promote exports. We explainthe motivations, advantages, and drawbacks below.

The advantages of undervaluation from China's point of view include:

- Giving a boost to China's exporters because the dollars exporters earnconvert into more renminbi than they would otherwise.[9] As an example, in March 2019 Chinese exporters who earned a dollar, wouldbe given in exchange 6.7 RMB at their bank. Hypothetically speaking,if the RMB were to appreciate to say 5.0 RMB = US $1, then the Chinese exporter would earn only 5 RMB from their export. This illustrates how undervaluation can help exporters.

- Making foreign direct investment (FDI) more attractive to outside investors, since their currencies, say the US dollar, convert into more renminbi with which to buy land, factories, or any local asset. The cost of establishing FDI in China is reduced in, say, dollar terms, thereby increasing FDI from the rest of the world.

- Causing investment and jobs to pour into China's export sector,turning it into the "factory of the world," due to the expectation of allegedly continued future undervaluation by the Chinese centralbank.

- Making imports headed into China more expensive in renminbi,thereby protecting domestic Chinese firms from import competition and retaining investment and jobs in the country.

- Boosting investment and jobs overall, critical for a population of 1.4 billion people.

The drawbacks of undervaluation for China:

- Offering effective protection against imports reduces competition, which can also reduce the efficiency and competitiveness of local firms.

- Can create excess demand for jobs and escalate wages in a country with a limited labor supply, which in turn could increase inflation. This did not happen in China for many decades because of its large population.[10] However, with the one-child policy having an effect starting in 2015, reports of labor shortages have emerged. Chinese labor costs have escalated sharply, threatening China's "factory of the world" position.[11]

We next discuss overvalued currencies which are more likely to be foundin emerging countries (although examples of overvaluation also occur in developed economies, such as Norway and Switzerland).

Advantages of overvaluation (for countries like India, Thailand, Egypt, or Nigeria as of early 2019):

- Imports are cheaper in the local currency. This can be crucial for import-dependent populations or where basic necessities like food, medicines, or energy must be imported for the local market.[12]
- Political stability increases. To the extent that the government handles or subsidizes imports of necessities, the politicalconsequences of allowing devaluation would be detrimental to the incumbent government. This is because, following devaluation, basic necessities, including energy, may still have to be imported anyway, costing more in the local currency, and possibly contributing to unrestand protests.
- Especially in import-dependent economies, importing at the overvalued exchange rate is cheaper than local production, keeping price increases and inflation under control.

Drawbacks of overvaluation:
- Exports are reduced because companies converting their foreign currency earnings, say, US dollars, at the overvalued exchange rate, do not earn enough local currency, in Egyptian pounds, Nigerian naira, or Indian rupees, to justify their costs. For instance, one dollar earned by an Indian exporter in March 2019 converted into 70 rupees, but if the exchange rate had been 78 rupees per dollar, the exporter's earning would have been 11 percent greater.
- Imports may appear artificially inexpensive compared with local substitute products, thereby dampening investments and jobs in the sectors that could have produced equivalent goods and services locally, to compete against imports.
- FDI coming into a country with an overvaluated currency is somewhat reduced because foreign currencies like the US dollar convert into fewer units of local currency, naira or rupees, with which to buy local assets such as land, factories, and so forth.

Comparing currency values is complicated because the comparison involves converting different moneys into one reference currency such as theUS dollar whose value itself fluctuates. Also, living standards and the cost of living vary dramatically across nations and complicate comparisons and analyses.

Farok J. Contractor, Ph.D.

The advantages of undervaluation from China's point of view include:

- Giving a boost to China's exporters because the dollars exporters earnconvert into more renminbi than they would otherwise.[9] As an example, in March 2019 Chinese exporters who earned a dollar, wouldbe given in exchange 6.7 RMB at their bank. Hypothetically speaking,if the RMB were to appreciate to say 5.0 RMB = US $1, then the Chinese exporter would earn only 5 RMB from their export. This illustrates how undervaluation can help exporters.

- Making foreign direct investment (FDI) more attractive to outside investors, since their currencies, say the US dollar, convert into more renminbi with which to buy land, factories, or any local asset. The cost of establishing FDI in China is reduced in, say, dollar terms, thereby increasing FDI from the rest of the world.

- Causing investment and jobs to pour into China's export sector,turning it into the "factory of the world," due to the expectation of allegedly continued future undervaluation by the Chinese centralbank.

- Making imports headed into China more expensive in renminbi,thereby protecting domestic Chinese firms from import competition and retaining investment and jobs in the country.

- Boosting investment and jobs overall, critical for a population of 1.4 billion people.

The drawbacks of undervaluation for China:

- Offering effective protection against imports reduces competition, which can also reduce the efficiency and competitiveness of local firms.

- Can create excess demand for jobs and escalate wages in a country with a limited labor supply, which in turn could increase inflation. This did not happen in China for many decades because of its large population.[10] However, with the one-child policy having an effect starting in 2015, reports of labor shortages have emerged. Chinese labor costs have escalated sharply, threatening China's "factory of theworld" position.[11]

We next discuss overvalued currencies which are more likely to be foundin emerging countries (although examples of overvaluation also occur in developed economies, such as Norway and Switzerland).

Advantages of overvaluation (for countries like India, Thailand, Egypt, or Nigeria as of early 2019):

- Imports are cheaper in the local currency. This can be crucial for import-dependent populations or where basic necessities like food, medicines, or energy must be imported for the local market.[12]
- Political stability increases. To the extent that the government handles or subsidizes imports of necessities, the politicalconsequences of allowing devaluation would be detrimental to the incumbent government. This is because, following devaluation, basic necessities, including energy, may still have to be imported anyway, costing more in the local currency, and possibly contributing to unrestand protests.
- Especially in import-dependent economies, importing at the overvalued exchange rate is cheaper than local production, keeping price increases and inflation under control.

Drawbacks of overvaluation:
- Exports are reduced because companies converting their foreign currency earnings, say, US dollars, at the overvalued exchange rate, do not earn enough local currency, in Egyptian pounds, Nigerian naira, or Indian rupees, to justify their costs. For instance, one dollar earned by an Indian exporter in March 2019 converted into 70 rupees, but if the exchange rate had been 78 rupees per dollar, the exporter's earning would have been 11 percent greater.
- Imports may appear artificially inexpensive compared with local substitute products, thereby dampening investments and jobs in the sectors that could have produced equivalent goods and services locally, to compete against imports.
- FDI coming into a country with an overvaluated currency is somewhat reduced because foreign currencies like the US dollar convert into fewer units of local currency, naira or rupees, with which to buy local assets such as land, factories, and so forth.

Comparing currency values is complicated because the comparison involves converting different moneys into one reference currency such as the US dollar, whose value itself fluctuates. Also, living standards and the cost of living vary dramatically across nations and complicate comparisons and analyses.

Figure 2. Is the rupee undervalued or overvalued?

Differential has been calculated as compounded annual growth between October 1998 to October 2018.

Source: RBI, IMF · Get the data · Created with Datawrapper

Source: Rajadhyaksha, N. (2018, October 8). Is the rupee undervalued or is it overvalued? *LiveMint.*

Portions of this article are reproduced from "Does a Strong Currency Help, or a Weak One?" By Farok J. Contractor, YaleGlobal, Tuesday, March 5, 2019.

Notes

1. Sutter, R. (2010). *US - Chinese relations: Perilous past, pragmatic present.* Lanham, MD:Rowman & Littlefield.

2. Wallace, C. (2019, February 22). China agrees to stop currency manipulation, Trumpsays. *Forbes.*

3. Venketas, W. (2019, January 15). Forex market size: A trader's advantage. *DailyFX.*

4. The expression "majority of currencies on the planet" is numerically true – by country. But recall that the dollar, euro, and yen dominate daily foreign exchange transactions. Hence as a fraction of overall global foreign exchange turnover, the majority of trades are in free-floating currencies. Albeit small, the fraction of daily trades in emerging market currencies – where governments intervene more heavily -- is rapidly growing.

5. Engel, C. (2016). Exchange rates, interest rates, and the risk premium. *American Economic Review, 106*(2), 436-474.

6. Kuepper, J. (2018, November 15). What is a currency intervention? *The Balance.*

7. Blanchard, O., Adler, G., & Carvalho, I. (2015). *Can foreign exchange intervention stem exchange rate pressures from global capital flow shocks? (Working Paper No. 21427).* Cambridge, MA: National Bureau of Economic Research.

8. Aitken, R. (2018, August 16). Turkish lira 'currency crisis' not over, could hit 8 against U.S. dollar. *Forbes.*

9.   Gwiazda, A. (2017). The sluggish internationalization of the Renminbi. *Bank i Kredyt*, 5, 483-493.

10. Holz, C. A., & Mehrotra, A. (2016). Wage and price dynamics in China. *The WorldEconomy, 39*(8), 1109-1127.

11. Yan, S. (2017, 27 February). 'Made in China' isn't so cheap anymore, and that could spell headache for Beijing. *CNBC*.

12. Shatz, H. J., & Tarr, D. (2000). *Exchange rate overvaluation and trade protection - lessonsfrom experience (Working Paper No. WPS 2289)*. Washington, DC: World Bank.

13. Jiang, C., Bahmani-Oskooee, M., & Chang, T. (2015). Revisiting purchasing power parityin OECD. *Applied Economics, 47*(40), 4323-4334.

14. Rajadhyaksha, N. (2018, October 8). Is the rupee undervalued or is it overvalued? *LiveMint*.

15. Kenton, W. (2019, February 11). Real effective exchange rate – REER Definition. *Investopedia*.

16. Rajadhyaksha, N. (2018, October 8). Is the rupee undervalued or is it overvalued? *LiveMint*.

17. A Turkish company that took out a 5-year US dollar-denominated loan in 2013 received 2.2 Turkish lire for every dollar it borrowed. But in 2018 when the loan had to be repaid, it took 5.5 Turkish lire from the company's cash flows to repay that one dollar. Many could not pay and went insolvent.

CHAPTER 9

Ten Quick Facts About US Trade:
Deficits, Dumping, and Discords[*]

Acting on his campaign rhetoric that <u>China is "raping our country,"[1]</u> Don Trump recently announced a 25 percent tariff on steel, 10 percent on aluminum, 30 percent on solar panels, and 20–50 percent on washing machines – <u>products he alleged are being "dumped" by the Chinese[2]</u> – and threatened a "trade war" against that country.

The objective of this article is to present 10 salient facts (not opinions) about US trade in the wake of the aggressive stance taken by the Trump administration. I seek to supply clear answers and unbiased perspectives to questions such as:

- How bad is the problem, really?
- How much does China figure in the problem?
- How has the US managed to sustain a trade deficit against the rest of the world and China since 1975—the past 43 years?
- What exactly is "dumping"?
- Who "wins" and who "loses" from international trade?
- Is China "stealing" intellectual property and technology from Western companies?

My hope is to simplify the national dialogue and clear up the ambiguity accompanying the increasing numbers of press reports about a topic that affects all Americans.

See my related blog post: <u>WWMS? (What Would Milton Say?):</u>

<u>https://globalbusiness.blog/2018/04/14/wwms-what-would-milton-say/</u>

---

[*] Reprinted from Farok J. Contractor (2018), Ten Quick Facts about US Trade: Deficits and Discords, *Rutgers Business Review*, 3(2), 103-120.

FACT 1: In 2017, the US "suffered" a deficit of $337 billion with China (and it has been getting worse each year).

As Figure 1 illustrates, the overall trade deficit the US had with China amounted to $337 billion in 2017. In goods (merchandise) alone, the deficit was even worse at $376 billion. The one small bright spot is that the US "enjoys" a surplus of $39 billion in services, which reduced the overall deficit to "only" $337 billion.

Figure 1. US vs. China – Merchandise and Services Trade (2017)

FACT 2: The US applies a weighted mean tariff on all imported products of only 1.6 percent.

According to the World Bank, on average, the tariff (customs duty) collected by US customs is only 1.6 percent,[3] which goes some way to explain why the US is, by far, the world's biggest importing nation. But most advanced countries *also* have average tariffs below 5 percent. And China's (according to the same World Bank source) is also only 3.5 percent. Hence, tariffs *alone* (at least when they are so low) may not be an explanation of fundamental imbalances in trade.

FACT 3: It's not just China: the US has run deficits against the rest of the world for decades.

True, the US imports a huge amount from China. But Chinese-made imports (of goods and services) amount to $524 billion out of $2,895 billion imported from all countries, which amounts to 524/2895 = .181, or only 18 percent of total US imports. European imports are somewhat larger. So why single out China? (Answers below.)

For the "rest of the world" as a whole, the US "suffers" a deficit of $566 billion, as seen in Figure 2. In goods (merchandise) alone, the US deficit is an even more sobering: $796 billion (and growing). The one small bright spot is that the US "enjoys" a surplus, against the rest of the world, of $230 billion (and growing) in services, which reduces the overall deficit "suffered" by the US, against the rest of the world, to "only" $566 billion.

Figure 2. The US vs. Rest of World: Merchandise and Services Trade (2017)

FACT 4: There are rather few countries where the US runs a surplus.

Most of the nations against which the US runs an overall surplus are small countries, and US surpluses are also rather small, as seen in Table 1.

Table 1. The Few Nations Where the US Has Tiny Trade Surpluses

	Countries	Surplus in $Billions
1	Hong Kong	32.5
2	Netherlands	24.5
3	United Arab Emirates	15.7
4	Belgium	14.8
5	Australia	14.6
6	Singapore	10.4
7	Brazil	7.6
8	Panama	6.0
9	Argentina	4.7
10	United Kingdom	3.3
11	Chile	3.1
12	Dominican Republic	3.0
13	Guatemala	3.0
14	Paraguay	2.6
15	Bahamas	2.5
	TOTAL OF 15 COUNTRIES	**148.3**

Source: US Census Bureau

Farok J. Contractor, Ph.D.

FACT 5: The US is by far the world's leading exporter of services.

The US exports more services than it imports from the rest of the world to the tune of a $230 billion surplus. This number has been growing annually, reflecting the fact that the US is a powerhouse of knowledge and intellectual property with one of the most entrepreneurial "startup" cultures of all nations.

From a comparative advantage perspective, it makes sense for low-end, routine products such as toasters and hand tools to be made in low-wage nations, while the US focuses on its strengths in technology and innovation.

Moreover, trade statistics do not fully capture, or reflect, the US's advantage in services. Apple, Inc. is one of the world's largest companies in terms of market capital value. Compared with a $649 retail value of an iPhone, Apple pays its subcontractor, Foxconn in China, only around $10 to assemble it, with parts shipped to Foxconn plants from Korea, Japan, Germany, and many nations to be assembled in China.[4] Once assembled, Foxconn ships the iPhone to the US at an invoice value of $220 ($210 imported parts value + $10 assembly fee). The $220 gets recorded as a US import from China—even though only $10 of the $220 invoice value was added in China. Meanwhile, the $649 – 220 = $429 gross margin (or retail value minus import cost) enjoyed by Apple appears nowhere in the trade data, even though Apple has exported and reimported its services and technology through its brilliant design of the iPhone's components and has orchestrated the global supply chain.

Critics could "blame" China and Apple for an import of $220 x 15 million iPhones = $3.3 billion, even though the Chinese value-added component was only $10 x 15 million iPhones = $150 million.

In the 21st century, the world economy (that is to say, of all nations) is slowly transitioning from agriculture to manufacturing, and from manufacturing to services—which bodes well for the US economy in the long run, provided:

(1) US companies continue to be the leaders in R&D and innovation.
(2) Other nations do not capture or "steal" American knowledge as rapidly as US firms generate new technology (more on this below).

166

FACT 6: There is no denying that China has a principal role in the US merchandise deficit.

As we see from the figures above, in goods or merchandise *alone*, China accounts for 47 percent of the USA's trade deficit: $376 billion for China compared with $796 for the world as a whole. Combining goods *and* services,[5] China accounts for 59 percent of the USA's overall trade deficit: $337 billion for China compared with $566 for the world as a whole. The overall proportion, or percentage, for China is larger because of the US lead in services exports.

In short, tens of millions of Chinese toil for between $2–4 per hour on behalf of American consumers, making toasters, knickknacks, furniture, and basic electronics (to give some idea of low-technology products), while a few million Americans work in skilled jobs earning $30 per hour, or more, to produce Boeing aircraft, design the latest iPhone, construct financial packages using advanced math, and also, yes, producing soybeans and pork. (The US farmer riding his/her $600,000 GPS-guided harvester or combine [6] over his/her 500-acre laser-leveled farm is typically not only a multimillionaire in assets, but also an educated mechanic, biochemist, and financial planner dabbling in agricultural futures, and who is also very knowledgeable in meteorology, among other skills—which explains the US trade success in agricultural exports.)

Thus far, with wages still much below the US, China leads in making basic products such as microwave ovens and garments.

FACT 7: The US trade deficit has been partially financed for four decades by the rest of the world (including China).

A trade deficit simply means that the US imports and consumes more from the rest of the world than it sells to the rest of the world. Every year that this happens, foreigners outside the US end up with net extra dollars in their hands. For example, in Figure 1 reproduced below, Chinese companies sold/earned $524 billion from exports to the US in 2017. What happened to the $524 billion they earned? Some of it was used by the same or other Chinese companies to buy American items from the US: $130 billion in goods + $57 billion in services, or a total of $187 billion imported from the US.

Even so, that meant that Chinese companies ended up in 2017 with $524 – 187 = $337 billion surplus in their accounts. Some of this surplus was used by the Chinese to buy products from third countries. But even after that, many billions of surplus dollars were left over, unutilized in China, in 2017. The Chinese do not need or use dollars in their country, considering them as only pieces of paper (or electronic entries). The surplus dollars are handed over by Chinese firms to Chinese banks in exchange for their own currency (the RMB, or renminbi yuan). Each year, the surplus dollars then end up in the Chinese Central Bank (the PBOC, or People's Bank of China).

Figure 1 (Repeated). The US vs. China: Merchandise and Services Trade (2017)

Source: US Census Bureau, Foreign Trade Division

What does the PBOC do each year with the surplus dollars? To keep them in cash form or electronic cashable entries is pointless. Instead, what the Chinese Central Bank does is very kindly reinvest the annual surplus dollars in US assets—mainly US Treasury securities, pieces of paper that the US government issues as bonds, notes, and bills in exchange for taking in dollars from investors. That way, reinvesting the hundreds of billions of surplus dollars back into the US produces these results:

- The dollar remains strong (instead of the Chinese selling off the billions of dollars in the open foreign exchange market—which would devalue the dollar sharply and make imports from China and elsewhere more expensive).

- The continued strength of the US dollar keeps US consumers happy (and they continue to "enjoy" reasonably well-made Chinese products at low or throwaway prices).

- Tens of millions of jobs within China that depend on the US market continue to be preserved—Chinese export factories continue to churn out a flood of exports.

- With strong buying of, faith in, and demand for US Treasury bonds, US interest rates remain low[7] for the American consumer's auto loans and mortgages, leaving American household money left over for discretionary purchases, such as Chinese-made TV sets.

- The US government budget, which has also run a deficit for most of the last 35 years, has been partially financed by foreigners like the Chinese. That is to say, over the past 35 years, by issuing pieces of paper called "Treasury Securities – US Bonds, Notes, and Bills" in return for real dollars, the US government has each year spent more than it took in from domestic tax revenue, enabling the US government to continue to fund Social Security, disability, and other expenditures, such as defense. But this has run up a cumulative total of $19 trillion in debt.

Table 2. US Government Debt (End 2017)

Total Treasury Securities (US Bonds, Notes, and Bills)

Approximate Total Outstanding Debt Instruments Issued to All Investors = **$19 trillion:**

- Domestic Investors = **$12.5 trillion**
- All Foreign Holdings = **$6.3 trillion**
    - China and Hong Kong = **$1.4 trillion**
    - Japan = **$1.1 trillion**

Trade deficits the US has run against the rest of the world for 43 years are a direct correlate of the government deficits the US government has also run for most of the past 43 years.

The "game" can continue, as long as three conditions are fulfilled:

- Investors (both foreign and domestic) continue to have faith and give up real current dollars to the US government in return for pieces of paper called treasury bills and bonds. (Often, the interest rates are so low that in inflation-adjusted terms the real return can be zero or negative. Yet thus far, faith remains in US government debt as a safe haven.)

- Foreign workers continue to toil on behalf of the US consumer for low wages, such as $1–4 per hour.

- Employment in the US remains at high or tolerable levels.

For the most part, with the exception of a few recessions, the above three conditions have prevailed for three to four decades. Faith remains. The game continues.

FACT 8: All policies create "winners" and "losers": but in international trade, "winners" vastly outnumber "losers."

I use the terms "winners" and "losers" only as a rhetorical device. Those who have "lost out" in the economic changes in recent times deserve every consideration, respect, and help, because they are our fellow human beings.

Losers: Don Trump rode to the White House in 2016 because of victories in a few key states where the earnings of a disaffected few million US workers in mature industries, such as coal, steel, and aluminum, declined in the past decade because of global competition.[8] Moreover, additional millions of Americans have had flat earnings since the Great Recession of 2008. This is psychologically devastating in a nation where, for over 200 years, the expectation has been that children would be better off than their parents' generation. Global competition has somewhat dampened that expectation.

Winners: But many millions more Americans are vastly better off today than their parents—in income, assets, health, education, and prospects—compared with, say 1980, when globalization took off around the world.[9] Unemployment in 2017–2018 was at a record low level of only 4.1 percent.[10] Retirees and those who consciously opted out of work enjoy the highest level of benefits and health care ever. The average American enjoys the highest after-tax purchasing power in the world. In per capita income, the US ranks 8th out of 193 nations, with small countries like Monaco, Switzerland, Qatar, and Denmark being ranked higher. But this is misleading because of

- Effectively lower taxes in the US than in those nations; and
- Far lower prices, in general, for almost all products because of
    – a dynamic, competitive economy where firms compete to keep prices low, and
    – low-cost imports.

Effectively, Americans enjoy the highest standard of living in the world, in material terms. In an earlier article, I compared the benefit to US consumers of buying imported items with the benefit of purchasing the same items manufactured domestically in the US. Chinese imports alone save American consumers $295 billion in additional costs—or an extra $2,380 per household, per year, in Americans' pockets.[11]

The benefits of international trade and investment have benefited billions of persons around the world. The World Bank reports that grinding poverty declined from 43 percent of humanity in 1980 to only 9 percent in 2017, despite an increase in world population from 4.5 billion to 7.6 billion humans.[12] An additional 2 to 3 billion have been lifted completely out of poverty into a middle-class existence. This wonderful result is partially due to the tide of globalization.

However, it is true that inequality and disparities have increased in the US, and the country is more psychologically tense and fragmented than other nations, as well as when compared with its own past. The "losers" have become more vocal in expressing their discontent, seething in abandoned coal mines or closed steel plants or in the shadows of gleaming skyscrapers and the high-tech economy that has left many of them abandoned as bewildered bystanders.

The backlash against international trade is not because it has lifted global standards of living, with winners far outnumbering losers in the US and around the world. The "gain" far outweighs the "pain." Rather, the backlash is because the ethic of hyper-competition that has infected companies, and even governments, has made us neglect the pain felt by the bewildered millions left behind. In the rush toward economic "progress," enlightened societies need to compassionately devise cushions, safety nets, counseling, and training for those negatively affected.

FACT 9: Dumping is supposed to be "selling below cost": but in almost all cases, the dumping company is not losing money.

(For more details and an illustrated numerical example, see my October 23, 2018 blog post, <u>What Is "Dumping"?: https://globalbusiness.blog/2018/10/23/what-is-dumping/</u>)

"Dumping" is reviled as a practice in which unscrupulous importers are said to be (a) selling "below cost," (b) thereby unfairly hurting competing local producers.

But is dumping really selling below cost? No, in most cases it is not. The selling price of the imported item may be set low, but it almost always is above the variable cost of production and distribution. This is true in manufactured goods, and especially true in the knowledge economy.

All multinational companies practice international price differentiation.

Most international marketers price the same software, or camera, or washing machine, steel, medicine, aluminum, or whatever item, according to what each nation's customers can bear, often with enormous price variations. The same college textbook retailing for $225 in the US may be sold for $35 in Thailand—and the publisher still makes an incremental profit because the cost of paying for royalties, printing, and distributing one extra textbook may only be $9.

A bottle of pills costing $100 at a US pharmacy may be sold by the same drug company in India for less than $10. Since the variable cost of manufacturing the bottle of pills is only $2 (not counting the sunk R&D and fixed costs, which may indeed be in the millions), even at $10 the pharmaceutical company is still making an incremental profit in India of $10 − 2 = $8 per bottle. The $100 price at the US pharmacy does not create a $100 − 2 = $98 profit: $100 in the US not only covers the $2 variable cost, but the $98 margin then generously covers the millions spent on

R&D and the fixed costs. Only then what is left over may be deemed as profit for the drug company.

In a low-income country, despite a very low price as long as it is above the variable cost floor, the company is making an incremental profit. This assumes that the fixed costs (and R&D amortization) are already covered by higher prices in the company's domestic and other foreign markets.

It is important to realize that we are not speaking here of counterfeit items or knockoffs. The genuine product made by the multinational company itself (or one of its foreign subsidiaries) is being deliberately sold by the company at dramatically different prices in different nations.

Tide detergent in China is sold for less than one-fifth the US price, to give just one of thousands of such examples from around the world. If a multinational company senses that consumers are willing to pay more in a particular nation, they will set the price much higher—for the same genuine item made by the company or one of its subsidiaries—than in a low-income, price-sensitive country. Global price differentiation is ubiquitous and is a common practice that maximizes the multinational company's overall global revenue and profits.

Each country, for the most part, is a separate and segmented market, so that a low price in one nation does not generally affect price levels in other nations.[13] What ultimately matters is that across all countries in the world together, all sales revenues cover all costs—not only the variable costs, but also R&D amortization and fixed costs.

Is dumping a situation where unscrupulous importers are said to be selling "below cost"?

Chinese steel and aluminum imports, allegedly dumped according to the Trump Administration, are a recent example.[14] Excess capacity was installed in China (in huge factories, far more than the domestic Chinese market demand required). This was aided by cheap loans and land given by the Chinese central and provincial authorities, driven by a "build it and they will come" mentality.[15] As long as the domestic Chinese market's fixed costs are covered, and profits are made, the Chinese steel and aluminum producers can then sell in the US market at very low prices, which are likely still above their variable cost floor per ton. The Chinese companies are probably not really losing money.

Is dumping a situation where competing local firms can be hurt?

Yes, in many cases this is so. Low prices because of Chinese imports have hurt US-based steel and aluminum producers in the US, as well as all over the world, who do not have the spare

172

production capacity or access to all country markets and so cannot play the same multi-country price differentiation game. [16] This has resulted in layoffs and closures in the US and Europe. Pain and hurt indeed.

Benefits and costs of low-priced imports.

But let us not forget that this so-called dumping has also resulted in a multibillion-dollar benefit to the US and European economies, so that cars, appliances, machinery, and any product that uses steel or aluminum can be bought at a lower cost. The economy-wide benefits of cheap steel and aluminum in Europe and the US—resulting in cheaper cars, appliances, and machinery for consumers there—likely considerably exceed the pain, suffering, and costs borne by shareholders and workers in the closed steel and aluminum factories.

As is often the case, the economy-wide benefits of international trade are much larger in the aggregate. But the benefits are diffused, hard to measure, and small for each car or appliance buyer. If kitchen aluminum foil costs 50 cents less, or if a toaster is $1 cheaper, or if a car costs $100 less for each buyer because of imported steel or aluminum, each individual customer is unlikely to notice the benefit, even though over the entire population each small individual benefit may add up to hundreds of billions saved. Nor is the consumer enjoying cheaper products likely to say anything to their congressperson or member of parliament. By contrast, because the pain and loss suffered in a handful of steel or aluminum companies are concentrated in a few voting districts, their voices can sometimes be louder and more strident, and have more political impact, compared with the mass of silent consumers.

FACT 10: China is hungry for Western technology and company secrets.

In China, an emerging country that is leveraging itself up from its previous backwardness and poverty into technological capability and affluence, company aspirations and objectives are no different from those of firms in other nations: they would all like to benefit from learning their rivals' technology and methods.

During the 1780s, English firms that had Arkwright-designed spinning wheels, jennies, and frames succeeded in having the British government pass draconian laws threatening severe punishment to anyone exporting textile machinery, designs, or tools to the United States, which then used manual methods. Despite the threatened punishments, by committing designs to memory or drawing them on small scraps of hidden paper, emigrants leaked the technology to America, which became a strong textiles rival of England by 1794. Samuel Slater was one such emigrant who became rich in the US by leaking British secrets to the Americans, thereby transferring English technology.[17] The English called him a traitor.

Samuel "Slater the Traitor"

Source: Wikipedia

For centuries, China itself closely guarded the secret of sericulture, thereby enjoying a world monopoly in silk production until 552 AD, when two Nestorian monks visited China in the name of religion and smuggled silkworms back to Byzantium in hollow walking sticks.[18] For millennia, Chinese tea was a monopoly, with spies regularly trying, but failing, to smuggle tea bushes out of China. It was not until the 1860s that an adventurous Scotsman, Robert Bruce, noticed a plant on the southern slopes of the Indian Himalayas that looked very much like the Chinese bush *Camellia sinensis*.[19] Today, India and other countries produce multiple quantities of tea compared with China.

Companies and individuals trying to learn or steal their rivals' secrets is nothing new. However, there is a big difference with regard to China—namely, conscious help for Chinese companies from their government in two respects:

(1) Chinese government regulations that prevent foreign firms from investing and doing business in China without taking on a local Chinese company as a partner, and implicitly or explicitly suggesting that the welcome for the foreign investor will be better if they share their technology with the Chinese partner.

That said, we should quickly add several qualifiers to the above general observation:

a. Over the years, China has pedaled back from many such restrictions and today allows subsidiaries fully owned by foreign multinationals (i.e., without any local Chinese partner) in an increasing number of sectors.

b. European and American companies are not naïve and know how to shelter their deepest secrets from their Chinese partners even while working with them in China.

c. For decades after World War II, the Japanese followed exactly the same regulatory practices, learning Western technology through joint ventures and licensing agreements, leveraging themselves into a cutting-edge position. No American administration appeared to be overly concerned at that time.

d. US and European firms are not static in their R&D. The best defense for a company is to undertake innovations (R&D) in a dynamic way so as to remain a few generations ahead of their rivals or Chinese partners. That way, by the time the local partner learns a technology, the foreign partner is a step or two ahead.

(2) Cyber-espionage is undertaken by most large governments. Here again, there is a difference or asymmetry in favor of China. The US government probably has superior cyber-drilling capabilities. But it is unlikely that the US government has a conscious program to steal commercial secrets to benefit US firms, and US laws would frown upon such behavior, if not prohibit it. By contrast, the Chinese government makes no secret of its nationalist desire to help Chinese companies, to say nothing of the fact that 45 percent of Chinese industry consists of state-owned enterprises (SOEs), anyway.[20]

This is not really a "trade" issue, but the Trump Administration has chosen to include it as part of the overall discussion on the international business relationship with China.

Conclusion

What underlies everything is the notion of comparative advantage—the idea that countries are generally better off when they specialize in producing and exporting what they are good at and importing items that do not offer the country a comparative advantage. A simple analogy would be two neighboring farmers. One farmer has superior knowledge in repairing and maintaining farm machinery, while the other has superior knowledge in plant genetics, fertilizers, and pesticides. Both farmers would be better off trading their expertise with each other instead of trying to handle their own operations independently. It does not matter that one farmer draws more benefit from the other's knowledge than he offers in the knowledge he shares. There will always be such inequality or asymmetry in trade. The salient point—the core argument of international trade—is that **both** farmers will be better off compared with where they were before their trading relationship.

The China-US trading relationship is mutually beneficial despite a seemingly frightening deficit. American firms and consumers enjoy reasonably well-made products and components at far lower prices than would be the case if the items were manufactured in the US. The $187 billion in goods and services the US exports to China support tens of thousands, or perhaps more than one hundred thousand, American jobs. The soberingly high trade deficit of $337 billion is very kindly reinvested by the Chinese in US assets—principally in US Treasury instruments—which keeps the dollar strong and the US consumer happily buying. A corollary effect of the recirculated dollars is to help fund the US government deficit and keep interest rates here low, which also helps to keep American mortgage and auto loan interest rates low.

This is not necessarily goodwill on the part of the Chinese, but self-interest, since this policy keeps US customers happy and buying Chinese products while maintaining export-oriented jobs in China. At the same time, US entrepreneurship, new products and services, and new generations of technology have maintained almost full employment here except in recessionary years. Chinese imports do keep lower-skill wages low in America, which is a negative for the bottom 20 percent of the US workforce. But all in all, it has been a win-win situation for both nations over the last 25 years.

To put the China trade in a larger global perspective, we saw above that imports from China amount to only 18.1 percent of US imports from all countries.

The world has laboriously built up an intricate trading system that results in interdependencies that constrain and cause discomfort. Certainly, as this article shows, there will be "winners" as well as some "losers" within a nation as it opens itself up to more international trade. But the key argument is that, on average, a nation is better off because the benefits that accrue to the winning firms and consumers generally significantly exceed the pain, suffering, and angst borne by the losers.

Averages are cold, heartless statistics, of course. A great society needs to be more heedful about the suffering caused by international trade to certain sections of their population and provide ameliorative relief to those affected while enjoying the overall benefits of trade that accrue to all within the nation. So, although a nation's participation in international business will indeed produce gains as well as pains, on the whole, the country will be better off.

NOTE: Also see pertinent 1978 commentary from the late Nobel Prize-winning economist Milton Friedman—his words still resonate today.[21]

Notes

[1] During his speech in Fort Wayne, Indiana, May 2016.

[2] See Wikipedia: Trump tariffs (economic policy of Donald Trump).

[3] See the World Bank: Tariff rate, applied, weighted mean, all products (percent).

[4] Apple, Inc. does not divulge this proprietary data. However, by piecing together leaked information from various sources, one can put together an overall rough picture.

[5] The business press does readers a disservice in not routinely including services (a large and growing component of world trade) in their reporting on world trade. This often distorts the overall picture and confuses readers and politicians.

[6] See Dodson, D. (2014). How much is that combine in the window? *The News-Gazette* (April 2).

[7] Higher demand for a bond raises its price, which reduces the effective interest rate earned from the bond. With very high demand, government bonds can become so pricey that the interest rate can even become zero or fall into the negative zone on an inflation-adjusted basis. Yet some investors will still buy the bond as a "safe haven" for sheer speculation or, for governments like China, in order to keep jobs in China and exports flowing out to the US consumer.

[8] Hillary Clinton received almost 3 million more votes than did Trump. However, the state-by-state US electoral college system sometimes gives the presidency to the other candidate. Trump won big in states most affected by global competition.

[9] See, for example, Bernanke, B. and Olson, P. (2016). Are Americans better off than they were a decade or two ago? *The Brookings Institution* (October 19). Also see Shapiro, B. (2017). The myth of the stagnating middle class. *National Review* (January 18).

[10] A 4 percent unemployment statistic is considered the minimum possible, or tantamount to a full-employment economy, because even with great demand for workers approximately 4 percent will be temporarily traveling between jobs.

[11] Contractor, F.J. (2017). Disrupting US-China relations will incur high costs. *Yale Global* (February 28). For more detail, see Contractor, F.J. (2017). What's at stake in China-US relations? An estimate of jobs and money involved in the bilateral economic tie. *GlobalBusiness.blog* (March 10).

[12] See the World Bank: Poverty Overview. [13] This is a reasonable assumption in many cases, although sometimes a "gray market" may emerge where unauthorized third parties buy the item in a low-price nation then transfer it to the high-price nation to make a profit, thereby undercutting the company's own profit margins and distribution network in the high-price nation. Generally, the gray market is not a significant problem for multinational companies.

[14] China dismay as Trump signs off steel, aluminum tariffs. *DW.com*, September 3, 2018.

[15] This is a saying popular in US culture, based on the 1989 movie *Field of Dreams*. Also see AFI's 100Years…100 Movie Quotes compiled by the American Film Institute.

[16] China being a relatively closed market that foreign firms cannot enter, US and European companies simply cannot play the same game in China in order to neutralize the Chinese rivals' multi-country price discrimination advantage.

[17] Heath, N. (2011). Samuel Slater: American hero or British traitor? *BBC News* (September 22).

[18] White, F. (2014). How did silk get out of China? *History Answers* (August 4).

[19] Contractor, F.J. (2011). How a soothing drink changed fortunes and incited protests. *Yale Global* (March 9).

[20] Contractor, F.J. (2015). Chinese cyber-espionage on US companies: The asymmetry in the analogy of the "pot calling the kettle black." *Globalbusiness.me* (September 28).

[21] Contractor, F.J. (2018). WWMS? (What would Milton say?). *GlobalBusiness.blog* (April 14).

CHAPTER 10

Does Just One Product – the iPhone –
Cause an $11 Billion Trade Deficit for the US?

Trade Statistics Alone Can Frighten and Mislead

In my July 11, 2018 blog post, <u>The US-China Trade Spat: How the Public, Media, and Politicians Can Be Deceived by Data:</u> <u>https://globalbusiness.blog/2018/07/11/the-us-china-trade-spat-how-the-public-media-and-politicians-can-be-deceived-by-data/</u>, I described how taking data and statistics out of the context of the larger picture can be not only frightening, but misleading.

Naturally, a company like Apple, Inc. does not disclose proprietary information about its costs and revenues. We do have some information about the iPhone 7, but later models likely follow a similar pattern, and the main argument of this article remains valid – how deceptive it is to look at trade data alone. Most iPhone components are sourced by Apple from other countries. Components from South Korea, Japan, Germany, China, and some from the US flow from these sources to be assembled by a Chinese firm called Foxconn. But most of this component trade flow is *not counted* in the bilateral US-China trade statistics. All that is counted in the US-China trade data are the bilateral (a) $258 invoiced amount of the finished or assembled iPhone7 (shipped by Foxconn from China to the US) *vs.* (b) $75 worth of US-made components (shipped from the US to China for assembly there).

Trade Data Paint a Lopsided Picture

Once assembled, the finished iPhone7 is sold, or exported, to Apple for an estimated export invoice value of $258. Here's what the trade data look like:

TABLE 1: TRADE STATISTICS COMPARISON	
Import from China: (61 million iPhone 7s imported from China) x ($258 each)	= $15.74 billion **import**
Export from US to China: (61 million USA-made components) x ($75 each)	= $ 4.58 billion **export**
Trade deficit because of the iPhone 7 *alone:* ($15.74 – 4.58)	= **$11.16 billion trade deficit**

Sources: Kif Leswing, The parts in an iPhone 7 only cost $219, according to a new estimate, *Business Insider*, September 20, 2016; Adam Jourdan, Designed in California, made in China: how the iPhone skews U.S. trade deficit, *Reuters*, March 21, 2018.

Caveats: Like most firms, Apple Inc. maintains confidentiality about its procurement countries and costs. Hence the above numbers are the best estimates made by journalists and others in the industry. Some of the estimates diverge, but the general conclusions remain valid.

A Production Value-Added Comparison Shows a Very Different Picture

The iPhone7—just one product—is therefore supposed to create a frightening trade deficit of $11.16 billion. But this is highly deceptive! Apple pays Foxconn only around $10 for the assembly work. That $10, plus some other minor components sourced from China, makes the value added in China only around $39. ($219 represents components from other nations imported by China and then assembled into the iPhone 7.) Nevertheless, when the iPhone is assembled and shipped to the US, its approximate $258 invoice value is counted in the trade data as the value of the "iPhone imported from China."

TABLE 2: PRODUCTION VALUE-ADDED COMPARISON: CHINA VERSUS THE US	
FOR EACH iPhone 7	**FOR ALL 61 MILLION iPhone7s**
Value added in China: (assembly $10 + other China-sourced components $29) in each iPhone7 = $39	$39 x 61 million = $2.38 billion
Value of US-made components: exported from the US to China to be assembled into each iPhone7 = $75[1]	$75 x 61 million = $4.58 billion
"Value-added" comparison: the US has a "surplus" of $75 – 39 = $36 for each iPhone7	$36 x 61 million = **$2.20 billion surplus**

By comparing the bottom-line numbers in TABLE 1: TRADE STATISTICS COMPARISON with TABLE 2: PRODUCTION VALUE-ADDED COMPARISON, we can see how misleading it can be to look only at trade data. These data seem to show that the iPhone7 alone causes an $11.16 billion trade *deficit*, whereas the value-added comparison shows a *surplus* for the US of $2.20 billion.

Figure 1

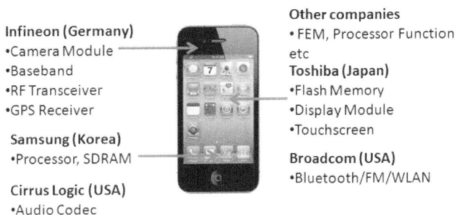

Assembled in China by FoxConn for US $6.50

Infineon (Germany)
•Camera Module
•Baseband
•RF Transceiver
•GPS Receiver

Samsung (Korea)
•Processor, SDRAM

Cirrus Logic (USA)
•Audio Codec

Other companies
• FEM, Processor Function etc

Toshiba (Japan)
•Flash Memory
•Display Module
•Touchscreen

Broadcom (USA)
•Bluetooth/FM/WLAN

This figure does not necessarily represent the iPhone 7 and is used for illustration purposes only.

Should We Count the Value of Apple's Research, Designs, and Marketing?

Table 2 shows only the "Production Value Added" comparison between China and the US. The picture is actually even more complicated. Trade and production value-added data do not include a multinational company's centralized research and development (R&D) expenditures or marketing overheads. Apple's R&D and marketing campaigns are done in the US by a huge staff of scientists, IT experts, and marketers at its Cupertino, California headquarters. The $258 invoiced amount for the iPhone7 assembled in China and exported to Apple USA does *not* include Apple's R&D and marketing—these are not counted in trade statistics. But if we include Apple's R&D and other overheads, then the overwhelming bulk of the value would appear to be added in the US. Retail price ($649) *minus* ($258 China invoiced export value[2]) *plus* ($75 components exported from the US to China) = $466 value added in the US.

What a Service Economy Looks Like

After all, being a "service economy" driven by creativity and innovation, the real strength of US companies is in their R&D, which is a long-term job creator. What is the real value Apple Inc. contributes? The company hardly makes anything itself. Instead, Apple is correctly identified as a world-beating R&D organization, a creator of high-tech designs, and an orchestrator of global supply chains in which components from a dozen or more nations flow to China to be assembled there, and the finished products are then exported from China to the rest of the world's markets—all under the supervision and control of Apple.

Figure 2

This figure does not necessarily represent the iPhone 7 and is used for illustration purposes only.

Roughly speaking, the $649 retail value of the iPhone7 *minus* the $258 assembled production cost, or $649 – 258 = $391, may be described as Apple's "gross margin." The gross margin includes dividends distributed to shareholders. But much of the rest of the "margin" may be described simply as returns on "thought"—the ideas and creativity of the scientists, engineers, marketers, and distributors of iPhones.

Similarly, even for each component, we could break down its value between the raw materials that went into making the component versus the thought and service overheads that went into designing that component. The mere "raw material" component of an iPhone may add up to less than $5 (even including some "rare earth" elements). The rest of the value is simply in thought.

Such is the high-tech, service economy we live in today. The iPhone may be an extreme example. But for the US-China trade as a whole, analysts estimate that the trade deficit "suffered" by the US would shrink by at least 36 percent on a production value-added comparison.[3] And the perceived role of American companies' value added would increase far more if we also included their R&D, branding and marketing, and services contributions (which do not necessarily enter into the trade or production data).

Related:

- For a detailed discussion of how deceptive it is to look at data and statistics alone without seeing the larger picture, see my July 11, 2018 blog post, The US-China Trade Spat: How the Public, Media, and Politicians Can Be Deceived by Data: https://globalbusiness.blog/2018/07/11/the-us-china-trade-spat-how-the-public-media-and-politicians-can-be-deceived-by-data/

- Xinhua, China's leading official news agency, conducted a 30-minute interview with me on June 18, 2018—see my July 10, 2018 blog post, The US-China Trade Spat: My Interview with Xinhua – June 18, 2018: https://globalbusiness.blog/2018/07/10/the-us-china-trade-spat-my-interview-with-xinhua-june-18-2018/.

Notes

[1] This is the most problematic estimate. Apple Inc. will not disclose the information. Journalists like Kif Leswing (see Table 1 sources) publish a breakdown of parts probably made in the US. However, even that is uncertain since the US component manufacturer will have sourced some subcomponents from other countries. Because of the confidentiality of Apple's costing, different analysts' numbers vary somewhat. However, the broad conclusions of this piece remain valid.

[2] The subtracted amount of $258 includes the $75 worth of components sourced from the US, which is why the $75 is added back into the calculation for the overall US value added.

[3] Louis Kuijs, Research Briefing | China: Impact of US trade action on China to be manageable, *Oxford Economics*, March 20, 2018. Also see Roger Fingas, Apple's iPhone may be creating misleading numbers for US trade deficit with China, *AppleInsider.com*, March 21, 2018.

CHAPTER 11

Trump Administration Labels China a "Currency Manipulator": What's behind the accusation, and who's right?[*]

At 5 o'clock in the morning on August 5, 2019, unable to sleep, Trump tweeted about China—not for the first time accusing it of being a "currency manipulator,"[1] and describing this as a "major violation." (See Figure 1 below.) Treasury Secretary Mnuchin followed with an official announcement later that day.[2]

What triggered Trump's reaction was that the renminbi yuan (RMB)[3] had devalued and breached the 7.0 RMB per US dollar (USD) rate for the first time since 2008.

Figure 1: Trump Tweet of August 5, 2019

Source: Twitter

---

[*] Reprinted from Farok J. Contractor (2019), Trump Administration Labels China a "Currency Manipulator": What's behind the accusation, and who's right? *Rutgers Business Review* 4(2), 93-102.

The term "currency manipulator" has no regulatory import or effect. It is only an accusation that further escalates the building tension between China and the US. Indeed, on August 5, 2019, the Chinese currency (RMB) had devalued to a rate of 7.05 per USD. This means that a dollar converts into more RMB than before, thereby increasing the Chinese exporters' margins and—irritating to Trump—insulates them from the effects of the Trump tariffs.

American administrations, going as far back as Ronald Reagan, have argued that the RMB exchange rate is under the control of China's central bank—the People's Bank of China (PBoC)—which follows the orders of the Chinese government. Since 2012, market forces have been allowed to have an influence. However, the PBoC has the ultimate say, and every morning, it fixes or announces a rate that all traders must obey.

Figure 2: RMB Exchange Rate 2008 – 2019:
Yuan hits lowest level since 2008 – 1 USD now buys more than 7 yuan

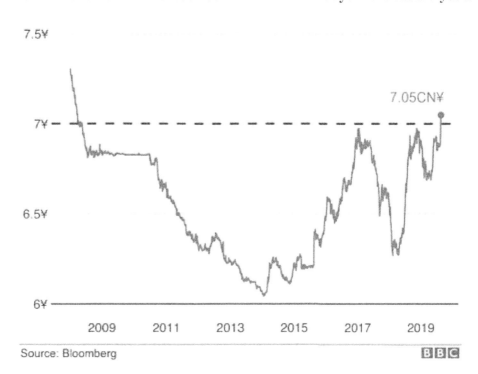

Source: Bloomberg & BBC. *BBC.com*, August 6, 2019:
Yuan fall: Why is China's currency getting weaker?

This article shows in a simple calculation how a further devaluation of the RMB could completely neutralize the Trump tariffs. Then it reviews how China's leadership, going back 40 years, managed their currency's exchange rate to jump-start the Chinese export engine and make China the "factory of the world."

A Simple Calculation of the Tariff – Exchange Rate Tradeoff

Simple calculations (shown below) illustrate how the exchange rate between the RMB and the USD can profoundly affect the profit or loss of Chinese exporters, US importers, and the pocketbooks of American consumers. (In a previous article,[4] I calculated the extra cost to the average US household at $2,380, or a total additional outlay for the US economy of $295 billion each year—if hypothetically all consumer items imported from China were replaced by US domestic production.)

Let's do some simple calculations, starting with the June 2018 exchange rate of 6.5 RMB/USD, as shown in Tables 1A, 1B, and 1C. (Trump began to impose tariffs on China the following month.)

As we will see, it would take only a small further devaluation of the RMB by the Chinese government—to 7.15 RMB/USD—in order to nullify a 10 percent tariff.

TABLE 1A

As recently as June 2018, the exchange rate was 6.50 RMB = 1 USD:

- If Chinese exporters invoice a shipment at $100, they earn (100 x 6.50) = **650 RMB.**

- But with a 10 percent tariff, the cost to US importers or consumers is $100 + $10 = **110 USD.**

- If Chinese exporters absorb the burden of the tariff so that US importers or consumers pay only $100, how much would they earn?
    - Put x + (0.10) x = $100. Hence, x = $90.91. The Chinese exporter would have to invoice or charge only $90.91—well below $100—in order to keep the import cost (including tariff) to the US importer at $100.
    - $90.91 converted at the Chinese bank means the Chinese exporter gets only 90.91 x 6.5 = **590.91 RMB**—which is well below the 650 RMB calculated above.

TABLE 1B

On August 5, 2019, the exchange rate was 7.05 RMB = 1 USD:

- If Chinese exporters invoice a shipment at $100, they earn (100 x 7.05) = **705 RMB**—which is more than the 650 earned in June 2018 (see Table 1a).

- But with a 10 percent tariff, the cost to the US importer or consumer is $100 + $10 = 110 USD.

- If Chinese exporters absorb the burden of the tariff so that US importers or consumers pay only $100, how much would they earn?
    - The Chinese exporter would have to invoice or charge only $90.91—well below $100 in order to keep the import cost (including tariff) to the US importer at $100.
    - $90.91 converted at the Chinese bank means the Chinese exporter gets 90.91 x 7.05 = **640.92 RMB**—which is only a bit below the 650 RMB earned before June 2018.

TABLE 1C

In the future:

Question:

If the RMB exchange rate devalues further, at what exchange rate would the Chinese exporter earn the original 650 RMB, while the US importer still pays only $100 (including tariff)?

Answer:

7.15 RMB per USD because $90.91 x 7.15 = 650 RMB.

Hence, a 7.15 RMB/USD exchange rate nullifies the Trump tariff of 10 percent (i.e., a 7.15 exchange rate restores the US consumer's cost to $100, while at the same time restoring the Chinese exporter's earning to 650 RMB).

Farok J. Contractor, Ph.D.

Will the Chinese Devalue Their Currency Further to Counteract US Tariffs?

Some economists, such as those at *Capital Economics,* expected the yuan to devalue further and *"end the year at 7.30 per US dollar."*[5] But further devaluations are by no means certain since the Chinese government is beset with contrary pressures and is issuing mixed signals. On Monday, August 5, the PBOC, in a candid statement, said that the devaluation was driven by *"unilateralism and trade protectionism measures and the imposition of tariff increases on China."*[6] But the next day, a more conciliatory and high-minded statement was issued, saying *"China has refused to engage in a competitive devaluation despite the US escalating trade tensions from 2018, nor has it used [the exchange rate] as a tool to address [the trade conflict]."*[7] This reflects the contrary pressures facing the Chinese and its central bank.

Pressures to Devalue or Not to Devalue

Pressures to devalue come from the fact that perhaps one in seven jobs in the organized sector are in export-oriented companies. Creating and maintaining jobs has been the number one priority of the Chinese regime ever since 1949 (although this pressure is now easing as the population begins to plateau). There are likely well over 100 million jobs related to China's export sector, including the 16 million Chinese jobs I estimate that are devoted to exports to the US.[8] Export-oriented Chinese firms competing everywhere are forced to keep abreast of the latest global technologies, and upgrading to world-class technologies is a national goal.

What are the pressures to *not* devalue? The PBoC does control the exchange rate by fiat, but it increasingly also wishes to present to the world an image of a responsible economic superpower (and not a reactor to, or tit-for-tat imitator of, what they consider the erratic policies of the US government).

Besides accusations of an undervalued currency from various past US presidents, there have been similar complaints from the European Union. "Undervaluation" is another term for *"too much devaluation."* For further details, see my article, *"What Do We Mean by Undervalued or Overvalued Currencies?"* [9]

Another deep background pressure to not devalue comes from the PBoC's aversion to, and prevention of, capital flight. There is enormous middle- and upper-class wealth bottled up inside China,[10] which seeks to diversify its assets by converting part of its wealth into other currencies or into an apartment in Manhattan, Vancouver, or Sydney. Moreover, there remain some financial and tax benefits by "round-tripping" funds from China to Hong Kong and back to the mainland again.[11] The PBoC's rules restrict unbridled selling of RMB for US, Canadian, or Australian dollars, but the selling pressure from the asset-diversification desires of Chinese individuals and companies has been so strong that the RMB has been devalued since 2014. (See Figure 2.)

Another reason to not devalue is that after a devaluation the cost of imports to the Chinese economy in RMB would rise commensurately (and China imports $1.731 trillion worth, not too far behind the US total). Higher local RMB import costs could also, conceivably, trigger inflation.

While today the Chinese are on the cusp of, or in a balance between, competing considerations regarding the RMB exchange rate, historically this was not the case. Below, we discuss the long history of the currency and the strategic and deliberate use of devaluations and undervaluation of the RMB, which remained Chinese policy for 25 years until 2005.

A Policy of Undervaluation (1980 – 2005) That Made China the "Factory of the World"

At the death of Mao Zedong in 1976, the Chinese population already stood at 931 million. Although the population growth rate had declined to 1.5 percent per annum (it had approached an explosive 3 percent in the 1970s), that still meant that up to 14 million young new job seekers entered the labor market each year. If there was one historical memory the regime remembered, it was the social danger of hordes of disaffected young persons without a job. With the ascent of Deng Xiaoping, the Chinese began to liberalize their domestic economy and began a conscious policy of devaluing the RMB, in order to jump-start the Chinese export engine and create good jobs.

At first incrementally through 1989, and then dramatically in the 1990s, the RMB was devalued to benefit Chinese exporters. Starting with a mere 1.80 RMB per USD in August 1981, by January 1994 one dollar earned by the exporter converted into as much as 8.72 RMB at the Chinese bank[12]—an almost fivefold increase in the exporter's revenues. With the spirit of Chinese entrepreneurship, talent, the mobilization of (often state-supported) capital, and the willingness to "price low," factories mushroomed to fulfill the eager foreign import demand. As many as 200 million workers may have moved from the interior to the eastern seaboard provinces, where most manufacturing is done. And China became the "factory of the world."

TABLE 2

The Long 25-Year RMB Devaluation/Undervaluation (1980 – 2005) That Made China the "Factory of the World"

Date(s)	RMB/USD Fx Rate	Regime Leader(s)
Aug. 1981	1.80	Deng Xiaoping
Sep. 1986 – Nov. 1989	3.73	Deng Xiaoping
Dec. 1993	5.82	Jiang Zemin / Xhu Rongji
Jan. 1994	8.72	Jiang Zemin / Zhu Rongji
Jun. 1995 –Jun. 2005	8.27	Hu Jintao
Jan. 2014	6.05	Xi Jinping
Dec. 2016	6.93	Xi Jinping (Trump begins Presidency)
Nov. 2018	6.93	Xi Jinping
Aug. 5, 2019	7.05	Xi Jinping

A Policy Change After June 2005: The RMB was Allowed to Appreciate and Kept in the 6.0 – 7.0 Range

However, after June 2005, under pressure from American and European administrations, accusing China of undervaluing its currency (i.e., devalued too much), the PBoC began to grudgingly allow an appreciation or strengthening of the RMB. Note in Figure 3 that the RMB was appreciated from 8.27 in June 2005 to 6.05 per dollar in January 2014, after which it devalued again, breaching the 7.0 level on August 5, 2019. For the past 11 years, from 2008 to 2019—despite what Trump may assert—the Chinese had kept their currency more or less stable in the 6.0 to 7.0 range. (See Figures 2 and 3.) However, as of August 2019, with tariffs and additional threatened tariffs, it is unclear as to where the RMB will go.

Figure 3: China/US Foreign Exchange Rate

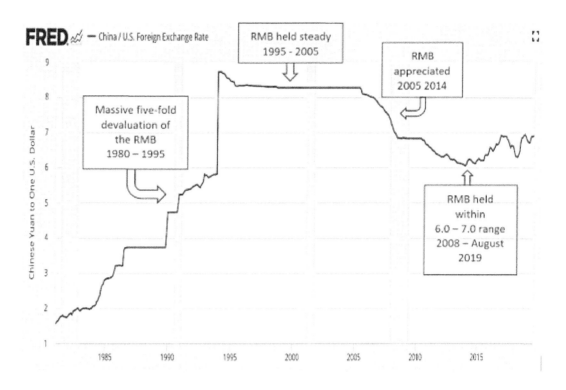

Source: <u>Federal Reserve of the US</u>

Conclusion: Both China and the West Have Benefited Greatly

China's opening up to the world has transformed that country. Perhaps 700 million Chinese have been lifted out of poverty into an at least tolerable existence, with another 600 million of them now considered middle-class or affluent by international standards. This is not entirely attributable to globalization; their domestic market has also grown. With the export experience that forced Chinese firms to compete with western companies, they were quick learners and absorbed western technology (to the point where many Chinese companies are considered a technological threat by the Trump administration).

We should not neglect to mention that consumers in the US and EU (whose combined population is around 838 million) also benefited greatly by being able to buy reasonably well-made Chinese products, purchased at a much lower cost than if the items were made domestically. The annual consumer benefit of Chinese imports to the US consumer is at least $295 billion (as I observed above), and since this does not include industrial or intermediate goods, the overall benefit to the US economy may well exceed $400 billion annually.

Farok J. Contractor, Ph.D.

Of course, Chinese imports have also displaced some American and EU jobs (in manufacturing, not in services). US manufacturing jobs today number only around 40 percent of such jobs in 1980. During the same period, US manufacturing output ($value) zoomed by 250 percent (and the US remains, far and away, the most competitive and productive producing nation on earth).

How can this discrepancy be explained? Studies by economists at Boston Consulting Group, the Wharton School, and the Center for Business and Economic Research at Ball State University conclude that *"...only 13 percent of the overall job losses in manufacturing had resulted from trade."*[13] The real explanation for the sharp decline in manufacturing jobs—and yet accompanied by a big surge in manufacturing output—is in automation, robotics, and information technology, in which US companies have massively invested since 1980.

Critics will aver that, whether it is automation or globalization, the net result is the same—loss of jobs, especially in rust-belt US states and in parts of Europe. This is true, and part of the anti-globalization backlash.[14] However, many of the displaced have found new jobs and the "overall" unemployment rate in the US and Europe is at low levels. The word "overall" is, of course, cold comfort to someone who has lost a job and now perhaps works harder, at lower pay. But such is the nature of the modern economy. A segment of the population in the US and in Europe is worse off. But "overall" or "on average" all three regions—China, the US, and Europe—have greatly benefited over the past 40 years.

Notes

[1] See my May 24, 2016, post, Update: Is China a "currency manipulator"? Donald Trump says so. This post was an update of my original post of November 16, 2015.

[2] Mohsin, S. (2019). U.S. Labels China a Currency Manipulator, Escalating Trade War. *Bloomberg* (August 5).

[3] The Chinese currency is officially called the renminbi yuan (RMB). However, an alternative appellation, Chinese yuan (CNY), is also used.

[4] Contractor, F.J. (2018). Ten Quick Facts about US Trade: Deficits and Discords. *Rutgers Business Review,* 3(2).

[5] Chiu, J. and Russolillo, S. (2019). China's Yuan Breaches Critical Level of 7 to the Dollar, Prompting Trump Critique. *Wall Street Journal* (August 5).

[6] Swanson, A., Stevenson, A., and Smialek, J. (2019). China's Currency Moves Escalate Trade War, Rattling Markets. *New York Times* (August 5).

[7] Tang, F. (2019). China says 'no such thing' as currency manipulation despite US claim it depreciated yuan exchange rate. *South China Morning Post* (August 6).

[8] Contractor, F. J. (2017). What Is at stake in China-U.S. Relations? An Estimate of Jobs and Money Involved in the Bilateral Economic Tie. *Rutgers Business Review*, 2(1), 1–22.

[9] Contractor, F.J. (2019). What Do We Mean by Undervalued or Overvalued Currencies? *Rutgers Business Review*, 4(1).

[10] According to Credit Suisse, the two greatest concentrations of world wealth are in the US and China, with 31 percent and 16 percent of the total world's wealth, respectively. No other nation comes even close.

[11] Contractor, F.J. (2016). Tax Avoidance by Multinational Companies: Methods, Policies, and Ethics. *Rutgers Business Review*, 1(1).

[12] Significant devaluations were engineered under the commercially minded and canny Shanghainese leadership of Jiang Zemin and his deputy Zhu Rongji.

[13] Cocco, F. (2016). Most US manufacturing jobs lost to technology, not trade. *Financial Times* (December 2).

[14] See my May 8, 2017, post, What Is Globalization? How to Measure It and Why Many Oppose It (Part 1).

CHAPTER 12

7 Reasons to Expect US Manufacturing Resurgence[*]

The US may be a service economy, but it's still the world's largest manufacturer. There are many reasons to remain bullish on US manufacturing and the American worker, suggests Farok Contractor, professor of management and global business at Rutgers Business School. US firms invest in high-tech equipment, and the US worker is tops in adding value per hour on products. Recent economic difficulties also help fuel a manufacturing resurgence: falling wages allow the US to compete with low-cost China; anxious Americans work long hours; high energy prices and an uptick in natural disasters could prompt multinationals to relocate factories closer to the big US market. Contractor also points to factors that could stall the resurgence: US students show little interest in science or engineering. And because American workers enjoy great mobility, US manufacturers hesitate to provide apprenticeships that provide state-of-the-art training. Tough economic conditions could usher in new serious attitudes on career and education choices. – YaleGlobal Online, August 7, 2012.

Lower wages, high productivity – despite disinterest in science – boost US manufacturing.

Some 2.8 million American jobs – 70 percent of them in manufacturing – have been lost since 2001 because of the US trade deficit with China, according to a recent Economic Policy Institute study: https://www.epi.org/publication/growing-trade-deficit-china-cost-2-8-million/. Indeed, consumers visiting a Wal-Mart or Macy's are hard-pressed to find much made in America.

It's true that the share of manufacturing in the US GDP is now only 12 to 15 percent, and the country is predominantly a service economy. But the nation is still the world's biggest manufacturer, with unrivaled productivity in terms of manufacturing value-added per employee or per hour worked (Table 1). American manufacturing wages average $34

---

[*] Reprinted from Farok J. Contractor, 7 Reasons to Expect US Manufacturing Resurgence, *YaleGlobal Online*, August 7, 2012.

an hour, some 21 times the average in Chinaat $1.60 an hour. But each US worker adds $145,000 in value, far more than German, French or Japanese employees, and more than 10 times that of the Chinese worker who contributes $13,700.

The predominant explanation is US manufacturers' investment in automated equipment. Also, American labor is better trained than the Chinese. Similar productivity rankings can be seen in dollar value-added per hour: The US worker is on top with $73 in value-added per hour worked; theChinese worker adds only $7.19 of value per hour; Japanese, German, and French workers contributeup to $63. China outperforms the US and Europe only in "value added per dollar wages paid" – but only because hourly wages are so low in China.

Seven factors converging by 2012 suggest that US manufacturing could see a strong resurgence. Jobsonce offshored are now returning in industries including automobiles and even unlikely areas likefurniture and televisions.

Comparisons of Manufacturing Productivity: US, Europe, Japan, China, 2010

All Sectors		Manufacturing Only									
GDP (Market Value)	GDP PER HOUR WORKED (Market Value)	% OF GDP IN MANUFACTURING	Mfg. Value-added at Market Prices	Persons Employed in Mfg.	Mfg. Value-added (Market) Per Hour Per Employee	Hours Worked in Mfg.	Mfg. Value-added (Market) Per Hour Worked	Compensation in Mfg.	Compensation Per Hour Worked in Mfg.	Mfg. Value-added (Market) Per Wages Paid	Actual Market Exchange Rate in US Dollars
Dollars Trillions	Dollars	%	Millions of Dollars	Thousands	Thousands of Dollars	Millions	Dollar Value Per Hour	Millions of Dollars	Dollars Per Hour	Value-added Per Dollar Wages	In US Dollars
Year											
US 2010	14.7	59.3	12	1,717,500	11,876	145	23,384	73	889,502	34	1.93	1.000
Germany 2010	3.2	60.3	21	614,760	7,307	84	10,371	59	464,929	47	1.32	1.326
France 2010	2.3	68.9	11	231,318	2,948	78	4,228	54	173,679	41	1.33	1.326
Japan 2010	5.6	49.7	22	1,230,120	10,083	122	19,442	63	587,677	31	2.09	.01139
China 2010	5.8	n/a	36	1,611,000	118,000	13.7	224,200	7.19	358,720	1.6	4.49	.1474

Productivity Measures in Red

Sources: For the US, Germany, France and Japan, compiled by the author from IMF, World Bank, Bureau of Labor Statistics and other sources. For China, figures were compiled from a variety of sources

> *Wages of the bottom half of American workers have significantly declined* in real terms over the past decade, as well as in comparison with othernations, while those of US manufacturing rivals, including China and Japan, have risen.

> *American workers are working longer, faster, with greater anxiety,* than ever before. Because of greater automation, flexibility, domestic US outsourcing, and the fear of being laid-off, surviving US manufacturing workers have seen little or no increases in wages in the past eight years, and their output has increased with productivity in output per employee at an all-time high. Americans put in 1800 hours per year, about the same as Japanese workers (Table 2). Top is South Korea, with its corporate culture that prevents employees from going home until the last boss has departed. The Frenchand Germans, by comparison, put in 19 percent less time than Americans.

> *The dollar has weakened* against several major currencies over the past decade, making imports more expensive and producing in or exporting from the US more competitive, by comparison. The US is not just the world's biggest importer but also the second-largest exporter of merchandise goods (Table 3). In 2001 – the year China joined the World Trade Organization – the renminbi yuan,RMB, was 8.27 per dollar. By 2012 the currency had appreciated by more than 30 percent to 6.3 RMBper dollar. For many Chinese exporters, a breakeven exchange rate, when their exports to the US are no longer competitive, is between 5.5 to 5.8 yuan per dollar. As the RMB continues to appreciate against the dollar, more Chinese firms will abandon exports and focus on their domestic market,growing at 8 percent per annum.

> *China is experiencing significant wage inflation.*On the eastern seaboard, where most of China's manufacturing takes place, several companies have experienced labor shortages and wage bills have increased by 20 percent per year.

> *Fuel prices have more than doubled.* For productswith significant transportation costs, the rise in energy costs can add significantly to the cost of imports. Shipping large appliances is expensive, soHaier, a leading white goods manufacturer based in China, opened a South Carolina plant where components, shipped across the Pacific Ocean, areassembled by American workers.

> *Delivery and Flexibility Pressures.* For productsrequiring flexibility in the face of fickle fashion changes or assembly operations that require components shipped within a few days to accommodate schedules, such pressures have drivencomponent producers to co-locate near US assembly operations.

> *Natural disasters and disruptions in recent years have spooked global supply chains*: Volcanoes in Iceland, overflowing rivers in Thailand, and tsunamis in the Pacific Ocean idled assembly plants in the US and Europe because parts from affected

regions could not be shipped. Years of cost savingsat Toyota, from sourcing components from faraway locations, were wiped out by a few weeks of losses from assembly operations idled by 2011 floods in Thailand.

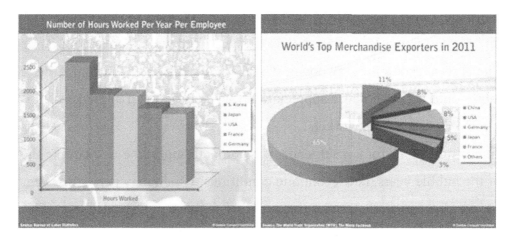

Of course, all indicators are not positive. Three factors could inhibit the US resurgence:

> *The culture devalues science or engineering education.* "Nerds," "geeks," or "wonks" are at the bottom of thesocial totem pole compared to sports, film, and media celebrities. A culture that emphasizes quick results and instant gratification deters students from tackling math, engineering, and other challenging subjects.

> *Too many students pursue a general college degree.* According to a survey released by the Manpower Group in May 2012 (https://www.manpowergroup.jp/company/r_center/w_paper/pdf/shortage.pdf), talent shortages persist in skilled trades, engineers, and IT staff, with "nearly half of U.S. employers struggling to fill mission-critical positions." In OECD countries an average of 23 percent of college degrees are in engineering, science, or mathematics. But in the US such degrees comprise only 15 percent – and ofthese, foreign students earn a quarter of the degrees at the undergraduate level and some two-thirds at the doctoral level.

> *US companies lack an apprenticeship system.* In other OECD nations like Germany, alternative paths in education lead to diplomas or certificates in technical areas, with employees trained by the company in a particular technology and then retained in well-paying careers. Some US companies are trying this approach, highlighted by G. Bussey in an April *Wall Street Journal* article.For example, General Electric is sending new employees for crash courses in hands-on manufacturing or sponsoring two-week summer campsat universities on lean manufacturing for high-school students.

But don't hold your breath. Few American companies are providing apprenticeships and only in selected areas of the country. Unlike Germany, the US is a very mobile society. The average household moves every five years. In an environment where companies can easily sack workers andwhere workers leave for better opportunities, firms are loath to invest in worker training, only to see skilled workers leave for competing companies. The current economic slowdown, which is reducing such churn in American society and jobs, could lead to a better appreciation for the benefits of apprenticeship programs for both companies and workers.

The time is propitious for a resurgence of manufacturing in the US. Unlike the exuberance of the bubble years, new economic conditions, which may persist for years to come, suggest more sober social attitudes, more career-focused college majors, more buckling down to learn harder subjects,less churn in jobs, and greater willingness to settle for somewhat lower wages in return for company investment in worker training and greater job security. In short, some aspects of the future may look like the old days when Detroit was king and skilled technical jobs meant reasonably secure careers with a moderate middle-class living standard.

STUDY QUESTIONS AND MODEL ANSWERS

Chapters 6 – 12 (Part II)

1. Do both trading nations always secure more or less equal benefits by engaging in international trade? Discuss this issue. Give a numerical example to illustrate your arguments.

2. Once trade opens up between two nations, what are the consequences of trade expansion on prices of the exported item and the imported item? What internal adjustments will have to be made in each country in terms of allocation of resources and expansion or contraction of sectors?

3. State and describe the purchasing power parity theory. How do economists actually take empirical measurements to prove or disprove the theory? How good is the theory in predicting exchange rates in the short or long run? Discuss how and why.

4. What is an "overvalued" exchange rate? How can an exchange rate remain overvalued for extended periods of time? Next, discuss the effects of an overvalued exchange rate on the economy and trade of a nation.

5. What is an "undervalued" exchange rate? Discuss the effects of an undervalued exchange rate on the economy and trade of a nation.

6. Some regulated countries have multiple exchange rates, or even "unofficial" or "parallel" markets. Why do these multiple exchange rates coexist? In the context of an overvalued official exchange rate, accompanied by rationing of the official allocations of foreign currency, who demands and who supplies foreign currencies in the "unofficial" or "parallel" or "black" markets?

7. Taking an overview of world trade patterns in the last 50–100 years, why have the terms of international trade gone adversely against commodities and the primary sector and swung in favor of manufactures and services?

8. State and discuss the pros and cons of trade protectionism from the point of view of the policymakers in one country.

9. Since many jobs in advanced economies are offshored and outsourced abroad by their companies, and the service functions or products previously made at home are then imported, why is there not a War painful degree of unemployment in the advanced nations?

AN EXAMPLE OF A MODEL ANSWER

To what extent do the assumptions and expectations of comparative advantage theory conform to the actual practice and behavior of companies? That is, how relevant does the theory appear to a practicing manager?

The fundamental proposition of the theory, namely that international trade benefits the economies of both trading nations, is almost universally accepted to be true and is an empirically observed fact. The greater prosperity that much of humankind has enjoyed since the World War II stems in considerable measure from the fact that trade barriers (tariffs and non-tariff barriers such as regulations that prevented imports) were mutually reduced by most nations. World trade grew faster than the average growth rate for domestic economies. Hence, the widespread belief that free trade policies are good and that it is good to reduce trade barriers. The theory is also correct in its expectation that, as trade opens up and penetrates a nation's domestic economy, fundamental realignments will have to take place in the reallocation of factors of production – away from the import-competing sector, which will shrink, to the now-expanding export sectors, in which the nation has a manifest comparative advantage. This internal reallocation of factors and output mix may appear in some versions of the theory to be painless and instantaneous. The nation magically moves from point A to point B. In practice, of course, such transitions are often costly, protracted, and incomplete. Different industries emerge as winners and losers from the transition.

Many of the assumptions of the theory also appear to practicing managers to be childishly oversimplified and totally unrealistic for today's commerce. The classic theory implicitly or explicitly assumed: (a) Atomistic producers and buyers, each having little individual influence on the market. (b) Fixed (or at least temporarily fixed) factors of production. (c) Factors of production unable to cross national frontiers. (d) Technology as a "public good." (e) Hence, every firm in a sector is supposed to have an identical production function. (f) And homogeneous products and undifferentiated factors. Finally, the theory cannot even conceive of foreign direct investment (FDI) as a substitute for trade in reaching foreign customers.

By contrast, the world of the modern corporation is one of imperfect competition, proprietary knowledge, sometimes heavy transaction costs, mobile factors, and differentiated products. Many, if not most, industries are concentrated. Or at least it is safe to say that most companies have the discretion to set prices (within a range) as opposed to being passive price takers.

Products of companies are not homogeneous, but differentiated and even sometimes unique, by virtue of brand equity, design, intellectual property rights, national origin labels, and other means of differentiation that constitute the art of modern management.

For at least the last 20 years, national borders have become more porous to the migration of factors of production, first capital, and now even labor through the physical travel of humans or by the electronic transmission of the fruits of their labor.

The practicing executive or patent lawyer would laugh at the theoretical economist's depiction of technology as a public good, knowing that the essence of firm competitiveness is secret or proprietary knowledge and expertise. There is hardly an industry for which we can say that all companies within it have an identical production function and undifferentiated products.

The very essence of FDI is that a company coming from thousands of kilometers away is nevertheless able to outperform local companies by virtue of the knowledge that is embedded in its personnel, its administrative routines, and its technological assets, which are superior, or at least different, from those of other firms. Sometime in the 1990s, an important benchmark was crossed in world economic history. The combined sales of FDI affiliates exceeded the value of total world exports. For the first time ever, FDI became more important than trade, and it will continue to become more important in the future. Instead of shipping products, the global corporation is increasingly shipping thoughts and mental organizational maps across national borders.

Finally, the world of comparative advantage theory is a world of nation-states, each able to police its borders. Comparative advantage theory's unit of analysis is a country. As a political entity, the nation-state is still viable. But a nation cannot anymore provide a very clear-cut economic unit of measurement. Regional supranational economic groupings are manifest in industry clusters that spill beyond national borders. The region, rather than the nation, the firm, or the economy as a whole, provide more interesting units of analysis to the researcher.

To conclude, the theory of comparative advantage is still very much valid in the 21st century and continues to drive policy thinking around the world. The main prescription of the theory is to lower barriers to trade – something deemed beneficial to both nations. This is illustrated by the continued signing of trade treaties, both bilaterally and multilaterally. In brief, trade treaties are agreements where the participating nations agree to phase out their tariffs and regulations that impede imports from the other nation/s. While the policy prescription of classic trade theory are correct and still valid, the old assumptions it rests upon have been eroded. Moreover, since the year 2016, governments have been paying more attention to the other side effect of international trade expansion, namely the loss of jobs and discontent in domestic industries that are no longer sheltered by protective tariffs and regulations.

Part III. Foreign Exchange Rates: Their Impact on International Operations

Section A. Hedging Foreign Currency Receivables and Payables

Includes Representative Problems 1–4 (With Solutions) in Foreign Exchange Risk Management in Chapter 13

Additional Problems from Chapter 13 Are Discussed in Part IV

Section B. Interest Rates and Foreign Exchange Rates

CHAPTER 13

Representative Problems (With Solutions) in Foreign Exchange Risk Management:

- **INTRODUCTION TO FOREIGN EXCHANGE RATES**

- **MANAGING TRANSACTION EXPOSURE: PROBLEMS 1 – 4**

The Following Problems Are Discussed in Part IV

- **ECONOMIC EXPOSURE OR INCOME STATEMENT EFFECTS: PROBLEMS 5 – 8**

- **CASE 2 GUIDELINES – PROBLEM 6:** *MOLTO DELIZIOSO:* **PRICING AND PROFITS FOLLOWING BREXIT DEVALUATION**

- **OPTIMUM PRICING IN FOREIGN MARKETS: PROBLEMS 9 – 11 AND SUPPLEMENTAL PROBLEM 12**

Farok J. Contractor, Ph.D.

INTRODUCTION TO FOREIGN EXCHANGE RATES

Foreign Currency Per USD

Currency	Date	Spot Rate	1 Month	2 Months	3 Months	4 Months	5 Months	6 Months	7 Months	8 Months	9 Months	10 Months	11 Months	12 Months
USD/CNY	May 10, '19	6.8251	6.8934	6.8933	6.8934	6.8934	6.8934	6.8934	6.8934	6.8934	6.8934	6.8934	6.8935	6.8935
USD/EUR	May 10, '19	1.1229	1.1258	1.1288	1.1316	1.1346	1.1373	1.14	1.1429	1.1459	1.1487	1.1514	1.1541	1.1567
USD/CAD	May 10, '19	1.3472	1.3462	1.3452	1.3443	1.3435	1.3426	1.34194	1.3411	1.3401	1.3394	1.3387	1.3381	1.3374
USD/JPY	May 10, '19	109.76	109.5011	109.2138	108.9711	108.6883	108.444	108.1999	107.9407	107.6313	107.3853	107.1413	106.9037	106.6745
USD/GBP	May 10, '19	1.3010	1.303	1.3051	1.307	1.309	1.3107	1.3125	1.3143	1.3163	1.3179	1.3195	1.3209	1.3224
USD/SGD	May 10, '19	1.3631	1.3625	1.3619	1.3611	1.3603	1.3595	1.3588	1.3581	1.3574	1.3567	1.356	1.3554	1.3547
USD/NOK	May 10, '19	8.7466	8.7364	8.7271	8.7188	8.71	8.7027	8.6958	8.6891	8.682	8.676	8.6709	8.6661	8.661
USD/AUD	May 10, '19	0.6992	0.6997	0.7001	0.7006	0.7012	0.7017	0.7022	0.7027	0.7032	0.7037	0.7042	0.7046	0.7051
USD/DKK	May 10, '19	6.6485	6.6304	6.6116	6.5943	6.5753	6.5585	6.5415	6.5239	6.5052	6.4884	6.4714	6.4557	6.4398
USD/INR	May 10, '19	69.91	70.19	70.455	70.695	70.9607	71.185	71.416	71.6778	71.9011	72.1375	72.3765	72.6255	72.8889
USD/MYR	May 10, '19	4.159	4.1594	4.1594	4.1594	4.1594	4.1594	4.1594	4.1594	4.1594	4.1594	4.1594	4.1594	4.1594

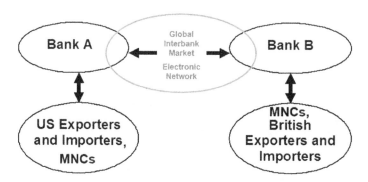

The Global Network of Banks and Companies

On May 10, 2019, These Rates Exist Simultaneously for the British Pound

- Spot Rate: £ 1 = $1.3010
- One Month Forward   £ 1 = $1.3030
- Three Months Forward £ 1 = $1.3070
- Six Months Forward   £ 1 = $1.3125

All bank transactions involve legally binding promises
- In the case of Spot Rates to deliver the agreed upon amounts of currencies (at the spot rate) within 48 hours.
- In the case of a One-Month Forward transaction to deliver the agreed upon amounts of currencies (at the May 10 one-month forward rate) approximately one month later around June 10.
- In the case of a Three-Month Forward transaction to deliver the agreed upon amounts of currencies (at the May 10 three-month forward rate) approximately three months later around August 10.
- In the case of a Six-Month Forward transaction to deliver the agreed upon amounts of currencies (at the May 10 six-month forward rate) approximately six months later around November 10.

Case 1: US Exporter Receives an Order on May 10: Shipment to Be Made on November 10: Payment will be £ 1,000,000.

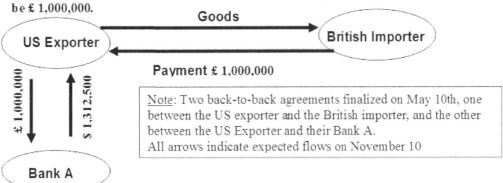

Case 2: US Importer Places an Order on May 10: Shipment Expected on November 10: Payment will be £ 2,000,000.

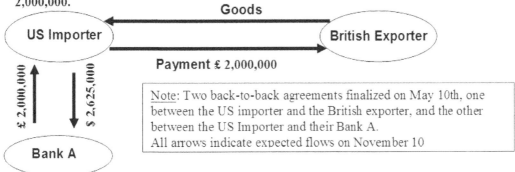

Case 3: British Importer Places an Order on May 10: Shipment Expected on November 10: Payment will be $ 6,000,000.

Case 4: British Exporter Places an Order on May 10: Shipment Expected on November 10: Payment will be $ 4,000,000.

Is There a Risk to the Banks? Netting Out Effects

Within their own client base, each large bank or institution has hundreds, perhaps thousands, of clients. For any particular date in the future, some of each bank's clients are demanding foreign currency, while other clients are wanting to supply (deliver to) the bank with the same foreign currency. Hence, within a large bank's own client base there is the likelihood of substantial "netting out" of exposure for any currency, for any future date.

Of course, there is no guarantee that such a "netting out" will happen, or be complete. In that case what can a bank do? Answer: Go to the interbank market and find another bank or party in the interbank forward market with whom they can sell/buy the particular currency. See the examples below for Bank A and Bank B.

<u>What Is the Exposure of Bank A and Bank B?</u>

Case 1: Bank A agrees to receive **£ 1,000,000** from its client
Case 2: Bank A agrees to deliver **£ 2,000,000** to another client

Net Exposure of Bank A: Net Deliverable of £ 1,000,000

Case 3: Bank B agrees to deliver **$6,000,000** to its client
Case 4: Bank B agrees to receive **$4,000,000** from another client

Net Exposure of Bank B: Net Deliverable of $2,000,000

But no bank needs to carry much exposure. A bank can go to the interbank foreign exchange market before closing time on May 10, and get rid of their net exposure (for November 1) in advance.

EFFECT ON INTERBANK MARKET ON MAY 10

- Bank A buys 180-days forward **£ 1,000,000** from some other bank or party in the interbank market. In return, Bank A promises delivery (to the other party in the interbank market) on November 1 **(£ 1,000,000)(1.6867) = $1,686,700.**

- Bank B buys 180-days forward **$2,000,000** from some other bank or party in the interbank market. In return, Bank B promises delivery (to the other party in the interbank market) on November 1 **($2,000,000)/(1.6867) = £ 1,185,747.**

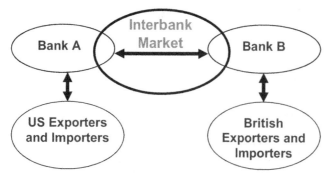

The actions of Bank A and Bank B in the interbank forward market on May 10th are opposite of each other – in terms of supply and demand – and substantially neutralize each other. Similarly, the actions of all other banks and financial institutions in the interbank market on the afternoon of May 10th, will mean that the forward supply and demand for a particular currency will be in balance at a certain market rate. Each bank can get rid of its own net exposure for any future date, and not carry any risk.

<u>NOTES TO READERS</u>:

To understand the logic and mechanics of the money market hedge, refer to Chapter 14 –

"Underlying Logic and Assumptions

for Money Market Hedges"

———————————

To understand why there is a difference between the spot and forward rate, refer to Chapter 15 –

"Interest Parity Theorem:

Why Is There a Difference Between the Spot and

Forward Rate for a Currency?"

PROBLEMS 1 – 4
PROBLEM 1

On July 9th, an American import-export company concluded two separate but simultaneous orders, one to import 1,000,000 Singapore Dollar (SGD) worth of optical instruments from Singapore and the other involving export of 5,900,000 Norwegian Krone (NOK) worth of apple pies to Norway. In both cases shipments are expected in the second week of January. Payments will be made in SGD and NOK respectively, upon presentation of shipping documents. Use the information for foreign exchange rates and interest rates in the boxes below. For classroom purposes, for a six month period, cut the annual interest rates in half. (In real life, just ask your bank). What is the best way to "hedge" (eliminate) the currency risk?

Annual Interest Rates			
	$	SGD	NOK
Deposit	5	1	4
Borrowing	8	3	6

Foreign Exchange Rates In $/Other Currency		
	SGD	NOK
Spot	.8235	.1401
30-Day	.8242	.1394
90-Day	.8288	.1389
180-Day	.8341	.1382

PROBLEM 1 SOLUTION

> **HEDGING THE IMPORT OF OPTICAL INSTRUMENTS (Calculations Made on July 9th)**

a. **FORWARD MARKET HEDGE:**

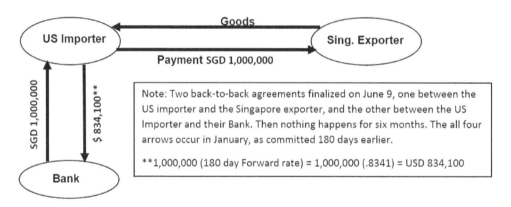

b. **MONEY MARKET HEDGE:**

Important Note: For classroom purposes, take the annual interest rates in the statement of the problem and cut them in half for a six-month term. Also assume that all firms have borrowed money (carry debt) for their normal operations

Objective: To deliver SGD 1,000,000 to the Singapore export company in January: Read the solution to this problem in the printed version (in the readings collection) which describes what happens going forward in time. Going forward in time the US importer (i) borrows an additional USD 819,403 from their bank in July for six months, (ii) takes the USD 819, 403 to the July Spot Market and converts them into SGD 995,025 in July, (iii) begins a six-month deposit of SGD 995,025 in July which earns an additional SGD interest of (.005 or one half of one percent), so that with the interest the value of the deposit six months late in January (Principal + Interest earned) or (995,025 (1.005)) = exactly SGD 1,000,000. In January (v) they pay the Singapore exporter SGD 1,000,000 out of the matured SGD deposit. Meanwhile, the USD loan (borrowing) has to be repaid for a total repayment of 819,403 (1.04) = USD 852,179. So the cost of the import in January is USD 852,179.

But where did those numbers come from? For that, we have to work backward in time.

To deliver SGD 1,000,000 to the exporter in January, begin the SGD deposit in July with SGD (1,000,000)/(1.005) = 995,025 SGD needed in July. Where does the US company get 995,025 SGD in July? From the Spot market conversion. (995,025)(Spot rate) = (995,025)(.8235) = USD 819,403 needed in July. Where does the US import firm get USD 819,403 in July? By borrowing an additional USD 819,403 for six months, starting in July. Next January, the USD loan (borrowing) has to be repaid for a total USD loan repayment of 819,403 (1.04) = USD 852,179. So the cost of the import in January is USD 852,179.

In this story, the Forward Market Hedge makes the cost of the import cheaper (USD 834,100) than the cost of the import using the Money Market Hedge (USD 852,179). So the forward market hedge is better.

HEDGING THE EXPORT OF APPLE PIES TO NORWAY (Calculations Made on July 9th)

c. FORWARD MARKET HEDGE:

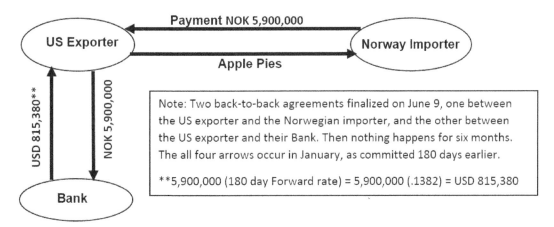

Note: Two back-to-back agreements finalized on June 9, one between the US exporter and the Norwegian importer, and the other between the US exporter and their Bank. Then nothing happens for six months. The all four arrows occur in January, as committed 180 days earlier.

**5,900,000 (180 day Forward rate) = 5,900,000 (.1382) = USD 815,380

d. MONEY MARKET HEDGE:

Important Note: For classroom purposes, take the annual interest rates in the statement of the problem and cut them in half for a six-month term. Also assume that all firms have borrowed money (carry debt) for their normal operations

Objective: To lock in the January USD value of the apple pie export six months in advance.
Read the solution to this problem in the printed version (in the readings collection) which describes what happens going forward in time. Going forward in time (i) the US exporter goes to a bank in July and borrows NOK 5,728,155 for six months. (ii) In July they take the NOK 5,728,155 to the Spot Market and convert them into USD (5,728,155)(Spot rate) = (5,728,155)(.1401) = USD 802,515 in July. (iii) Now that the US firm has USD early, their own currency, they use the USD 802,515 to lower their normal USD debt balance by that amount, enjoying an additional saving of USD borrowing interest (i.e. borrowing interest cost that they now do not need to incur). Reducing their USD borrowing by USD 802, 515 for six months saves the US firm interest of (802,515)(.04) = USD 32,100 by January. So the total value of the Money Market Hedge operation is (USD received from the Spot Market conversion in July + USD borrowing interest cost saved) = 802,515 + 32,100 = USD 834,615

But where did those numbers come from? For that, we have to work backward in time..
Recall that the US firm or exporter having borrowed NOK from a bank will have to repay NOK to the same bank six months later? How will they do that? By promising the bank a repayment in January of NOK 5,900,000 which they can pay the bank from the 5,900,000 NOK they will get from the apple pie importer in Norway. (i) So to replay exactly 5,900,000 NOK in January they need to start in July by borrowing (5,900,000)/1.03 = 5,728,155 NOK in July. Then the rest of the story is the same as above. (ii) In July they take the NOK 5,728,155 to the Spot Market and convert them into USD (5,728,155)(Spot rate) = (5,728,155)(.1401) = USD 802,515 in July. (iii) Now that the US firm has USD early, their own currency, they use the USD 802,515 to lower their normal USD debt balance by that amount, enjoying an additional saving of USD borrowing interest (i.e. borrowing interest cost that they now do not need to incur). Reducing

their USD borrowing by USD 802, 515 for six months saves the US firm interest of (802,515)(.04) = USD 32,100 by January. So the total value of the Money Market Hedge operation is (USD received from the Spot Market conversion in July + USD borrowing interest cost saved) = 802,515 + 32,100 = USD 834,615.

In this story, the Forward Market Hedge (USD 815,380 received in January) is less than the value received using the Money Market Hedge (USD 834,615 in January). So the money market hedge is better in this story.

> **To gain additional insights on the so-called "Money Market Hedges," please first read the chapter entitled:**
>
> **UNDERLYING LOGIC AND ASSUMPTIONS FOR MONEY MARKET HEDGES**
> **FOR IMPORTER (Foreign Currency Payable) AND EXPORTER (Foreign Currency Receivable)**
> **Then come back and read, if you need to, Expanded Solution / Reading for Problem 1, below.**

PROBLEM 1 EXPANDED SOLUTION

On July 9th, an American import-export company concluded two separate but simultaneous orders, one to import 1,000,000 Singapore Dollar (SGD) worth of optical instruments from Singapore and the other involving export of 5,900,000 Norwegian Krone (NOK) worth of apple pies to Norway. In both cases shipments are expected in the second week of January. Payments will be made in SGD and NOK respectively, upon presentation of shipping documents. Use the information for foreign exchange rates and interest rates in the boxes below, and answer these questions:

Annual Interest Rates			
	$	SGD	NOK
Deposit	5	1	4
Borrowing	8	3	6

Foreign Exchange Rates In $/Other Currency		
	SGD	NOK
Spot	.8235	.1401
30-Day	.8242	.1394
90-Day	.8288	.1389
180-Day	.8341	.1382

While it is the same American company, the two deals, one for the import of optical instruments, and the other for the export of pies, are separate and are treated as separate transactions. In order to calculate the best alternatives, the executive/s in the American company does several calculations on July 9th. All data above are available on July 9th.

All calculations Below Are Done and Decisions Are Made on July 9th **For Final Outcomes Which Will Only Conclude on January 9th (ALL CALCULATIONS FOR JANUARY 9TH VALUES**

> **HEDGING THE IMPORT OF OPTICAL INSTRUMENTS (Calculations Made on July 9th).**

a. Forward Market Hedge
   Calculation (Result as of January 9th)

   Description: On July 9 (date), the American company executive, arranges to "buy SGD 1,000,000, 180 days forward." That is to say, on July 9th the American company makes a legally binding commitment to receive SGD 1,000,000 180 days later and in return commits to deliver to the counterparty in the forward market or bank (1,000,000)(0.8341) = $834,100, 180 days later. Once this commitment is made on July 9th, then nothing happens as far as the American company is concerned. Approximately six months go by. Then on approximately January 9 (date), $834,100.00 are debited from their account with the bank, SGD 1,000,000 are credited into their account (temporarily) and the SGD 1,000,000 are immediately, or fairly soon, remitted to Singapore. In any case, the American company knows ever since July 9th, that the cost of their import will amount to exactly $834,100 on January 9th.

b. Money Market Hedge (Basic Logic: Early Currency Conversion on July 9th itself)

<u>Calculation</u> (result as of January 9th)

<u>Description:</u> On July 9 (date), the American company executive, arranges to borrow $819,403**, for six months. Then on the same day (July 9), the $819,403 are converted into SGD 995,024.88, using the July 9th spot rate, and deposited in a SGD currency bank account, earning interest over the next six months, to yield a (Principal: SGD 995,024.88 + Interest: SGD 4,975.12) = Total SGD 1,000,000 value on January 9 (date). The SGD 1,000,000 on January 9 will pay for the import.

Meanwhile, the US Dollar loan comes due with a total loan repayment obligation (Principal of $819,403 + 4percent interest) $852,179.10 to be repaid to the bank on January 9th. So the total cost on January 9th will be $852,179.10

<u>CHOICES AVAILABLE ON JULY 9TH FOR OUTCOMES ON JANUARY 9TH</u>: The American executive makes the above calculations on July 9th because all the data above are known on July 9th. Pay $834,100 on January 9th (Forward Market) <u>OR</u> Pay $852,179.12 on January 9th (Money Market Hedge). **The forward market hedge is cheaper**. Hence the idea of using the Money market Hedge is dropped and only the Forward Market Hedge is implemented on July 9th.

** Why borrow $819,403? We assume that companies do not have extra cash. If it wants to implement the Money Market Hedge – which requires early currency conversion -- it will have to borrow that much additional Dollars for six months. How do they know they have to borrow $819,403 for six months? Because they know that, in order to have the SGD deposit mature to exactly SGD 1,000,000 on January 9th (six months later) the SGD deposit will have to start with 1,000,000/1.005 = SGD 995,024.88 on July 9th. Next calculation: In order to begin a SGD deposit on July 9th with SGD 995,024.88 they will need to convert in the July 9th Spot Market $(995,024.88)(0.8235) = $819,402.98 into 995,024.88 SGD. So this calculation shows that $819,403 will have to be borrowed starting July 9th, for six months.

HEDGING THE EXPORT OF PIES (Calculations Made on July 9th)

c. <u>Forward Market Hedge</u>
   <u>Calculation</u> (Result as of January 9th)

   <u>Description:</u> On July 9 (date), the American company executive, (knowing that they will receive NOK 5,900,000 from Norway on January 9th) arranges to "Sell NOK 5,900,000, 180 days forward." That is to say, on July 9th the American company makes a legally binding commitment to deliver NOK 5,900,000 to the counterparty in the forward market or bank, 180 days later, and in return will receive from the counterparty or bank $815,380 on January 9th, 180 days later. Once this commitment is made on July 9th, then nothing happens as far as the American company is concerned, except that they are getting the export consignment ready to ship. Approximately six months go by. Then on approximately January 9 (date), the export shipment is made, and NOK 5,900,000 received from the Norwegian importer are (temporarily) credited into their account and almost immediately again debited because NOK 5,900,000 have to be paid out on January 9th, to fulfill the Forward Market commitment made six months earlier. In turn, the counterparty or bank (in the Forward Market commitment) credits the American company's account with $815,380 on January 9th fulfilling their earlier promise. In any case, the American company knows ever since July 9th, that the Dollar value of their export will amount to exactly $815,380 on January 9th.

On January 9 (date), $815,380 are credited to the American company's account.

d. <u>Money Market Hedge</u> (Basic Logic: Early Currency Conversion on July 9th itself)

   <u>Calculation</u> (result as of January 9th)

   <u>Description:</u> On July 9 (date), the American company executive, arranges to borrow NOK 5,728,155.30**, for six months from a bank. Then on July 9th (date), NOK 5,728,155.30 are converted into (5,728,155.30)(0.1401) = $802,514.55, using the spot rate, and used their own American business, (which means that, for the next six months, the American company would retire/reduce $802,514.55 worth of ordinary dollar debt they would otherwise have carried for the next six months – thereby *saving or not having to pay* $(802,514.55)(0.04) = $32,100.58 in borrowing interest). Hence the total value of the Money Market Hedge is not only $802,514.55, but because $802,514.55 was received early -- on July 9th – there will be an additional saving of interest amounting to $32,100.58 which adds up to a total value, as of

January 9th, of $802,514.55 (received) + $32,100.58 (saved) = a total value of $834,615.13, on January 9 (date).

CHOICES AVAILABLE ON JULY 9TH FOR OUTCOMES ON JANUARY 9TH: The American executive makes the above calculations on July 9th because all the data above are known on July 9th. Receive $815,380 on January 9th (Forward Market) OR receive $802,514.55 on July 9th plus an additional saving of $32,100.58 by January 9th, to amount to a total value of $834,615.13 as of January 9th. **The money market hedge is higher**. Hence the idea of using the Forward Market Hedge is dropped and only the Money Market Hedge is implemented on July 9th.

INTERNAL NETTING?

e. A clever employee in the American firm notices that, by combining the two orders using the July 9th spot rates, the net foreign exchange exposure is much reduced. If so, should the company hedge at all? The import of optical instruments (SGD Payable) and the export of pies (NOK Receivable), partially cancel each other out in terms of the American company's overall foreign exchange risk: $834,100 **payable** vs. $834,615.13 **receivable**. But that is only if both import and export are hedged. If the import and export are left unhedged, over the next six months, the Dollar may or may not take the same direction (become weaker or stronger) with respect to both the SGD and the NOK. (i) There is no guarantee and over the six months a much bigger net exposure may result if both deals are unhedged, (ii) even if hedged, the netting or offset is only partial, and (iii) if both transactions are left un-hedged the exact final outcome cannot be known until January 9th when the January 9th spot rates will become known.

If the American company executive is risk averse and needs to know the exact January 9th outcome of both transactions in advance, then each transaction should be hedged separately, and then s/he can sleep in peace for the next six months, with exactly anticipated outcomes already known.

** The logic of the Money Market Hedge is to make the currency conversion early, on July 9th itself. By borrowing NOK in July and converting them into US Dollars on July 9th, the currency risk is eliminated thereby. The conversion is done at the known July 9th Spot Rate. How do they know they have to borrow NOK 5,728,155.30 for six months? And why would an American company borrow money in NOK? Because they know that they can repay a NOK loan from the NOK they are due to get from the Norwegian importer in January. So a NOK loan of NOK [(5,900,000)/(1.03)] = NOK 5,728,155.30 borrowed for six months starting in July, would mean that they would have to repay the bank NOK 5,900,000 in January – which they can repay, from the NOK 5,900,000 the Norwegian importer will pay them.

PROBLEM 2 –

TWO SEPARATE CASES, 2A AND 2B

(2A) An importer from Israel placed an order on an exporter in the US on March 11th. The goods are to be shipped on approximately September 11th, and payment of 1,000,000 Dollars will be due at that time.

On March 11th, an executive in the Israeli company was asked to hedge the company's foreign exchange exposure. Compute three alternative hedges, showing complete calculations. The data shown below were available on March 11th, to the executive. Which method is best?

___

(2B) An importer from Israel placed an order on an exporter in the US on March 11th. The goods are to be shipped on approximately September 11th, and payment of 3,500,000 Shekels will be due at that time.

On March 11th, an executive in the American company was asked to hedge the company's foreign exchange exposure. Compute three alternative hedges, showing complete calculations. The data shown below were available on March 11th, to the executive. Which method is best?

___

Annualized Interest Rates			March 11th
(For Three And Six Month Terms)			SPOT 3.4253 Shekels/$
Deposit	Borrowing		90 DAY 3.4433 Shekels/$
Dollars 3	7		180 DAY 3.4612 Shekels/$
Shekels 5	9		

PROBLEM 2 SOLUTIONS –

2A AND 2B

(2A) ISRAELI IMPORTER TO PAY $1,000,000 IN SEPTEMBER

Forward Market: 1,000,000 (3.4612) = 3,461,200 Shekels (September) ** Best Choice

Money Market : $\frac{1,000,000}{(1.015)}$ (3.4253) (1.045) = 3,526,540 Shekels (September)

___

(2B) AMERICAN EXPORTER TO RECEIVE SHEKELS 3,500,000 IN SEPTEMBER

Forward Market: $\frac{(3,500,000)}{(3.4612)}$ = $1,011,209.90 (September)

Money Market : $\frac{3,500,000}{(1.045)} \frac{1}{3.4253}$ (1.035) = $1.012,030.20 (September) ** Best Choice

PROBLEM 3 –

TWO SEPARATE CASES, I AND II

On February 27th, a Brazilian importer placed an order on a Chinese company, valued at 50,000,000 Chinese Renminbi Yuan -- CNY (or 30,030,000 Brazilian Real at that day's exchange rate). Payment is to be made upon shipment by the exporter, expected to take place at the end of August. Assume that the exchange rates given below apply without transactions costs, and assume that each firm, Chinese and Brazilian, considers its opportunity cost of capital to be the borrowing rates shown for Yuan and Real, respectively.

In international trade transactions, the order is denominated in either the importer's or exporter's currency, depending on the negotiation:

Case I.   50,000,000 CNY, OR
Case II. As 30,030,000 Real.

In each (mutually exclusive) case, one or the other of the firms bears the exchange risk.

For each case,

(i) Calculate hedging alternatives
(ii) Which one will be chosen and why?

Annual Interest Rates for 3-Month or 6-Month Terms		
	DEPOSIT	BORROWING
CNY	2percent p.a.	10percent p.a.
Real	4percent p.a.	12percent p.a.

Exchange Rates Offered By Banks at 4:00 p.m. on February 27th		
	Real/CNY	CNY/Real
Spot	.6006	1.6650
30-Day	.6060	1.6502
90-Day	.6174	1.6197
180-Day	.6339	1.5775

PROBLEM 3 SOLUTIONS –

CASE I AND CASE II

Case I. 50,000,000 CNY Payable by Brazilian Importer in August

The Brazilian importer is doing the calculations, and wants to fix the Real cost of the import in advance. All calculations and arrangements to be locked in between the Brazilian importer and their bank in February, but the outcomes shown in the numbers below are all for August.

Forward Market Hedge: In February "Buy 50 million CNY 180-days Forward." Hence, $(0.6339)(50,000,000)$ = **31,695,000 Real payable to bank in August**. The Brazilian importer promises in February to pay 31,695,000 Real to the bank in August and the bank promises to deliver to them 50,000,000 CNY in August, which they can use to pay for the import.

Money Market Hedge: Borrow 29,732,672 Real (for a six- month loan) in February; convert the borrowed Real into $29,732,672/(0.6006)$ = 49,504,950 CNY in February; and then deposit 49,504,950 CNY in a CNY deposit account for six months, so that with the interest earned, it becomes $(49,504,950)(1.01)$ = 50,000,000 CNY in August from which the exporter can be paid. Meanwhile the six month Real loan will come due in August, for a total repayment to the bank of $(29,732,672)(1.06)$ = **31,516,632 Real in August** which is the "known in advance" cost of the import. The MM Hedge is the cheaper choice for the importer.

Case II. 30,030,000 Real Receivable by Chinese Exporter in August

The Chinese Exporter is doing the calculations, and wants to fix the CNY revenue of the export in advance. All calculations and arrangements are to be locked in between the Chinese exporter and their bank in February, but the outcomes shown in the numbers below are all for August.

Forward Market Hedge: In February "Sell 30,030,000 million Real 180-days Forward." Hence, $(1.5775)(30,030,000)$ = 47,372,325 CNY receivable from bank in August. The Chinese exporter promises in February to pay 30,030,000 Real to the bank in August (from the export proceeds) and the bank promises to deliver to them **47,372,325 CNY in August**.

Money Market Hedge: Borrow 28,330,188 Real (for a six month loan) in February; convert the borrowed Real into $28,330,188(1.665)$ = 47,169,763 CNY in February; and then use the 47,169,763 CNY to reduce the company's outstanding CNY debt level for six months, so that with the interest saved (from the debt reduction), the total value becomes $(47,169,763)(1.05)$ = **49,528,251 CNY in August**. Meanwhile the six month Real loan will come due in August, for a total repayment to the bank of $(28,330,188)(1.06)$ = 30,030,000 Real in August which can be paid from the 30,030,000 Real that the Brazilian importer will remit to the Chinese exporter in August. *The MM Hedge is the better choice for the exporter.

PROBLEM 4

Impex Inc. of New Jersey, an international export/import company, does considerable trade with Fredonia, buying and selling goods of both nations. On Monday, July 27, they finalize two deals. (1) To buy, 100,000 fredos worth of straw hats from a Fredonian firm. (2) To export 160,000 fredos worth of wrenches made by Dirty Devil Hardware of Bayonne, NJ. Impex, acting as intermediary, quotes to its U.S. clients in dollars, relieving them of exchange risks. Assuming that both the above deals have expected shipments at the end of January, with payment due on presentation of shipping documents at that time, how can Impex insulate itself against exchange risks? Using the data below, calculate the consequences of three types of hedges. Which one will be chosen? Assume the opportunity cost of capital to be the company's borrowing rate.

Exchange Rates: $/Fredo	
Spot	.0400
30-Day	.0380
60-Day	.0375
90-Day	.0350
180-Day	.0300

Short Term Interest Rates* (Annual percent Rates)		
	In $	Fredos
Borrowing	10	32
Deposit	6	28

* Valid for 3 or 6 months

Calculate hedges based on

A) Covering the net Fredo exposure
B) Hedging (a) The import transaction separately,
  (b) The export transaction separately,
    and then netting the dollar amounts.

This problem illustrates how in less efficient markets, or markets subject to capital controls or heavy government intervention (such as in frontier market nations), the difference in various hedging outcomes can be large.

PROBLEM 4 SOLUTION

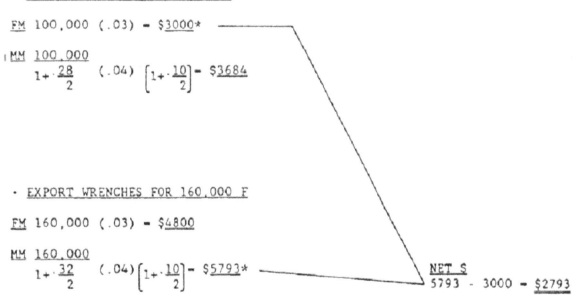

A. __Net 60,000 F Receivable__

$\underline{FM}$ 60,000 (.03) = $\underline{\$1800}$

$\underline{MM}$ $\dfrac{60,000}{1+\cdot\frac{32}{2}}$ (.04) $\left[1+\cdot\frac{10}{2}\right]$ = $\underline{\$2172}$

B. __Treat Each Separately__

· __IMPORT HATS WORTH 100,000 F__

$\underline{FM}$ 100,000 (.03) = $\underline{\$3000}$*

$\underline{MM}$ $\dfrac{100,000}{1+\cdot\frac{28}{2}}$ (.04) $\left[1+\cdot\frac{10}{2}\right]$ = $\underline{\$3684}$

· __EXPORT WRENCHES FOR 160,000 F__

$\underline{FM}$ 160,000 (.03) = $\underline{\$4800}$

$\underline{MM}$ $\dfrac{160,000}{1+\cdot\frac{32}{2}}$ (.04) $\left[1+\cdot\frac{10}{2}\right]$ = $\underline{\$5793}$*

$\underline{NET\ \$}$
5793 - 3000 = $\underline{\$2793}$

In Alternative A. the firm nets the Fredo exposure (160,000 – 100,000 = 60,000 Fredos net exposure), and this is the common sense thing to do which yields a net receivable of $2172. But in Alternative B, by 'hedging' each separately, the firm gets a superior result of a net $2793 receivable.

While this is a hypothetical case, as noted above, what it illustrates is that in very thin or imperfect markets the differences between various alternatives can be substantial. Therefore, it is all the more important to calculate the outcomes of all choices and pick the best one

<u>NOTES TO READERS:</u>

To understand the logic and mechanics of the money market

hedge, refer to Chapter 14 –

"Underlying Logic and Assumptions

for Money Market Hedges"

To understand why there is a difference between the spot and

forward rate, refer to Chapter 15 –

"Interest Parity Theorem:

Why Is There a Difference Between the Spot and

Forward Rate for a Currency?"

PROBLEMS 5 – 8
PROBLEM 5

Multinational company operations are affected by both Balance Sheet exposure as well as Income Statement exposure. The Balance Sheet is but a historical summary or the net *stock* of past transactions of the firm The income statement reflects the real, on-going "economic adjustment" type of impact on a firm arising from a currency devaluation or revaluation. The Income Statement is concerned with *flows* within each time period.

The Problem

The last income statement of the Chilean subsidiary of a U.S. multinational is given below at a time when $1 = 500 Pesos. Let us assess the Impact of a possible Peso devaluation to say 600 Peso = $1. On the revenue side as well as on the cost side there is a mix of currencies (in Peso and $) although the accounting figures below are all shown in Peso equivalents.

IN LOCAL CURRENCY (PESO millions)

	P (in $per unit)	P (in Pesos per unit)	Quantity (No. of Units in millions)	Revenue (Peso Millions)
SALES REVENUES				
Local	-	1100	2000	2.200,000
Export to US	2.00	1000	1500	1.500,000
TOTAL REVENUE				3,700,000
COSTS				
Labor				800,000
Interest and Depreciation				900,000
Materials				
- Chilean				600,000
- Imported				1,000,000
TOTAL COSTS				3,300,000
PROFITS				400,000

Additional Data

The item is a consumer product with Price Elasticities of Demand: (Chilean = 1.0) (US = 2.0)

Consider two marketing strategies that the firm can adopt:

Strategy I: No Change Scenario - Keep the $unit price to U.S. consumers the same as before, as well as the Peso price to local customers, kept constant.

Strategy II: "Pass-Through" Scenario - Keep the price in Pesos the same for local consumers, but pass on the full effect of the currency shift onto export market customers, by changing the $export unit price.

For the above two strategies write the post-devaluation income statements in each case at 600 Pesos = $1 (assuming other things stay the same).
a) Would a Peso devaluation be good or bad for the subsidiary?
b) Which pricing strategy would you choose?
c) What are the implications for sourcing strategy?
d) In general, what factors affect the "bottom line" in cases like this?

221

e) Having done this before/after "snapshot" analysis, next take a medium-run perspective over several months or a year following a devaluation. What assumptions (for "holding other things constant") may have to be modified?

PROBLEM 5 SOLUTION

Strategy I: Keep Prices to All Customers the Same as Before in Their Own Currencies

Unit Prices (**P**)	• Local	1100 Pesos/unit
	• Export to US	$ 2.0 / unit
		= 1200 Pesos/unit[1]
Quantity (# of units **Q**)	• Local	2000 units
	• Export	1500 units[2]
	TOTAL	**3500** units

Income Statement In Pesos

			P		**Q**
Revenue	• Local	2,200,000	1100 Pesos/unit	X	2000 units
	• Export to US	1,800,000	$ 2.0 (600) = 1200 Pesos per unit	X	1500 units
		4,000,000			
Costs	• Labor	800,000			
	• Interest & Depr.	900,000[3]			
	• Materials				
	- Local	600,000			
	- Imported	1,200,000[4]	1,000,000 (600/500)		
		3,500,000			
Profit		**500,000** =			
		$ 500,000/600			
		= $ 833.33			

[1] Keeping the same Dollar price per unit of $ 2.0 now means more Pesos. Since the Peso has devalued. $ 2.0 is now equivalent to 2.0 x 600 = 1200 Pesos per unit.

[2] The US customer demand is the same as before, at 1500 units. Why? American customers only respond to $ price signals. Because in US $ the price has not changed the US export quantity does not change (even though the same Dollars now mean (600/500) more Pesos than before).

[3] In the short or medium term Interest and Depreciation costs can be treated as Fixed Costs, i.e., no change.

[4] The total quantity to be produced has not changed. Hence the quantity of imported materials will remain the same. But imported materials have to be paid for in Dollars. So the Peso cost of purchasing the same materials (even with the exact same Dollars) goes up by a factor of (600/500)

Strategy II: Reduce the $ Unit Price in the Export Market
(So as to pass on the full benefit of the Peso Devaluation to US Customers[5])

Unit Prices (**P**)		
	• Local	1100 Pesos/unit
	• Export to US	1000 Pesos/unit = $ 1.6666 / unit[5]
Quantity (# of units **Q**)	• Local	2000 units
	• Export	2000 units[6]
	TOTAL QUANTITY HAS INCREASED TO:	**4000** units

Income Statement In Pesos

			P		**Q**
Revenue	• Local	2,200,000	1100 Pesos/unit	X	2000 units
	• Export to US	2,000,000	$ 1.6666 (600) = 1000 Pesos per unit	X	2000 units
		4,200,000			
Costs	• Labor	914,286[7]	(800,000 x 4000/3500)		
	• Interest & Depr.	900,000			
	• Materials				
	- Local	685,714[8]	(6,000,000 x 4000/3500)		
	- Imported	1,371,429[9]	1,000,000 (600/500)(4000/3500)		
		3,871,429			
Profit		**328,571** = $ 328,571/600 = $ 547.62			

[5] In order to pass on the full benefit of the Peso devaluation to US customers, the company brings its Peso price per unit back from 1200 Pesos per unit (in previous Strategy I) down to 1000 Pesos per unit (in Strategy II). (See Footnote 1 for comparison).

[6] But bringing the Peso price down to 1000 Pesos per unit now means only $ 1000/600 = $ 1.6666 per unit. Previously, in Strategy I, US customers were paying $ 2.00 per unit. So US customers see a sixteen and two-thirds percent reduction in their unit price -- down from the previous $ 2.00 to the new $ 1.6666. Percentage wise, the price drop amounts to [(Old Price – New Price)/(Old Price)] 100 % = [(2.0 – 1.6666)/(2.0)] 100 = 16.6666 % drop in unit price as seen by US customers in Dollars.

Happy to see a sixteen and two-thirds percent drop in the Dollar unit price, US customers now demand 16.6666 x 2 = 33.33 % more quantity, because the Price Elasticity of Demand in the US = 2. Hence New Q_{US} = Old Q_{US} (1 + .3333) = 1500 (1.3333) = 2000 units.

[7] Assume that labor will be paid the same wages in Pesos per hour. But because of the increased production quantity (4000 total units instead of the old 3500 units) the wage bill for the company will increase by a factor of (4000/3500). So multiply the old wage bill by the quantity increase factor. i.e., (800,000 x 4000/3500).

[8] The cost of locally procured materials increases because of the larger quantity by a factor of (4000/3500).

[9] The cost of imported materials in Pesos increases as a result of two factors (i) larger quantity (4000/3500) and (ii) Foreign exchange (600/500).

How to Calculate the New Quantity in Strategy II

Price Elasticity of Demand (US customer) = ε_{US}

$$\varepsilon_{US} = 2.0 = \left[\frac{\%\text{ Increase in } Q_{US}}{\%\text{ Decrease in } {}^{\$}P_{US}} \right]$$

%Increase in Q_{US} = (2.0)(%Decrease in ${}^{\$}P_{US}$) = (2.0) (16.66% decrease in ${}^{\$}P_{US}$)
= 33.33% Increase in Q_{US}

So, New Q_{US} = (1.3333)(Old Q_{US}) = (1.3333)(1500 units)
= 2000 units

Comparing Elastic and Inelastic Demand

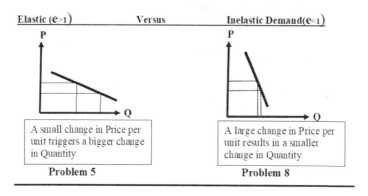

Elastic (e>1)	Versus	Inelastic Demand(e<1)

A small change in Price per unit triggers a bigger change in Quantity

Problem 5

A large change in Price per unit results in a smaller change in Quantity

Problem 8

PROBLEM 5 POINTS FOR DISCUSSION

1) **What are the strategy implications of the above analysis for**
   - Export pricing policy?
   - Sourcing?

For this company (only, and not in general) the export price should not be changes since Scenario I works out better for the Chilean firm in its currency the Chilean Peso.

Pesos being devalued against Dollars makes imported components or materials more expensive in peso terms. This may be a time to reexamine the possibility of sourcing local, from a local supplier. That may not always be a feasible or risk-free idea, but worth investigating.

2) **Will the effects of an exchange rate change *always* result in better profits? Should the unit export price *always* be changed?**

General Answer: No. One cannot generalize. It varies from one firm to another.
Four variables affect the "bottom line" – variables which are not the same from one company to another:

   a. The mix of exports versus local sales, or the mix of currencies on the Revenue side.
   b. The mix of imports in total inputs, or the mix of currencies on the Cost side.
   c. The proportion of Variable versus Fixed costs.
   d. Elasticities of demand faced by the firm in various market segments.

3) **The above exercise was a simple Before/After short-term calculation. But what about longer-run effects? Consider Purchasing Power Parity (PPP) theory, which says that the devaluation is (in the long run) to be accompanied by local inflation.**
   For longer run analysis, set up a spreadsheet and estimate numbers for Revenues, Costs and Profits for each year in the future Year 1, Year 2, Year 3, etc.. For each future year PPP Theory may also supply estimates for the exchange rates to be used.

CASE 2 GUIDELINES — PROBLEM 6:

MOLTO DELIZIOSO: PRICING AND PROFITS
FOLLOWING BREXIT DEVALUATION
(Case from Harvard Publishing)

♛IVEY | Publishing

Farok J. Contractor wrote this case solely to provide material for class discussion. The author does not intend to illustrate either effective or ineffective handling of a managerial situation. The author may have disguised certain names and other identifying information to protect confidentiality.

> Readers may obtain the complete text of the above case by Farok J. Contractor from the Harvard Case Collection, https://store.hbr.org/product/molto-delizioso-pricing-and-profits-following-brexit-devaluation/W17205, or consult Rutgers Libraries.

GUIDELINES

1. Recalculate the income statement shown in case Exhibit 1 using the post-Brexit exchange rate of £1.00 = €1.16,[8] assuming that there are no change in prices charged by the company to UK buyers. Assume that fixed costs remain fixed and variable costs vary proportionally to volume or quantity sold. Calculate profit in both pounds and euros.

2. Recalculate the income statement shown in case Exhibit 1 using the post-Brexit exchange rate of £1.00 = €1.16, assuming that the UK subsidiary increases its price to UK buyers to £235 per unit. Assume that fixed costs remain fixed and variable costs vary proportionally to volume or quantity sold. Assume that UK purchasers' consumer behaviour is somewhat elastic and that market research suggests their elasticity = 1.1. Use the simple point elasticity formula:

   Price Elasticity ε = percent Decrease/Increase in Quantity Demanded
                        percent Increase/Decrease in Price per Unit

   Calculate profit in both pounds and euros.

3. Recalculate the income statement shown in case Exhibit 1 using the post-Brexit exchange rate of £1.00 = €1.16, assuming that the UK subsidiary increases its price to UK buyers to £235 per unit. Assume that fixed costs remain fixed and variable costs vary proportionally to volume or quantity sold. Assume that UK purchasers' consumer behaviour is somewhat elastic and that market research suggests their elasticity = 0.8. Use the simple point elasticity formula:

   Price Elasticity ε = percent Decrease/Increase in Quantity Demanded
                        percent Increase/Decrease in Price per Unit

   Calculate profit in both pounds and euros.

4. Which of the three options above should Montague choose? What is the perspective of the Italian headquarters?

---

[8] £ = GBP = United Kingdom pound; € = euro; currency amounts are in £ unless otherwise specified; US$1.00 = £0.77 on July 6, 2016; US$1.00 = €0.90 on July 6, 2016.

PROBLEM 7

INCOME STATEMENT	Quantity (in millions)	Unit Price (in Pesos)	Pesos	Total
Export Sales	1.00	1.00	1,000,000	
Domestic Sales	2.00	1.00	2,000,000	
Total Revenues				3,000,000
Imported Materials	0.20	1.00	200,000	
Locally Purchased Materials	1.00	1.00	1,000,000	
Local Labor (man-hours)	0.50	1.00	500,000	
Fixed Costs				
- In Dollars			300,000	
- In Pesos			300,000	
Total Costs				2,300,000
Cash Flow (in Pesos)				700,000
Cash Flow (in Dollars)				$700,000

The Income Statement of the subsidiary of a U.S.-headquartered firm is shown above, before the occurrence of a peso devaluation from 1 peso = $1, to 1 peso = $0.80.

The plant sells to both domestic (local market) as well as U.S. export markets, and sources its raw materials in both countries. This is indicated above.

ASSUME THAT:

a) For various macroeconomic reasons, the devaluation is accompanied by a 10percent inflation, causing domestic raw material and labor prices to rise 10percent.
b) As a result, the company raises its peso selling price by 10percent for all customers, domestic and foreign.
c) Local demand is completely inelastic and, hence, no change in quantities is demanded. However, U.S. demand is elastic, with coefficient of elasticity e = 2.5 (See footnote**).

**Coefficient of elasticity $e = 2.5 = \dfrac{dQ/Q}{dp/P}$

This means that every 1percent decrease in the $price paid by U.S. consumers will make them increase quantity consumed by 2.5percent.

Hint: First calculate the post-devaluation post-price increase, dollar price to U.S. consumers. Then calculate the increase in U.S. demand from elasticity. Then calculate the percent increase in total demand and apply that percent increase to all raw material and labor.

PROBLEM 7 SOLUTION

INCOME STATEMENT	Quantity (in millions)	Unit Price (in Pesos)	Pesos	Total Pesos
Export Sales	1.30	1.10	1,430,000	
Domestic Sales	2.00	1.10	2,200,000	
Total Revenues				3,630,000
Imported Materials	0.22	1.25	275,000	
Locally Purchased Materials	1.10	1.10	1,210,000	
Local Labor (man-hours)	0.55	1.10	605,000	
Fixed Costs				
- In Dollars			375,000	
- In Pesos			300,000	
Total Costs				2,765,000
Cash Flow (in Pesos)				865,000
Cash Flow (in Dollars)				$ 692,000

Rewrite the entire Income Statement as follows:

1. First, make changes under the "Unit Price (in Pesos)" column for all inputs and outputs (being careful with the imported raw materials price).
2. Next, make changes under the "Quantities or Units" column. (Be careful about export demand, and remember that raw materials and labor go towards total demand. Find the percent increase in total demand over the old figures; then apply that percent increase over all raw materials and labor)
3. Make appropriate changes in the "Fixed Costs."
4. The rest is simple arithmetic.

**Coefficient of elasticity $e = 2.5 = \dfrac{dQ/Q}{dp/P}$

This means that every 1percent _decrease_ in the $price paid by U.S. consumers will make them _increase_ quantity consumed by 2.5percent.

Hint: First calculate the post-devaluation post-price increase, dollar price to U.S. consumers. Then calculate the increase in U.S. demand from elasticity. Then calculate the percent increase in total demand and apply that percent increase to all raw material and labor.

PROBLEM 8

The Income Statement of the Bulgarian subsidiary of a U.S. multinational company is shown below, assuming the exchange rate for the Bulgarian Lev is 2 Lev = 1 US Dollar. The subsidiary imports material from the U.S., sold to it by the parent firm, and also exports back to the U.S. 400 units of finished product, through the parent firm. Eventual customers in the US manifest a price elasticity of demand of 0.7 for this product. 600 units of finished product are sold in Bulgaria itself.

If the Lev exchange rate changes to 1 USD = 1.8 Lev, the company may need to reassess its pricing policy for the US market, (while leaving Bulgarian prices unchanged because of competition and other industry factors in Bulgaria). While theoretically there is a wide range of possible export prices, for this example assume either

(I)   No change in US $prices paid by U.S. Customers
(II)   Full increase of U.S. Dollar devaluation passed on to U.S. customers in the shape of a
        commensurately higher U.S. Dollar Unit Price

For your spreadsheet formulae, assume, for the moment, a simple linear production function[9] for both labor and material inputs. Ignoring, temporarily[10], transport costs, tariffs, corporate taxes, and distribution margins, and/or parent company markups[11] on supplied material or on finished product, calculate the value of the subsidiary's profits under

a)   Strategy I above
b)   Strategy II above.   Which is better? Choose one[3].

Before US Dollar Devaluation (1 USD = 2 Lev)			
SALES REVENUE	**Lev '000s**	**Quantity Q**	**Unit Price P (in Lev)**
Local Sales	1200	600	2.0
Export Sales	800 (= 400 USD)	400	2.0 (= 1 USD)
	2000	1000	
COSTS			
Labor	300		
Materials			
- Local	500		
- Imported	400 (= USD 200)		
Fixed Costs			
- In Lev	300		
- In USD	300 (= USD 150)		
Total Costs	1800		
Profit	200 (USD 100)		

---

[9] Assume a simple linear relationship between production and needed labor and material purchases. However, you realize that in practice, the relationship need not be linear. The financial analyst should confer with the plant manager and purchasing department, to obtain the exact relationship.

[10] In actual practice, introduce into your spreadsheet, additional columns for each cost such as transport, tariff, taxes and distribution margins. However, for this discussion this would be a needless distraction from the principles we wish to learn.

[11] Astute students will also realize that combining the parent company's perspective with the subsidiary's, may result in a pricing decision that is different from the preference of the subsidiary alone (if parent company markups are sufficiently high, for instance).

PROBLEM 8 SOLUTION

Exposure of the Income Statement to Exchange Rate Changes

	Before Exchange Rate Change (1 USD = 2 Lev)			After Exchange Rate Change (1 USD = 1.8 Lev) Strategy I			After Exchange Rate Change (1 USD = 1.8 Lev) Strategy II		
	Lev '000s	Quantity Q	Unit Price P (in Lev)	Lev '000s	Quantity Q	Unit Price P (in Lev)	Lev '000s	Quantity Q	Unit Price P (in Lev)
SALES REVENUE									
Local Sales	1200	600	2.0	1200	600	2.0	1200.00	600.00	2.0
Export	800 (= 400 USD)	400	2.0 (= 1 USD)	720 (= 400 USD)	400	1.8 (= 1 USD)	737.78	368.89	2.0 (= 1.11 USD)
	2000	1000		1920	1000		1937.78	968.89	
COSTS									
Labor	300			300			290.67		
Materials									
- Local	500			500			484.45		
- Imported	400 (= USD 200)			360 (= USD 200)			348.80 (= USD 193)		
Fixed Costs									
- In Lev	300			300			300.00		
- In USD	300 (= USD 150)			270 (= USD 150)			270.00 (= USD 150)		
Total Costs	1800			1730			1693.92		
Profit	200 (USD 100)			190 (USD 105.55)			243.86 (USD 135.4)		

CONCLUSIONS:

(i)   A Dollar devaluation or Bulgarian Lev appreciation improves the US Dollar (USD) value of this company.

(ii) Strategy II is better than Strategy I for the subsidiary. (Combining the parent firm's perspective may produce a different conclusion).

Price Elasticity of Demand $\varepsilon_{US} = 0.7 = \left[\dfrac{\% \text{Decrease in } Q_{US}}{\% \text{Increase in } {}^{\$}P_{US}} \right]$

Hence % Decrease in Q_{US} = (0.7)(%Increase in ${}^{\$}P_{US}$)
= (0.7) (11.11% Increase in ${}^{\$}P_{US}$) = 7.7777% Decrease in Q_{US}

So, New Q_{US} = (1 − 0.0777) (Old Q_{US}) = (0.9222) (400 units)
= 368.89 units

Where Does the 11.11% Increase in ${}^{\$}P_{US}$ Come From?

Answer: In order to restore the Bulgarian company to its original price level in Lev, i.e., a unit revenue of 2.0 Lev per unit, the new Dollar price needs to be set at (2.0/1.8) = $ 1.1111 per unit ...

(where 2.0 is the target Lev per unit and 1.8 is the new exchange rate).

$ 1.1111 is 11.11% higher than the old $ 1.0 per unit.

PROBLEMS 9 – 10

PROBLEM 9

Among the many vineyards surrounding the picturesque Chilean town of Viña Del Mar, one company, Rodrigo Baltazar, S.A. (Balco) exports wine in bulk containers to a US importer.

Planning a five year import agreement with Balco, the two companies agreed that the US bottling and branding would be in the hands of the American importer. It was agreed that invoicing will be done in US Dollars.

The US market is huge (in the order of 4.5 billion bottles consumed each year) but has become fiercely competitive, with wines from all over the world, including large volumes from California, vying for the consumer's attention. Market research projections for this Chilean wine in the US market are estimated below:

$Import Price per Metric Tonne[1]	US Market Demand Estimate (Tonnes sold)
--	--
5600	40,000
5200	50,000
4800	60,000
4400	70,000
4000	80,000
3600	90,000
3200	100,000
2800	110,000
--	--
Etc.	Etc.

A) Analysts expect the Chilean Peso, over the next five years of the agreement, to range between 700 and 900 per US dollar. Calculate the optimal selling price and corresponding quantity of units sold, assuming a variable cost[2] in the Chilean vineyard and bottling operation to be 2 million pesos per tonne, and fixed costs to be 60 billion pesos per year, using the two alternate exchange rate assumptions (i) the 900 Pesos/$rate as well as (ii) a 700 Pesos/$rate.[3]

B) Sketch the Revenue and Cost curves at the two exchange rates.

C) Being so dependent on exports to the large US market, (and since the invoicing is to be done in US dollars) Balco felt it worthwhile to calculate what would happen in an extremely gloomy scenario under which the US Dollar would weaken significantly. They wish to know at what Peso to $exchange rate their profits would shrink to zero (or breakeven).

---

[1] 1 Metric tonne is approximately equivalent to 267 US gallons (depending on the alcohol and sugar content). However, for this problem do not worry about this conversion as our unit of analysis will remain in metric tonnes. The metric system is used by all countries of the world except the US and Burma. Consequently, US and Burmese importers have to calculate the conversions.

[2] For simplicity's sake assume, for now, that the variable cost per tonne will not change, regardless of exchange rates. This requires us to assume that all of Balco's material and component costs are local in Chile and are invariant to exchange rate changes. Of course, in real life this is not true because all producers, these days, depend not just on locally sourced inputs but also imported components and inputs whose costs in local currency would vary with the exchange rate. We would then need to create additional separate columns in the spreadsheet for each type of input and its cost in local currency – and then convert the total into a US dollar variable cost total. But here, for our calculation, we wish to keep things simple. So we assume that the variable cost will not change, regardless of exchange rates.

[3] In your calculations, you may wish to convert some of the figures into millions, in order to avoid a large number of zeros.

PROBLEM 9 SOLUTION

Figures in Millions

Import Price Per Tonne	Quantity (Tonnes)	US Dollar Revenue	Revenue in Chilean Pesos at 900 P/$	Revenue in Chilean Pesos at 700 P/$	Total variable Cost (Pesos)	Contribution Margin at 900 P/$	Contribution Margin at 700 P/$	Fixed Costs	Balco Profit at 900 P/$	Balco Profit at 700 P/$
5600	40,000	224	201600	156800	80000	121600	76800	60000	61600	16800
5200	50,000	260	234000	182000	100000	134000	82000	60000	74000	22000
4800	60,000	288	259200	201600	120000	139200	81600	60000	79200	21600
4400	70,000	308	277200	215600	140000	137200	75600	60000	77200	15600
4000	80,000	320	288000	224000	160000	128000	64000	60000	68000	4000
3600	90,000	324	291600	226800	180000	111600	46800	60000	51600	-13200
3200	100,000	320	288000	224000	200000	88000	24000	60000	28000	-36000
2800	110,000	308	277200	215600	220000	57200	-4400	60000	-2800	-64400
2400	120,000	288	259200	201600	240000	19200	-38400	60000	-40800	-98400

Figures in Millions

Import Price Per Tonne	Quantity (Tonnes)	US Dollar Revenue	Revenue in Chilean Pesos at 900 P/$	Revenue in Chilean Pesos at 700 P/$	Revenue in Chilean Pesos at 615.4 P/$	Total variable Cost (Pesos)	Contribution Margin at 900 P/$	Contribution Margin at 700 P/$	Contribution Margin at 615.4 P/$	Fixed Costs	Balco Profit at 900 P/$	Balco Profit at 700 P/$	Balco Profit at 615.4 P/$
5600	40,000	224	201600	156800	137849.6	80000	121600	76800	57849.6	60000	61600	16800	-2150.4
5200	50,000	260	234000	182000	160004	100000	134000	82000	60004	60000	74000	22000	4
4800	60,000	288	259200	201600	177235.2	120000	139200	81600	57235.2	60000	79200	21600	-2764.8
4400	70,000	308	277200	215600	189543.2	140000	137200	75600	49543.2	60000	77200	15600	-10456.8
4000	80,000	320	288000	224000	196928	160000	128000	64000	36928	60000	68000	4000	-23072
3600	90,000	324	291600	226800	199389.6	180000	111600	46800	19389.6	60000	51600	-13200	-40610.4
3200	100,000	320	288000	224000	196928	200000	88000	24000	-3072	60000	28000	-36000	-63072
2800	110,000	308	277200	215600	189543.2	220000	57200	-4400	-30456.8	60000	-2800	-64400	-90456.8
2400	120,000	288	259200	201600	177235.2	240000	19200	-38400	-62764.8	60000	-40800	-98400	-122765

Farok J. Contractor, Ph.D.

PROBLEM 10

---

*"The sluggish economy and thinner profit margins have raised the Yen threshold from 100
Yen to 115 Yen to the Dollar. Below that the average Japanese firms' profits will be wiped out"*
-- Masaaki Kano, JP Morgan Tokyo
Newsweek, November 15, 2002

This problem treats a crucial issue in international business, namely the "breakeven exchange rate." To many companies, especially in East Asia or Mexico, the US and EU are such huge markets that they may be the largest single component of the company's global total sales. For many Korean, Japanese, Mexican, Taiwanese, Thai, and Chinese firms, the USA alone may comprise 40 to 50 percent of their total sales. Such firms have a large exposure to the weakness or strength of the US Dollar.

For such vulnerable companies, calculating the "breakeven exchange rate" is a critical exercise. This asks the spreadsheet to generate (via a graph or a calculation) the exchange rate, between the dollar and their home currency, that would make export profits zero (other things being held constant). Many companies are anxious enough to make such a calculation on a monthly basis. For instance, for some Japanese firms their breakeven exchange rate is around 100 - 110 Yen = $1. (See the above quote from JP Morgan, Tokyo). But, as we know, the Yen strengthened against the US dollar for many years, one even reaching as high as 79 per dollar.

A specialty cheese, made from New Zealand mountain goats, caters to a tiny East-coast market. Sporadic imports, by other companies, amounting to 10,000 pounds per year, are sold for a high price of $8.00 per pound. But Mr. Jethro Dent, mail order entrepreneur and president of Gourmets Intercontinental, Inc., feels that a much larger market exists for this cheese. He suspects that 10,000 pounds extra can be sold for every one dollar drop in price. The cheese can be imported at 3.0 New Zealand Dollars per pound C.I.F. New York. The tariff on this cheese is 20percent, and it costs $0.60 per pound for repackaging, storing and mailing to mail-order customers. Furthermore, adding this product to the company's existing line would involve extra fixed costs of $10,000 per year. Take $0.75 = 1 New Zealand Dollar as the initial exchange rate.

i)   At what price per pound should Mr. Dent advertise the cheese in his next brochure?

ii) Thinking in the longer term, Mr. Dent is worried about the value of the US dollar. As the US dollar devalues, prices may have to be adjusted upward, and the quantity demanded, and profit margins, will shrink. But Mr. Dent wants to know what breakeven US $to New Zealand Dollar exchange rate would have to be reached in order for the firm to have to abandon this import business altogether (other things being equal).

232

PROBLEM 10 SOLUTION
Part (i)

UNIT PRICE $/lb	QUANTITY lbs	$ REVENUE	TOTAL VARIABLE COSTS (AT $3.30 PER POUND) T.V.C.	CONTRIBUTION MARGIN = (REVENUE - T.V.C.)	FIXED COSTS	PROFIT
9	0	0	0	0	10,000	-10,000
8	10,000	80,000	33,000	47,000	10,000	37,000
7	20,000	140,000	66,000	74,000	10,000	64,000
⇨6	30,000	180,000	99,000	81,000	10,000	71,000⇦
5	40,000	200,000	132,000	68,000	10,000	58,000
4	50,000	200,000	165,000	35,000	10,000	25,000
3	60,000	180,000	198,000	-18,000	10,000	-28,000
2	70,000	140,000	231,000	-91,000	10,000	-101,000
1	80,000	80,000	264,000	-134,000	10,000	-144,000
0	90,000	0	297,000	-297,000	10,000	-307,000

Part (ii)

Response to the Continued Devaluation of the US Dollar

Put x = Exchange Rate in US Dollar/NZ Dollar; P = Price per unit (US $/Lb.); Q = Quantity (lbs.)

Three simultaneous unknowns, x, P and Q require three simultaneous equations.

1) From First Graph below, put $P = 9 – 0.0001Q$ .... (1)

2) Put Revenue = Total Costs for "breakeven"
$$PQ = \text{Total variable Costs} + \text{Fixed Costs}$$
$$(9 - .0001Q)Q = [3(1.20)x + 0.60]Q + 10,000$$
$$(9Q - .0001Q^2) = 3.6xQ + 0.60Q + 10,000 \dots\dots\dots\dots\dots\dots\dots(2)$$

3) Put Marginal Revenue = Marginal Costs
Differentiate Equation (2) above with respect to Q on both sides
$$9 - .0002Q = 3.6x + 0.60 \dots\dots\dots\dots\dots\dots\dots\dots\dots\dots\dots\dots\dots(3)$$

Solving the above three equations simultaneously we get
P = 8; Q = 10,000; and x = 1.77 US Dollars/NZ Dollar

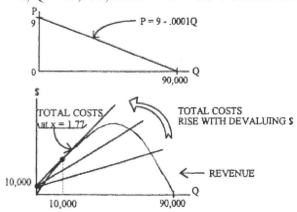

Conclusion is that it would take a huge US Dollar devaluation for the import business to be shut down. So no immediate worry.

Farok J. Contractor, Ph.D.

PROBLEM 11 PLUS SUPPLEMENTAL PROBLEM 12

PROBLEM 11

This problem reflects a crucial real-life issue facing tens of thousands of Chinese companies by 2015 when the RMB had appreciated by more than 33percent, over ten years, to a high level near 6.0 RMB/$. The RMB exchange rate is one of the most critical variables for the entire Chinese economy. The case is set in 2005, but looks forward ten years to the period after 2015. To see the history of the RMB exchange rate, see my article "Is China a Currency Manipulator?" in these readings and others on my website https://globalbusiness.blog/

Mr. Tony Wu, a Taiwanese businessman with contacts in the US retail trade, invested in a factory outside Shanghai to produce motorized scooters (small 2-stroke mopeds used by teenagers for recreational purposes and by retirees in the southern US states). The scooters are sold under the brand name "Zippy-Do©." The entire investment is intended for the American market, and will be sold through a range of retailers such as Target, Pep Boys, as well as some bicycle shops.

Inquiring Minds© a marketing consultancy based in Los Angeles conducted a series of market tests and focus group discussions, in early 2005, in several locations in the US, and determined that aggregate US demand for this item is quite elastic, especially in the USD 500 – 1500 range. The key element of the market research findings, presented to Mr. Wu, is shown in the table below.

Wholesale Unit Price per "Zippy" in USD	Annual Aggregate US Demand: Quantity (units or No. of Zippys)
100	135,000
200	130,000
300	125,000
400	120,000
500	110,000
600	100,000
700	90,000
800	80,000
900	70,000
1000	60,000
1100	50,000
1200	40,000
1300	30,000
1400	20,000
1500	10,000
1600	**0**

As the factory was getting ready to export the first shipments, Tony Wu and his accountant sat down to calculate the wholesale price they would negotiate with buyers in the US. The accountant estimated that the variable cost per "Zippy" would be 4500 RMB each (including the additional costs of transport, etc., delivered to the US). The fixed costs of the operation, because of expensive land and considerable tooling and equipment, were 100 Million RMB per annum. At that time, after bank commissions, the effective foreign exchange rate was 8.25 RMB per US Dollar.

(a) Calculate the optimum unit price in USD, and RMB profits at the 2005 rate of 8.25 RMB/$.

Sometime later, Mr. Wu had a neighbor in the *Heavenly Serenity Villas Estate* he lives in, one Mr. David Kiang, CEO of Sino Bank. At the ninth hole on the estate golf course, Mr. Kiang casually asked Tony Wu if he had assessed the consequences of an RMB revaluation on his business. *"You know, the US Treasury Secretary was once more in Beijing talking about how the RMB is undervalued and grumbling about the US trade deficit,"* he continued. *"Our government is resisting external pressures, but one never knows. Someday soon, the RMB may go to 6.0 or even stronger..."* he trailed off before walking back towards his golf cart. Tony Wu, who was basically an engineer and unfamiliar with finance, tried to hide his discomfort. With a furrowed brow, the first phone call he made on finishing the golf game was to his accountant -- to ask him what would be the effect of a revaluation to 6.0 RMB per dollar, and what the breakeven exchange rate was for his operation.

(b) Calculate the optimum unit price in USD, and RMB profits, at an assumed 2015 rate of 6.0 RMB/$.

(c) Estimate, roughly, the breakeven exchange rate by re-calculating in steps of 0.1 RMB per USD.

PROBLEM 11 SOLUTION

At 8.25 RMB/USD AND 6.0 RMB/USD

Wholesale Unit Price per "Zippy" in USD	Annual Aggregate US Demand Quantity (units)	USD Revenue (Millions)	RMB Revenue (Millions) at 8.25 RMB per USD	RMB Revenue (Millions) at 6.0 RMB per USD	RMB Total Variable Cost (Millions)	RMB Fixed Costs	RMB Profit at 8.25 RMB per USD	RMB Profit at 6.0 RMB per USD
100	135,000	13.5	111.375	81	607.5	100	-596.125	-626.5
200	130,000	26	214.5	156	585	100	-470.5	-529
300	125,000	37.5	309.375	225	562.5	100	-353.125	-437.5
400	120,000	48	396	288	540	100	-244	-352
500	110,000	55	453.75	330	495	100	-141.25	-265
600	100,000	60	495	360	450	100	-55	-190
700	90,000	63	519.75	378	405	100	14.75	-127
800	80,000	64	528	384	360	100	68	-76
900	70,000	63	519.75	378	315	100	104.75	-37
1000	60,000	60	495	360	270	100	125	-10
1100	50,000	55	453.75	330	225	100	128.75	5
1200	40,000	48	396	288	180	100	116	8
1300	30,000	39	321.75	234	135	100	86.75	-1
1400	20,000	28	231	168	90	100	41	-22
1500	10,000	15	123.75	90	45	100	-21.25	-55
1600	0	0	0	0	0	100	-100	-100

At 8.25 RMB/USD and 5.9 RMB/USD

Wholesale Unit Price per "Zippy" in USD	Annual Aggregate US Demand Quantity (units)	USD Revenue (Millions)	RMB Revenue (Millions) at 8.25 RMB per USD	RMB Revenue (Millions) at 5.9 RMB per USD	RMB Total Variable Cost (Millions)	RMB Fixed Costs	RMB Profit at 8.25 RMB per USD	RMB Profit at 5.9 RMB per USD
472.5	135,000	13.5	111.375	79.65	607.5	100	-596.125	-627.85
200	130,000	26	214.5	153.4	585	100	-470.5	-531.6
300	125,000	37.5	309.375	221.25	562.5	100	-353.125	-441.25
400	120,000	48	396	283.2	540	100	-244	-356.8
500	110,000	55	453.75	324.5	495	100	-141.25	-270.5
600	100,000	60	495	354	450	100	-55	-196
700	90,000	63	519.75	371.7	405	100	14.75	-133.3
800	80,000	64	528	377.6	360	100	68	-82.4
900	70,000	63	519.75	371.7	315	100	104.75	-43.3
1000	60,000	60	495	354	270	100	125	-16
1100	50,000	55	453.75	324.5	225	100	128.75	-0.5
1200	40,000	48	396	283.2	180	100	116	3.2
1300	30,000	39	321.75	230.1	135	100	86.75	-4.9
1400	20,000	28	231	165.2	90	100	41	-24.8
1500	10,000	15	123.75	88.5	45	100	-21.25	-56.5
1600	0	0	0	0	0	100	-100	-100

Farok J. Contractor, Ph.D.

PROBLEM 11 Solution (continued...)

At 8.25 RMB/USD and 5.835 RMB/USD

Wholesale Unit Price per "Zippy" in USD	Annual Aggregate US Demand Quantity (units)	USD Revenue (Millions)	RMB Revenue (Millions) at 8.25 RMB per USD	RMB Revenue (Millions) at 5.835 RMB per USD	RMB Total Variable Cost (Millions)	RMB Fixed Costs	RMB Profit at 8.25 RMB per USD	RMB Profit at 5.835 RMB per USD
100	135,000	13.5	111.375	78.7725	607.5	100	-596.125	-628.728
200	130,000	26	214.5	151.71	585	100	-470.5	-533.29
300	125,000	37.5	309.375	218.8125	562.5	100	-353.125	-443.688
400	120,000	48	396	280.08	540	100	-244	-359.92
500	110,000	55	453.75	320.925	495	100	-141.25	-274.075
600	100,000	60	495	350.1	450	100	-55	-199.9
700	90,000	63	519.75	367.605	405	100	14.75	-137.395
800	80,000	64	528	373.44	360	100	68	-86.56
900	70,000	63	519.75	367.605	315	100	104.75	-47.395
1000	60,000	60	495	350.1	270	100	125	-19.9
1100	50,000	55	453.75	320.925	225	100	128.75	-4.075
1200	40,000	48	396	280.08	180	100	116	0.08
1300	30,000	39	321.75	227.565	135	100	86.75	-7.435
1400	20,000	28	231	163.38	90	100	41	-26.62
1500	10,000	15	123.75	87.525	45	100	-21.25	-57.475
1600	0	0	0	0	0	100	-100	-100

BREAKEVEN IS AT 5.833 RMB/USD

At 8.25 RMB/USD and 5.8 RMB/USD

Wholesale Unit Price per "Zippy" in USD	Annual Aggregate US Demand Quantity (units)	USD Revenue (Millions)	RMB Revenue (Millions) at 8.25 RMB per USD	RMB Revenue (Millions) at 5.8 RMB per USD	RMB Total Variable Cost (Millions)	RMB Fixed Costs	RMB Profit at 8.25 RMB per USD	RMB Profit at 5.8 RMB per USD
472.5	135,000	13.5	111.375	78.3	607.5	100	-596.125	-629.2
200	130,000	26	214.5	150.8	585	100	-470.5	-534.2
300	125,000	37.5	309.375	217.5	562.5	100	-353.125	-445
400	120,000	48	396	278.4	540	100	-244	-361.6
500	110,000	55	453.75	319	495	100	-141.25	-276
600	100,000	60	495	348	450	100	-55	-202
700	90,000	63	519.75	365.4	405	100	14.75	-139.6
800	80,000	64	528	371.2	360	100	68	-88.8
900	70,000	63	519.75	365.4	315	100	104.75	-49.6
1000	60,000	60	495	348	270	100	125	-22
1100	50,000	55	453.75	319	225	100	128.75	-6
1200	40,000	48	396	278.4	180	100	116	-1.6
1300	30,000	39	321.75	226.2	135	100	86.75	-8.8
1400	20,000	28	231	162.4	90	100	41	-27.6
1500	10,000	15	123.75	87	45	100	-21.25	-58
1600	0	0	0	0	0	100	-100	-100

SUPPLEMENTAL PROBLEM 12

CASE: FREDONIA AUTOMOTIVE WORKS (FAW) © Farok J. Contractor

> This is a mini case illustrating the long-term exchange risks faced by global firms. At the same time, this case illustrates a crucial tax liability problem facing global companies in the 21st century. This involves the question of how to allocate central fixed costs (such as R&D expenditures) incurred in or around their home country, over the many other country markets in which the firm operates. In exporting, the price set for the item has to recover not only variable costs, but also recover some contribution towards fixed costs, in order to support ongoing R&D and other central overheads at corporate headquarters. But how to notionally slice the company's total fixed cost into portions, and allocate or charge a portion to each country's sales, is a vexing and unresolved problem in economics, and in tax accounting. This creates problems with tax authorities since declared profits in that country are to some extent, arbitrary. Currency shifts can also create the appearance of dumping, as illustrated in this case.
>
> This problem illustrates dimensions of transfer pricing, tax liability, overhead and fixed cost allocation across national borders, pricing, and dumping issues.

A company in Fredonia makes electric vehicles, some of which are exported to the US, while the sales in Fredonia and in the rest of the world amount to 1,000,000 vehicles. The variable cost per vehicle is 4000 Fredos and the total global fixed costs of the company are annually 5554,050,000 Fredos. Assume that all the manufacturing and costs are incurred in Fredonia, the home base of the multinational company. US market demand is shown below. Calculate the optimal price and quantity for the US market.

The US Market	$P Unit Price	Q (Quantity of Vehicles Sold in US Market)
The vehicles are exported by the parent company to its US subsidiary which, in turn, sells the vehicles to US customers. The US subsidiary faces a US corporate income tax of 30 percent.	2300	470000
	2500	450000
American market demand conditions are given at the right.	2700	430000
	2900	410000
For simplicity, assume for now that transport, tariff and other incremental US distribution costs can be neglected, and that the fixed costs of the US sales operations are subsumed in the global total fixed costs of the company	3000	390000
	3100	370000
	3200	350000
	3300	330000
	3400	310000
	3500	290000
	3600	270000

TranSGDer Pricing Policy: In order to appear fair and reasonable to tax authorities in all nations, corporate HQ in Fredonia initially sells cars to its US subsidiary at a unit tranSGDer price of (VC Per Unit + Pro rata Fixed Cost Per Unit) = (4000 + Pro rata FC Per Unit), where the pro rata fixed cost charge is calculated with the formula (Total Global Fixed Costs)/(Global Total Number of Vehicles Sold).

The initial exchange rate is 3 Fredos = $1. But later, the Dollar devalues to 2.5 Fredos = $1. Calculate the optimum price that the company should charge in the US per vehicle, under three **Tax Scenarios**:

1. Credit for US tax paid and losses are tranSGDerable to parent company. (For simplicity assume, for now, that the effective tax rates in the US and in Fredonia are the same).
2. Losses in the US operation are tranSGDerable to the parent firm, but no double tax avoidance treaty exists between the two nations.
3. Neither US tax credits, nor losses, are tranSGDerable to the parent company

SUPPLEMENTAL PROBLEM 12 SOLUTION

CASE: FREDONIA AUTOMOTIVE WORKS (FAW)

Introduction

Students should read the introduction below and then the calculations. Then return to the introduction and re-read it to absorb the significance of the issues raised.

This mini case addresses several key dilemmas facing multinational companies.

In modern, high-technology companies, there is a large gap between Selling Price and Variable Cost. The surplus of Revenues over Variable Costs is not profit but a "margin" from which the firm funds ongoing R&D, marketing and other overheads. Only then, what is left over may be considered as "profit." If revenues and variable costs occurred the *same* nation, there would be no accounting, tax, or tranSGDer-pricing issues.

However, multinational companies face an acute dilemma because of the geographical dislocation between where costs are incurred and the countries where sales are made and revenues earned. Many have large R&D or other overheads concentrated in the home or a few nations. By contrast, the firm may sell in over a hundred countries. The large centralized or concentrated expenditures in a few nations have to be amortized by recovery of "margins" from many. This poses several questions to company executives and accountants.

1) How shall we set an "optimum price" in a particular country market (which will, of course end up being different from one nation to another)? This is similar to Problems 7 – 11.

2) For accounting and tax reporting purposes in each nation, we have to calculate and report a country-by-country profit. This will require us to notionally slice the central R&D and other overheads incurred in the home nation, and allocate a notional slice, or "charge" against the margins earned in each nation. What principles, or accounting basis shall we use to make this "charge"?

3) But whatever basis our firm uses to make this worldwide calculation (across all subsidiaries and affiliates), for affiliates or subsidiaries in some nations this procedure will show profits while in other nations the same principle creates accounting losses.

4) Moreover, the whole calculation will vary from year to year, as exchange rates change.

5) How will this look to tax authorities in each nation?

6) How does this case illustrate the appearance of "dumping" resulting from price discrimination across countries? What exactly is happening in most cases of "dumping"? Finally, if "dumping" is selling below cost, how can such practice by a firm go on for years, or decades?

Assume the Year 1 exchange rate is 3.0 Fredos per $at the start, but one year later will change to 2.5 Fredos per $.

Start: Exchange Rate 3.0 Fredos = $1

At 3.0 Fredos = $1						In Millions of Fredos				
$P Price Per Unit in the US Market	Q (Quantity of Vehicles Sold US Market)	$Rev-enue in milli-ions	Total Revenue	Total Var. Cost	Actual Contribution Margin (Pre-tax) In US Market	Pro Rata Fixed Costs	Profit Of US Sub	US Tax at 0.3	Profit in US after tax	Actual Contribution Margin – US Tax
2300	470000	1081	3243	1880	1363	1775.79	-412.79			1363.00
2500	450000	1125	3375	1800	1575	1723.67	-148.67			1575.00
2700	430000	1161	3483	1720	1763	1670.10	92.90	27.87	65.03	1735.13
2900	410000	1189	3567	1640	1927	1615.00	311.99	93.60	218.39	1833.40
3000	390000	1170	3510	1560	1950	1558.33	391.67	117.50	274.17	1832.50
3100	370000	1147	3441	1480	1961	1500.00	461.00	138.30	322.70	1822.70
3200	350000	1120	3360	1400	1960	1439.94	520.06	156.02	364.04	1803.98
3300	330000	1089	3267	1320	1947	1378.07	568.93	170.68	398.25	1776.32
3400	310000	1054	3162	1240	1922	1314.32	607.68	182.30	425.38	1739.70
3500	290000	1015	3045	1160	1885	1248.59	636.42	190.92	445.49	1694.08
3600	270000	972	2916	1080	1836	1180.78	655.22	196.57	458.65	1639.445

The Total Fixed Costs in the home country of the multinational firm (FAW) are 5554,050,000 Fredos per year. Clearly, all of this cannot, and should not, be charged against the contribution margin generated in the US. Why? Because the company spends its R&D and other overheads, not just for the U.S. alone, but for its home market in Fredonia, as well as other markets around the world.

So only an appropriate (notional accounting) slice of the total fixed costs of 5554,050,000 Fredos per year may be charged against U.S.-derived contribution margin in order to calculate taxable US country profit. But what appropriate slice or fraction of the global total? And how to determine it? One common-sense approach is to "prorate" the total based on the Unit Sales in the U.S. divided by Worldwide Total Sales (including the U.S.). Here is one calculation, assuming 370,000 cars are sold,

Year 1 Optimum Price P = 3100 (without considering the tax issue) and Q = 370,000 cars :

$$(5554,050,000) \cdot \frac{\text{Number of cars sold in the U.S.}}{\text{Number of cars sold Worldwide}} = 5554,000,000 \cdot \frac{370,000}{1,370,000} = \boxed{1,500,000,000 \text{ Fredos}}$$

Under this calculation, 1,500,000,000 could be claimed as a reasonable share or fraction of the total home country fixed costs that may be charged again US market sales in order to calculate taxable profit in the US. See the pro rata Fixed Cost column in Table 1 above. But, depending on the sales price and volume in the US market, there could be other figures calculated. All the pro rata numbers are "notional" meaning that they are based on accounting and tax conventions that may not be universally accepted.

Year 1 Optimum Price P = 2900 (Considering Contribution Margin after US tax payments) and Q = 410,000 cars :

$$(5554,050,000) \cdot \frac{\text{Number of cars sold in the U.S.}}{\text{Number of cars sold Worldwide}} = 5554,000,000 \cdot \frac{410,000}{1,410,000} = \boxed{1,615,000,000 \text{ Fredos}}$$

Without considering US tax liability, the optimum Price is $3100 per car, since Contribution Margin (without US tax considerations) is maximized at this level. Considering US tax liability, the "Actual US Contribution Margin – US Tax" the optimum Price is P = 2900 per vehicle.

Moreover, as we will see below, the same common-sense prorating method for calculating the notional fixed cost charge against U.S. operations produces different numbers as the Fredo-$exchange rates change.

One Year Later: New Exchange Rate 2.5 Fredos = $1

The following year, the Total Fixed Costs in the home country of the multinational firm (FAW) remains the same -- at 5554,050,000 Fredos per year. Once again, the company asserts that it is spending this huge amount of Fredos 5.5 Billion on R&D and other overheads, in order to maintain its competitiveness against other global rivals. The Fredo 5.5 Billion is, as before, centralized, in the home market, or at most one or two other locations where the home office is located, and where R&D is performed. Such functions have to be centralized, the firm avers, because dispersing R&D to several nations is inefficient and costly, and research results can be poorer. But even though the 5.5 Billion

Fredos expenditure is centralized, the company recoups revenues, not just from its home market in Fredonia, but also from the US and a large number of other markets around the world.

The Dilemma of the Multinational Firm

The dilemma of the multinational company is that while large technological and administrative overheads have to be centralized in one or a few nations, it must extract revenues and pay taxes in a huge number of countries. But how to calculate the tax liability in each nation if the bulk of costs are centralized?

The policy of prorating central fixed costs appears fair. However, as we see in Table 2, the competitive nature of the US market and the weakening Dollar produces a situation where the actual (or *de facto*) fixed cost burden that can be charged to US sales, using the formula

$(5,554,050,000) . \dfrac{\text{Number of cars sold in the U.S.}}{\text{Number of cars sold Worldwide}}$

produces a calculation showing very low, or zero, tax liability to the US government.

TABLE 2

At 2.5 Fredos = $1						In Millions of Fredos				
$P Price Per Unit in the US Market	Q (Quantity of Vehicles Sold US Market)	$Rev-enue in milli-ions	Total Revenue	Total Var. Cost	Actual CM (assuming both US tax credit and losses tranSGDerable to parent **).	Pro Rata Fixed Costs	Profit Of US Sub	US Tax at 0.3	Profit in US after tax	Actual Contribution Margin – US Tax
2300	470000	1081	2702.5	1880	822.50	1775.79	-953.29			822.50
2500	450000	1125	2812.5	1800	1012.50	1723.67	-711.17			1012.50
2700	430000	1161	2902.5	1720	1182.50	1670.10	-487.60			1182.50
2900	410000	1189	2972.5	1640	1332.50	1615.01	-282.51			1332.50
3000	390000	1170	2925	1560	1365.00	1558.33	-193.33			1365.00
3100	370000	1147	2867.5	1480	1387.50	1500.00	-112.50			1387.50
3200	350000	1120	2800	1400	1400.00	1439.94	-39.94			1400.00
3300	330000	1089	2722.5	1320	1402.50	1378.07	24.43	7.33	17.10	1395.17
3400	310000	1054	2635	1240	1395.00	1314.32	80.68	24.20	56.48	1370.80
3500	290000	1015	2537.5	1160	1377.50	1248.59	128.92	38.67	90.24	1338.83
3600	270000	972	2430	1080	1350.00	1180.78	169.22	50.77	118.45	1299.24

Year 2 Optimum Price P = 3300 (without considering the tax issue) and Q = 330,000 cars :
(5554,050,000) . Number of cars sold in the U.S. = 5554,000,000 330,000 = 1,378,060,150
Fredos

       Number of cars sold Worldwide   1,330,000

Under this calculation, $1,378,060,150 could be claimed as a reasonable share or fraction of the total home country fixed costs that may be charged again US market sales in order to calculate taxable profit in the US. See the summary numbers in Table 2 above. But this produces a US tax liability calculation of only $7.33 million as compared with last year's figure of 138.3 million. A huge drop!

Year 2 Optimum Price P = 3200 (Considering Contribution Margin After US tax payments) and Q = 350,000 cars :
(5554,050,000) . Number of cars sold in the U.S. = 5554,000,000 350,000 = 1,439,925,925
Fredos

       Number of cars sold Worldwide   1,350,000

At this price, US sales show an accounting loss of $39.94 million, and zero tax liability. In short, FAW can claim that for this year, there is no tax owed to the US government – assuming that the notional pro rata numbers are accepted.

Paradoxically, we thus see in Table 2, that despite raising US prices, the company suffers a precipitous decline in profitability and consequently very low, or zero, US corporate tax liability which can raise suspicion with US tax authorities.

Tax Liability Suspicions
The company informs the U.S. tax authority (the IRS) that, having declared a loss, this year it owes the U.S. government no taxes. The IRS responds with suspicion. Politicians in the United States already complain that foreign firms operating in the U.S. underpay taxes compared with American companies, as a percentage of their sales in the U.S. The whole issue, of notionally charging a fraction of overheads, incurred in the home country of the multinational, against U.S. operating margins, to allegedly reduce (evade?) U.S. tax liability, is a thorny and potentially inflammatory issue.

This is not just a U.S. problem. *All* countries view the multinational company with suspicion, as a potential tranSGDer-price manipulator, seeking to lower tax liability. The multinational firm faces such suspicion simply because much of its overheads are centralized, while at the same time, they must declare taxable profits in a great many nations.

Firms like FAW respond that they are doing nothing wrong. In calculating US tax liability in Table 2 above they used the same prorating accounting formula that was acceptable the previous year. The firm responds that, this year the U.S. affiliate showed a loss because of a weakening dollar (or a strengthening Fredo). They are using the same formula as last year. Why blame them?

Politicians and tax accountants who have been following this story respond thus,

"FAW is selling as many as 330,000 - 350,000 vehicles in our nation and they show huge sales in the U.S. of over $1 Billion.. The company still makes a huge contribution marginand extracts earnings out of the US which, although less than last year, are still around 1,400 Million Fredos. Do they mean to tell us they will pay no taxes to the U.S." ? "Unacceptable," they cry!

Should a Company Withdraw from a Country Market If They are Reporting a Loss?

In the judgment of FAW's advisers, the Fredo was likely to remain strong for an indefinite period. In short, in accounting terms, there could be many years of "losses" ahead. Should they give up the U.S. market and withdraw?

The answer is an emphatic "No." In accounting terms, American operation may post breakeven levels or losses for several years. However, in real financial contribution, U.S. operations are throwing off a contribution margin that is very large and indispensable to run the global operation. True, this margin is less than prior years, but it is still huge since it is coming from as big a market as the U.S. To eliminate this margin would force the company to do drastically cut their global R&D budget, which would have disastrous consequences in the long run, since the company is competing against other rival global firms with large R&D budgets. In brief, foreign companies find that it is *impossible* to withdraw from large markets like the U.S. Besides, as their CFO observed, "The economics textbook says 'hang on in any market segment as long as the contribution margin is positive – as long as revenues more than cover the marginal costs of operating in that country."

But while US operations can continue to make needed contributions to central R&D and overheads, the company faces another accusation, that they are engaging in "dumping" behavior.

"Dumping"

To compound the troubles faced by firm, they received word that one of FAW's rivals in the U.S. was considering launching a "dumping" complaint against the foreign firm. "How can this be? " asked the subsidiary manager. "Didn't we actually just raise the price per car we charge to US customers this year?" (See Table 3). The CFO responded, "At $3,300 per unit, our U.S. price is now *higher* than last year, but *lower* than in the rest of the world in Fredo terms." In Table 3 (and in Tables 1 and 2) we see that the Year 2 price, $3,300, at the new exchange rate is 8,250 Fredos, whereas teh Year 1 price, $3,100 at the old exchange rate was 9,300 Fredos.

In fact, many foreign firms find they are unable to raise prices in the U.S. at all, or by any significant amount. Why? Because the U.S. is an open, fiercely competitive market, yet one which is so big and important that few foreign companies can afford to ignore it. For many firms such as FAW, the U.S. market is their biggest market segment in the world, and a slice big enough that it cannot be abandoned. (The reasons were outlined in the foregoing section).

"Dumping" superficially appears to be the case when a foreign company imports products into a nation and sells them "below cost." But what is "cost" in a multinational context? Should costs include only variable cost, or average cost including central overheads? In almost all cases, "dumping" is typically *not* a situation where a foreign firm is importing and selling below variable cost. That would indeed be predatory "dumping", and unsustainable in the long run. By comparison, many foreign firms seem to practice "dumping" for years, or decades on end – which would be impossible if they really were making losses. Ordinarily, "dumping" entails selling at prices *below* those the company charges for the same item in other countries --- but at a unit price well *above* the variable cost floor (for instance in this case, FAW is selling its car for 8,250 – 9,300 Fredos whereas its variable cost is only 4,000 Fredos). This is sustainable indefinitely, as long as less price sensitive customers who pay higher prices in other nations effectively cross-subsidize the lower price in more price-sensitive nations such as the U.S. This cross-subsidization is illustrated in Table 3 below.

For simplicity, let us assume that initially the price per unit charged to customers both in the U.S. as well as in the rest of the world was the equivalent of 9300 Fredos per unit at the Year 1 exchange rate of $1 = 3 Fredos (See Table 1). We assume that the contribution made by US customers is the same as contributions made by customers in the rest of the world. Following the devaluation of the dollar, despite raising the dollar unit price to $3300, this is now equivalent to only 8250 fredos at the new Year 2 exchange rate or $1 = 2.5 Fredos. (See Table 2). Let us assume that nothing has changed in the rest of the world and so the company continues to charge customers there 9300 Fredos per unit. Hence, even though the company has followed textbook principles, even though they have increased the U.S. price to $3300, they are now subject to an accusation of "dumping" since a price gap has opened up – US customers are paying the equivalent of Fredos 8250, while non-U.S. customers are still paying 9300 Fredos.

TABLE 3: Cross-Subsidization in Favor of the US Customer

	Year 1		Year 2		
	US Unit Price = $ 3100 = 9300 Fredos; (3.0 Fr = $ 1)		US Unit Price = $ 3300 = 8250 Fredos; (2.5 Fr = $ 1)		Global Total Profit in Billions of Fredos
	US Market	Rest of World	US Market	Rest of World	
Quantity	370,000 cars	1,000,000 cars	330,000 cars	1,000,000 cars	
Unit Sales Price	9300	9300	8250	9300	
			(Looks like "dumping")		
Where the money goes					
Per Car Contribution Towards Variable Cost	4000	4000	4000	4000	
Per Car Contribution Towards Fixed Cost	4054[9]	4054	4176[10]	4176[11]	
Per Car Contribution Towards Profit	1246[12]	1246	74[13]	1124[14]	
Global Total Profit	Fredos 1,707,020,000[15]		Fredos 1,148,420,000[16] (a big drop from the previous global total profit figure)		

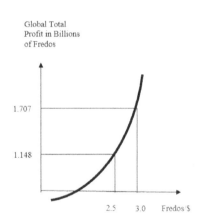

From what the company collects, the first category it <u>must</u> cover is variable cost, which is 4000 Fredos per car, constant over time, and constant over all customer groups. However, it may then collect less of a "contribution towards fixed costs" from some nations' customers, while collecting more from others. This, in effect, is the cross-subsidization game. The calculation of "contribution towards fixed cost" by each customer group is shown below:

a. (1,500,000,000)/(370,000) = 4,054 Fredos per car contribution towards fixed costs.

b. (5,554,050,000 – 1,500,000,000)/ (1,000,000) = 4, 054 Fredos per car contribution towards fixed costs

In b., the rest of the world's customers pick up the remaining burden of fixed costs that the U.S. customers have not picked up. Notice that in the first two columns, we assume for simplicity sake that both U.S. and non-U.S. customers are being treated equally. Their contributions are equal.

In the following year, after the Fredo strengthens, the actual contribution margin contribution from the US market declines. See footnotes to Table 3 for calculations. The rest of the world's customers pick up the remaining burden of fixed costs that the U.S. customers have not picked up. Customers in the rest of the world carry a disproportional burden. That is to say, they cross-subsidize the U.S. customer.

How Long Can the Cross-Subsidization Game Last?

Indefinitely, as long as each nation or market segment's price more than covers variable cost. However, before that limit is reached, there is another limit that the multinational firm faces, namely, over *all* its markets, total revenues must adequately cover *both* variable as well as fixed cost, so as to leave a decent overall profit. This perhaps more immediate constraint is illustrated for our company, FAW, in the calculation below:

- Last Year Global Total Profit: 1,707,020,000 Fredos.

- This Year Global Total Profit 1,148,429,000 Fredos.

There is a worrying drop in global total profits. Some companies find that they are on the horns of another dilemma. Fierce competition and/or a weakening dollar not only may make U.S. profitability zero (see Tables 2 and 3) yet they cannot withdraw from this market which then threatens to drag the *entire* company down to a level of poor profitability.

The Dollar devaluation not only pulls down US profits drastically, but also pulls down profit margins in the rest of the world by forcing car sales in the rest of the world to bear a higher fixed cost burden. The overall loss in global total profits is large.

CHAPTER 14

Underlying Logic and Assumptions for Money Market Hedges

UNDERLYING LOGIC AND ASSUMPTIONS FOR:

IMPORTER (Foreign Currency Payable) and

EXPORTER (Foreign Currency Receivable)

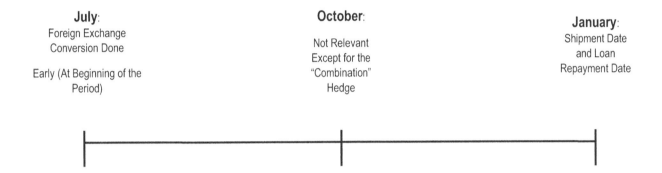

July:	October:	January:
Foreign Exchange Conversion Done	Not Relevant Except for the "Combination" Hedge	Shipment Date and Loan Repayment Date
Early (At Beginning of the Period)		

Basic Logic

Assume that an import or export deal is finalized in July, but by the time the goods are manufactured and shipped it will be January, six months later. At the beginning (in July), you do know the spot rate on that day in July when the agreement is "signed." But you do not know what the exchange rate will be at the end of the period (January). Hence, the outcome for the exporter or importer is unknown in their currency. This is called exchange risk for that particular transaction.

The "money market hedge" is the simple idea that if you convert "at the beginning" (at the date in July when the export/import deal is "signed"). you have converted at a known July Spot Rate and gotten rid of the exchange risk. The conversion is already done, early, at a known spot exchange rate.

Complications from Converting Early

But this means the currency has been converted six months too early, which may entail additional costs (or benefits).

IMPORT CASE: The importer (who has agreed to pay in the foreign currency six months later) will have to borrow additional amounts in their own currency in order to take their local currency amount to the exchange market in July and convert to the foreign currency early. (Keep in mind that most companies do not have extra cash lying around.) This early conversion in July itself gets rid of the currency risk.

EXPORT CASE: The exporter (who has agreed to receive the foreign currency six months later in January) can show – in July itself – the "signed" export document to a bank and borrow from the bank some foreign currency money, in July, against the export order as collateral. Then in July itself, knowing that day's spot rate, the borrowed foreign currency can be converted into the exporter's local currency. Hence, the outcome for the exporter, in their own currency is fixed or known in July itself.

But There Are Additional Costs and Benefits of Early Conversion

IMPORTER (FOREIGN CURRENCY PAYABLE SIX MONTHS LATER):

- Additional Costs: Because it is early, the importer has to take out an additional loan. The importer borrows in their own currency at the beginning of the period (July), then takes the borrowed amount (principal) to the foreign exchange market and converts it (at the known July spot rate) into the exporter's currency. They will have to repay the loan (principal plus interest) to the bank at the end of the six-month period (around the shipment date in January).

- Additional Benefits: Once the importer converts into the exporter's currency, they do not know what to do with this foreign currency (until the shipment date in January). After all, the import agreement calls for paying the foreign currency only at shipment, six months later, in January. However, they may be able to earn some deposit interest on that currency by depositing the foreign currency in a foreign currency account it until it is needed to pay for the shipment in January.

EXPORTER: (FOREIGN CURRENCY RECEIVABLE SIX MONTHS LATER):

- Additional Costs: The exporter borrows in the importer's currency at the beginning of the period (July), then takes the borrowed foreign currency (principal) to the spot exchange market in July and converts it (at the known spot rate) into their own currency. Of course, they will have to repay the foreign currency loan to the bank at the end of the period (around the shipment date in January). But they repay that loan out of the proceeds of the export shipment (which will be received in the foreign currency in January).

- Additional Benefits: The foreign exchange conversion, at the beginning of the period, yields them an amount in their own currency, six months earlier than normal, in July itself. Because the amount is received in their own currency, the export company can use this amount to augment their own cash flows (working capital) earlier than if they had waited until the shipment was paid for in January. We assume something that is true for most firms – that the export company carries a certain level of debt for operational purposes. Receiving the money early, from the spot exchange conversion in July, enables them to lower their ordinary domestic operations debt level below what it would otherwise have been over the ensuing time period (between July and January), thereby saving them some borrowing interest cost that the company otherwise would have had to pay.

THIS GENERAL LOGIC APPLIES NOT JUST TO EXPORTS AND IMPORTS, BUT ALSO TO MULTINATIONAL COMPANIES

The above logic is not just for importers and exporters, but **for any company that has foreign currency payables and receivables** (such as multinationals that expect future dividend or royalty flows in a foreign currency).

Farok J. Contractor, Ph.D.

GENERAL ASSUMPTIONS FOR HEDGING PROBLEMS
(ALSO IN REAL LIFE)

The calculations depend on assumptions that apply to most companies in real life:

- We make a general assumption that all companies are carrying a reasonable amount of debt already. Hence…

- Any operation that requires early payment or withdrawal will force the company to borrow additional amounts (see money market hedge for an importer).

- Any operation that results in early receipt of money will enable the firm to reduce the level of its debt, thus benefiting from a reduction (or savings) in the interest payment that would otherwise have been incurred (see money market hedge for an exporter).

- The basic idea of the money market hedge is to avoid a future currency conversion at an unknown rate by converting early or at the beginning of the time period at the known spot rate. However…

- The money market hedge for an importer is not the same as for an exporter.

- The importer borrows their own money, converts it to the exporter's currency, and then – because they have no better alternative – deposits the foreign currency into a deposit in that currency.

- The exporter's money market hedge, on the other hand, entails borrowing in the importer's currency and converting it into their own currency. Once they have their own currency, its best use is (not to deposit it in a passive bank account, but) to use it in their own business to reduce the level of their debt – thereby saving on the interest they would have paid for other borrowing in their own currency.

- So-called "combination" hedges are very rare, but, once in a blue moon, they may work out to be the best.

Moreover, in practice there are a few more minor or trivial considerations:

- In real life, buying and selling rates are not the same because of bank commissions or transaction costs. For teaching purposes, we will abstract from this by assuming that the exchange rates given can be used by the companies for either buying or selling. In real life, ask your bank what exact exchange rates to plug into the calculation for your transaction.

- In real life, interest rates will vary across banks in the same country, as well as across countries. We will use the simplifying assumption that the interest rates shown in the problems can be used by all parties. In real life, ask your bank what interest rates to plug into the calculation.

- Forward exchange markets are not always well developed in all currencies. However, your bank can make a special arrangement for forward delivery of currency even if the market is thin or inefficient. In some cases, such as the Chinese RMB, forward cover is obtainable, but through non-deliverable* forward commitments between the company and bank. Ask your bank.

---

* The net effect of non-deliverable forwards is the same as deliverable forwards because the company and bank settle the difference between the previously agreed upon forward rate and the spot rate on maturity.

CHAPTER 15

Interest Parity Theorem:
Why Is There a Difference Between the Spot and Forward Rate for a Currency?

$$\frac{X_S}{X_F} = \frac{(1 + i_{USD})}{(1 + i_{FC})} \text{ where } X_S \text{ and } X_F \text{ are in Foreign Currency (FC) per USD}$$

Table 1 shows spot and forward rates for selected currencies on May 10, 2019. Except for currencies controlled by their governments, global supply and demand determine exchange rates (with financial institutions acting as intermediaries or trading platforms). But what explains the difference between the spot rate (where currencies have to be exchanged immediately or within 48 hours) and the forward rate (where the promised exchanges take place say one, three, or six months later at the pre-agreed forward rate)?

Table 1: Spot and Forward Rates May 10, 2019

Currency	Date	Spot Rate	Foreign Currency Per USD		
			1 Month	3 Months	6 Months
USD/CNY	May 10, '19	6.8251	6.8934	6.8934	6.8934
USD/EUR	May 10, '19	1.1229	1.1258	1.1316	1.14
USD/CAD	May 10, '19	1.3472	1.3462	1.3443	1.34194
USD/JPY	May 10, '19	109.76	109.5011	108.9711	108.1999
USD/GBP	May 10, '19	1.3010	1.303	1.307	1.3125
USD/SGD	May 10, '19	1.3631	1.3625	1.3611	1.3588
USD/NOK	May 10, '19	8.7466	8.7364	8.7188	8.6958
USD/AUD	May 10, '19	0.6992	0.6997	0.7006	0.7022
USD/DKK	May 10, '19	6.6485	6.6304	6.5943	6.5415
USD/INR	May 10, '19	69.91	70.19	70.695	71.416
USD/MYR	May 10, '19	4.159	4.1594	4.1594	4.1594

Note: The numbers at the fourth and fifth decimal places actually change constantly depending on second-by-second changes in supply and demand for a currency.
Source: http://www.mecklai.com/Digital/MecklaiData/HistoryData_Forward?AspxAutoDetectCookieSupport=1

Actually, as illustrated in the Appendix, forward rate commitments are available for customized time periods up to one year and beyond for major currencies.

AN EXAMPLE ON MAY 10, 2019

Consider a money fund manager who needs to park $1 million for six months in safe US or equally safe Canadian treasury bills. Given the interest rates below (six-month treasury yields):

- US treasury bill yield: 2.39 percent annualized rate
- Canadian treasury bill yield: 1.60 percent annualized rate

Keeping the money in US treasury bills will result after six months: 1,000,000 [1 + (.0239/2)] = USD 1,011,950 six months later

Investing in Canadian treasury bills for six months (with return of money to USD six months later): Suppose that early in the trading day on May 10th the spot rate for CAD was 1.3472 CAD/USD and the forward rate for CAD was 1.3390 CAD/USD:

- On May 10: Using the spot rate, convert USD 1,000,000 into 1,000,000 (1.3472) = CAD 1,347,200 on May 10th
- On May 10: Deposit CAD 1,347,200 in a six-month Canadian treasury bill (equivalent to a six-month bank deposit).
- On May 10th, thinking ahead to November 10, 2019 (six months later): Our fund manager knows that the Canadian treasury bill will mature to give (1,347,200)[1+ (.0160/2)] = CAN 1,357,978 in November. But six months later, to re-convert CAN dollars back into USD is a risk because what the CAN/USD spot rate will be on November 10th is an unknown on May 10th.
  - But there is a way to get rid of this risk because, on May 10th, a forward conversion rate for November 10 is available, which is 1.3390 CAN/USD.
- On May 10: Arrange to sell "six months forward" CAN 1,357,978 at the forward rate of 1.3390. (Selling CAN six months *forward* means a legal commitment to deliver to CAN 1,357,978, on November 10th, to the counterparty or bank in the FX Market. The counterparty is also legally bound to honor the prearranged rate of 1.3390, and deliver to our trader USD 1,014,173 on November 10th). (But where did this USD 1,014,173 number come from? See below.)
- On November 10, 2019 (six months later): The previously committed "six-month-forward" contract at the 1.3390 rate will kick in or mature on November 10th. Our trader will deliver CAN 1,357,978 (from the matured treasury bill) and the counterparty or bank will deliver to our trader USD (1,357,978)/1.3390 = USD 1,014,173 six months later (in November).

- On May 10: After doing the calculations, investing in CAD appears better than investing in USD, because USD 1,014,173 is greater than simply keeping the money in USD which would yield USD 1,011,950.

BUT WHAT WILL HAPPEN LATER ON MAY 10TH?
The above hypothetical example will apply to only a few early traders. For the rest…

- On May 10: Seeing that investing in CAD is better than investing in USD (because USD 1,014,173 is greater than USD 1,011,950), not just our money fund manager, but _all_ money fund managers will seek to buy CAD spot, and sell CAD six months-forward – to the tune of hundreds of millions or billions.

- On May 10 (morning): At the same time, to avoid risk, most money managers will want to get back into their starting position in USD, by selling CAD six months forward." By later in the day on May 10th, the volume of "selling CAD six-months forward" or the greater demand for USD "six-months forward," will increase (bid up) the forward rate from 1.3390 to 1.34194 CAD/USD – the forward rate shown in Table 1 above. This can happen in minutes, or microseconds with computerized flash trading. Then the actual realization from moving into USD spot (on May 10th), depositing funds in CAD for six months, and reconverting back into USD six months later (November 10th) will be USD (1,357,978)/1.34194 = USD 1,011,951.

- On May 10: Once later in the day the supply/demand in the Canadian Dollar Forward Market has settled into the new equilibrium, the result is that
  - Keeping money in USD yields USD 1,011,950 six months later
  - Moving USD to CAD spot and taking a six-month-forward contract to get back into USD yields USD 1,011,951 six months later (i.e., **THE SAME RESULT**).

  That is to say, "Interest Parity" has been achieved or

$$1,011,950 = 1,011,950 \text{ or } \quad 1 + i_{USD} = \frac{[X_S\,(1+i_{FC})]}{X_F} \text{ or }$$

$$\frac{X_S}{X_F} = \frac{(1+i_{USD})}{(1+i_{FC})} \text{ where } X_S \text{ and } X_F \text{ are in Foreign Currency (FC) per USD}$$

THIS IS THE INTEREST PARITY THEOREM FORMULA

CONCLUSION

The Interest Parity Formula means that **the difference between spot and forward rates is simply explained by the difference between the short-term interest rates in the two countries in question.**

(Except for very brief intervals – minutes or microseconds – when the market is "off-equilibrium."[1])

OTHER CONCLUSIONS

Arbitrage opportunities (or doing better than your competitors by earning a slightly higher yield) occur every now and then.[1] However, the "early movers" with computers programmed for flash trading, can find small arbitrage advantages and do better than their slower competitors.

- BUT

In so doing, the forward rate[2] for the currency will adjust so that the arbitrage advantage disappears (in minutes or microseconds) for the rest of the traders/money managers.

- AND

"Interest Parity" is restored – until the next time that the US Federal Reserve or the Bank of Canada (Canadian Central Bank) announces a change in their short-term interest rates.

DOES THE INTEREST PARITY THEOREM WORK FOR MANY OR ALL CURRENCIES?

No! It only applies to only a few currencies such as the Canadian Dollar, Euro, Pound, and (maybe) the Yen where the foreign exchange market is

- Huge
- Efficient
- Has minimal or trivial transaction costs / commissions / taxes
- Has no convertibility restrictions imposed by governments
- Where government agents or "big fish" do not meddle with market forces.

---

[1] Often this happens when a country's central bank announces a change in their short term interest rate.

[2] And to a lesser extent the spot rate will also adjust, so as to restore things to the Interest Parity formula.

So, is the Interest Parity Theory only a theory applicable to a handful of currencies? **Yes and no.** Trading between just the US dollar, Canadian dollar, euro, pound, and yen comprise at least 75 percent of daily trading volume.[3]

So, the theory does apply to most exchanges.

WHAT ABOUT THE REMAINING 175-ODD CURRENCIES IN THE WORLD?

For the rest of the world's currencies, their forward rate reflects not only interest rate differentials, but also perceptions of risk and expectations of where spot rates for the currency may be headed, given economic and political news.

---

[3] The 24-hour volume of trades in all currencies now exceeds the equivalent of USD 5 trillion.

Appendix

Foreign Currency Per USD

Currency	Date	Spot Rate	1 Month	2 Months	3 Months	4 Months	5 Months	6 Months	7 Months	8 Months	9 Months	10 Months	11 Months	12 Months
USD/CNY	May 10, '19	6.8251	6.8934	6.8933	6.8934	6.8934	6.8934	6.8934	6.8934	6.8934	6.8934	6.8934	6.8935	6.8935
USD/EUR	May 10, '19	1.1229	1.1258	1.1288	1.1316	1.1346	1.1373	1.14	1.1429	1.1459	1.1487	1.1514	1.1541	1.1567
USD/CAD	May 10, '19	1.3472	1.3462	1.3452	1.3443	1.3435	1.3426	1.34194	1.3411	1.3401	1.3394	1.3387	1.3381	1.3374
USD/JPY	May 10, '19	109.76	109.5011	109.2138	108.9711	108.6883	108.444	108.1999	107.9407	107.6313	107.3853	107.1413	106.9037	106.6745
USD/GBP	May 10, '19	1.3010	1.303	1.3051	1.307	1.309	1.3107	1.3125	1.3143	1.3163	1.3179	1.3195	1.3209	1.3224
USD/SGD	May 10, '19	1.3631	1.3625	1.3619	1.3611	1.3603	1.3595	1.3588	1.3581	1.3574	1.3567	1.356	1.3554	1.3547
USD/NOK	May 10, '19	8.7466	8.7364	8.7271	8.7188	8.71	8.7027	8.6958	8.6891	8.682	8.676	8.6709	8.6661	8.661
USD/AUD	May 10, '19	0.6992	0.6997	0.7001	0.7006	0.7012	0.7017	0.7022	0.7027	0.7032	0.7037	0.7042	0.7046	0.7051
USD/DKK	May 10, '19	6.6485	6.6304	6.6116	6.5943	6.5753	6.5585	6.5415	6.5239	6.5052	6.4884	6.4714	6.4557	6.4398
USD/INR	May 10, '19	69.91	70.19	70.455	70.695	70.9607	71.185	71.416	71.6778	71.9011	72.1375	72.3765	72.6255	72.8889
USD/MYR	May 10, '19	4.159	4.1594	4.1594	4.1594	4.1594	4.1594	4.1594	4.1594	4.1594	4.1594	4.1594	4.1594	4.1594

Source: http://www.mecklai.com/Digital/MecklaiData/HistoryData_Forward?AspxAutoDetectCookieSupport=1

Part IV. Foreign Exchange Rates and Pricing in International Markets – See Part III, Chapter 13

Section A. Economic Exposure and Operational Planning

Includes Discussion of Representative Problems 5 – 8
(With Solutions) in Foreign Exchange Risk Management and
Case 2 (Problem 6) Guidelines Presented in Chapter 13, Part III

Section B. Optimal Pricing as a Function of Exchange Rates

Includes Discussion of Representative Problems 9 – 11 (With Solutions)
in Foreign Exchange Risk Management and Supplemental Problem 12
Presented in Chapter 13, Part III

NOTE TO READERS:

For Relevant Materials Not Included in This Textbook,
Refer to the Appendix: Additional Suggested Readings

Part V. Global Management in a Still-Fragmented World: Local vs. International

NOTE TO READERS:

**For Relevant Materials Not Included in This Textbook,
Refer to the Appendix: Additional Suggested Readings**

CHAPTER 16

Global Management in a Still-Fragmented World

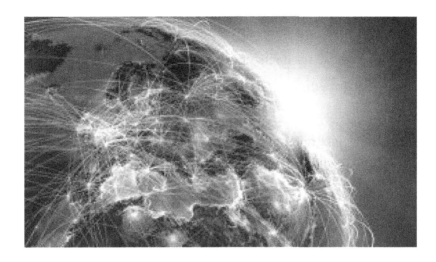

In this article, we look at the job of the global manager, which covers two broad domains:

- *Internal corporate strategy*—which must address the issue of how international firms need to strike a balance between global standardization of their products and processes and the benefits of local adaptation (while at the same time deciding what decisions to centralize and which to devolve to foreign subsidiaries).

- *External global strategy*—which must address the challenge of how multinational companies need to manage global pressures they are forced to deal with, such as corporate social responsibility, activist groups, non-governmental organizations (NGOs), governments, and multilateral agencies that push the firm in directions it may not otherwise pursue while also managing cultural differences.

Both concerns—internal strategy and management of external relations—are connected by the fact that the world is fragmented into about 200 nations exhibiting a huge variation in income, culture, language, and government. International Business involves the management and utilization of these differences across countries.

A Very Unequal but Interconnected World

The world remains fragmented and very unequal. The multinational corporation wishes to operate on a global scale, with as few impediments as possible in order to take advantage of global scale and scope. But political entities—countries—draw lines called borders, within which rules, institutions, culture, and income (purchasing power) are often different from those of their neighbors. (*Per capita* annual income ranges from more than $100,000 to below $500 per person, with as many as 66 nations whose residents' average income is below $3,000 per year).[1] Internet traffic has seen phenomenal growth, from 16 million users at year-end 1995 to 3 billion in 2014: 40 percent of humans are now connected.[2] However, cross-border traffic remains below 20 percent—and that percentage is dropping as "within country" links are growing even faster. There is no "global village," but rather a series of spatially dispersed villages that are (only somewhat) internationally connected.

Global Standardization vs. Local Responsiveness

Not too long ago, IBM specified a dress code for its office employees worldwide—a white shirt and tie. (IBM had relatively few women employees then.) IBM prided itself on its ability to replicate, in foreign subsidiaries, the standardized technology, protocols, and procedures it had developed at home. Moreover, the company believed a computer is a computer anywhere on the planet. Twenty years ago, companies saw considerable advantage in developing an efficient model in their home country (often after considerable research and development [R&D] outlay) and then reproducing that model in worldwide operations. The additional costs of local adaptation—to each country's tastes or requirements—were not seen as worth it. In its early days, MTV simply used material produced for the US market in foreign TV stations. Indeed, there are powerful arguments for replicating a standard template worldwide at lower cost than trying to tweak it—or trying to come up with a new design for each nation.

But what if the *benefits* of local adaptation (such as greater viewership or increased sales in each nation) are higher than the *costs* of local adaptation? MTV found that while it is costly to develop local talent and video content, these costs could be more than recouped from higher viewership and advertising revenue in many local cultures. IBM found that the computer hardware business fragmented or modularized into individual user PCs and that customized IT consulting—country by country, based on each nation's organizational styles and requirements—was more profitable than the hardware end of their business. Today, hardware is below 10 percent of IBM's global revenues.

Neither Global nor Local: A Balanced Perspective on International Business

To be sure, the allure of standardization and replication of a standard model across borders remains a powerful argument. Auto companies prefer, whenever possible, to have a standard car design sold across several or all nations, which would enable the firm to add economies of large scale, lower design and R&D costs, reduce inventories, and negotiate even larger-quantity discounts from component suppliers. But road conditions, regulations, and cultural preferences vary considerably across countries. A suspension that works on Germany's smooth roads may fail in India. Emission standards are not uniform. In low-labor-cost countries, where chauffeurs are easily hired and prestige dictates that the car owner be driven sitting in the back seat, companies such as BMW and General Motors have found that short legroom in back seats is a deterrent to sales. Such cases present considerable temptation to do additional R&D and retooling and come up with local or country-specific car designs.

However – if local adaptation is pushed too far – the incremental costs of country-by-country design adaptation (and loss of the efficiency gains from standardization, as mentioned above) often exceed the incremental revenues. Merely redesigning the suspension on a vehicle can cost tens of millions in additional R&D expenditures, retooling, inventories, and the loss of scale economies. The question then is, "Will higher sales in that country justify these additional costs?"

A key issue in international management, therefore, is the art and strategy of picking the optimum balance between one extreme of complete worldwide standardization on the one hand, and the other extreme of adaptation for each country market, as described in my article *"Globalization: What the Heck Is It?"[3]*, which gives an analytical approach to finding the optimum.

Another Key Job of the International Executive: Global Price Discrimination

For an astonishingly wide range of products and services – from consumer products such as cameras, to industrial goods such as servers, to services such as consulting – companies do not charge the same price for the exact same item. A year after Apple launched its iPhone5, its official list price in Apple stores (and authorized retailers) exhibited a greater than 50 percent variation[4] – $649 in the highly competitive US market, $791 in Hungary, and a high of $1,005 in Brazil. A camera sold for $300 in the US may go for $175 in Thailand and more than $500 in Switzerland. The price of the same drug in an emerging nation can be less than 10 percent of the cost in the US. A prescription for Plavix® that would cost a patient $152 in the US (where pharmaceutical company competition is weakest) would in the UK cost only $57,[5] and generic equivalents in India retail for under $3. Indeed, according to economics theory, companies would be sub-optimizing on global total profits if they charged the same price everywhere. Recall the context of international business: 194 countries have a huge variation in disposable income, culture, regulation, and intensity of internal competition. Each country is a separate fragment of the world to the marketer. And some "gray market" (parallel market) leakage across borders notwithstanding, customers in each nation buy locally at the price the multinational sets (see below).

In an affluent nation such as Switzerland, a firm would be unnecessarily giving up profits by setting camera prices low. The Swiss can afford it. For a regulated pharmaceutical industry in the US, with strict enforcement of patents and affluent customers covered by insurance, US drug prices are the highest in the world, and the large US market enables drug companies to recoup their frighteningly high R&D costs. By contrast, competition in the US mobile telephony business is intense, and firms such as Apple are forced to set prices for American consumers of mobile phones that are among the lowest in the world. Prices for many products in emerging nations are set low simply because otherwise there would be no buyers. (A low price does not necessarily mean no profits as long as the low price is still above variable cost. See below.) For cameras and consumer electronics, Americans pay below-global-average prices with multinational companies setting even lower prices in emerging nations where income levels are not high.

The task of the international marketing executive is to calculate, using market research and econometric models, the "optimum price" that maximizes profit in each country. However, then the firm has to be prepared to face the problems of accusations of "dumping" in some countries or price gouging in others, possible bad publicity, and the nuisance of "gray market"[6] leakage.

The Economics of Price Discrimination and Its Dilemmas

A drug prescription that wholesales for $100 or $1,000 may often have a direct manufacturing cost of less than $2. So, for a $100 revenue, is there an "obscene" profit of $100 – $2 = $98? No, the $98 is not profit, but a "margin" above the cost of manufacturing alone. Out of the $98 margin, pharmaceutical companies have to support marketing, distribution, and above all the R&D cost of drugs. The industry's association, PhRMA, puts the average cost of developing and launching a new drug compound at $1.3 billion each. Other breathless and improbable claims suggest a figure of $5 billion.[7] More tempered academic studies suggest lower figures in the hundreds of millions, although secrecy and sheer accounting complexity mean that very few data are actually made public.[8] Suffice it to say that medical R&D costs are high and that the odds of a compound being approved by the Food and Drug Administrations (FDAs) of nations are very low. Hence, the costs of hundreds of failed R&D efforts have to be sustained by the one successfully launched drug. Pharmaceutical companies already have higher R&D/Sales ratios than most industries could tolerate. Importantly, the outlay on R&D (for the few successes and many failures) has to be recouped in a short patent life of 20 years or less. So the largest fraction of the 98 percent gross margin ($100 wholesale minus $2 manufacturing cost) is put back into the R&D pot.[9]

But this is true not just for the drug business, but for most high-technology companies. One criterion I propose for a "high-tech" company is a "High Ratio of Fixed Costs over Variable Costs." Take semiconductors as an example. A semiconductor fabrication factory can cost $3 billion to set up. In addition, each new semiconductor design may cost millions in R&D. But once these fixed costs are incurred (i.e., treated as "sunk costs"), then the incremental cost of producing a chip may only be $10. A pharmaceutical firm may spend $300 million of R&D for a drug. But once that cost is incurred (sunk), the incremental or variable costs of manufacturing the drug may only be $2 per dose or prescription—trivial by comparison. Musicians and filmmakers may toil for years on their creative output. But the variable or incremental cost of producing the CD or DVD is only $0.50.

What does a "High Fixed Cost/Variable Cost Ratio" do for a multinational firm? It enables it to play the game of international price discrimination. A new movie release retailing for $17 in an affluent nation may be sold—at an official, company-set price—of only $4 in a poor emerging-country market. The official or company-determined $17 price in the affluent nation and the official $4 price for the same movie in a poor country are optimal for each of those markets. The millions spent on producing the movie and the master digital files are already gone—sunk costs. The $17 price over the variable cost to produce each 50-cent Blue-Ray disk or DVD (or to stream the download) equals $17.00 − $0.50 = $16.50 "contribution margin" to be applied toward amortization of the millions spent on producing the movie. But even the official $4 price in an emerging nation yields a contribution margin of $4.00 −$0.50 = $3.50. Better to earn the $3.50 margin in a poor country than have no sales in that nation because the price was set too high.

Farok J. Contractor, Ph.D.

Managing the Multinational Company's External Relations and Reputation Worldwide: The Pharmaceutical Industry Example and Life-Saving Drugs

According to the World Bank, 1.1 billion humans have a *per capita* income of $500 per year or less,[10] which is the cutoff for grinding poverty. Some 30-odd nations have *per capita* incomes averaging less than $1,000 annually. Probably more than 2 billion persons can be described as poor or resource-thin. When it comes to life-threatening diseases like AIDS, with a conservative estimate of 36 million infected[11] – the majority in lower-income nations – how can the international executive balance the need to recoup huge pharmaceutical R&D costs against the need of poor patients?

Antiretroviral (ARV) AIDS drugs, which can keep an HIV-positive person alive indefinitely, sell for an annual price of more than $12,000 in rich nations, although the variable cost of producing doses for one person is only $300 per year, as the case reveals. But three-quarters of humankind earns less than $12,000 in one year. Millions of them would die of AIDS-related complications unless the ARV patent holders (such as Bristol-Myers Squibb or Pfizer) agreed to sell the same patented drug at very low prices in poor nations. Initially, to protect their gross margins (on the grounds of supporting R&D costs and preventing the gray market), the patent holders refused to lower their prices. Twelve years later, in 2014, much of the pharmaceutical industry has—with great reluctance—agreed to the principle of global price discrimination.

In a recent example in 2014, Gilead Science, a US firm that has patented a hepatitis C drug with the brand name of Sovaldi, sells it in the US for $1,000 per pill. The total cost for the patient or insurance company is $84,000 for a 12-week course of treatment[12]. Op-Ed writers fulminated and tongues wagged, even in rich countries like the US, outraged at the high price. However, Gilead Science has agreed to license the patent to seven generic producers in India at a low enough royalty so that the price of the generic drug to the Indian consumer would be around $2,000 for the 12-week treatment. While $2,000 is a mere 2.4 percent of the US price of $84,000, it is still well above India's average annual per capita income of $1,170 per person.

While the issue began more than a decade ago, it has become increasingly critical to the future of the industry worldwide and illustrates some of the other key aspects of global management:

- *Managing Reputation and Customer Attitudes Worldwide*: How can the pharmaceutical industry justify high gross margins to an increasingly aware and tax-weary public that is already aging in Europe, Japan, and (later) in the US while their tax base is beginning to plateau or shrink?

- *The Role of NGOs and Activist Organizations*: Companies have to contend with pressure groups ranging from the American Association of Retired Persons (AARP) to third-world oriented NGOs (e.g., OXFAM) that pressure industries to lower prices or engage in "fair-trade" practices that do not really involve them directly. (For example, Starbucks, a retail coffee shop/restaurant chain, purchases coffee from importers and had little to do with the international supply chain or coffee farmers. But under pressure from OXFAM, Starbucks was forced to render assistance to coffee farmers in far-flung places such as Ethiopia that no Starbucks executive had previously visited. The ARV/AIDS drugs controversy was sparked by protests led by NGOs in South Africa and the United States.) Contract procurers such as Nike or The Gap now pay close attention to labor conditions in factories in Bangladesh or Indonesia that are neither owned nor controlled by the retailer.

- *The Role and Value of the Patent System*: Innovation in a capitalist context is motivated by the potential rewards of R&D—namely, a government-conferred monopoly to the patent holder, who can then charge high prices for 20 years (or less). Innovation drives modern economies and high-tech industries that bear the necessary risk-taking of entrepreneurship. An R&D outlay is a form of entrepreneurial risk—a leap in the dark with the final outcome unknown. And yet, there are situations in the pharmaceutical or telecommunication industries where the public interest and public awareness can run counter to the rewards of the patent system and where firms hoping for the "payoff" from their entrepreneurial efforts and patent awards are constrained by regulations and price caps.

- *Influence of Multilateral Bodies Such as the World Trade Organization (WTO), International Treaties, and Protocols*: Every treaty or membership in a global industry association brings with it benefits, as well as costs. The WTO started out as a forum for the mutual reduction of tariffs in order to promote growth in world trade.[13] Lower trade barriers increase exports and imports, which are generally held to be beneficial. Today, the WTO has expanded its ambit to include other issues such as intellectual property.

According to WTO rules, under the "compulsory licensing" provision, a government can unilaterally declare a medical emergency in a particular disease area (such as AIDS) and suspend patent-holder rights by bringing in generic drug producers in lieu of the patent holders. The generic producer agrees to sell the drug very cheaply at only a small margin over its variable cost since they do not have to amortize sunk R&D costs—and, by the way, may even pay an insultingly small royalty to the patent holder, which only rubs salt into the wound of the patent holder that has lost the ability to charge a high price in that country.

While membership in the WTO, or treaties such as the North American Free Trade Agreement (NAFTA), brings with it substantial benefits to exporters, many firms incur restrictions and additional costs. Importers in many sectors face heightened competition. Thousands of domestic firms go bankrupt because they cannot compete with imports, as happened in China and India after they signed the WTO treaty and lowered trade barriers. Treaty requirements often mean that a nation agrees to inspection of their industries and economy by outsiders to make sure the country's companies are adhering to the rules of the treaty. This is anathema to authoritarian governments such as China's. Nevertheless, gritting their teeth, the Chinese government joined the WTO in December 2001. While thousands of Chinese import-competing firms went out of business, Chinese exports quadrupled in the decade after signing the treaty. Much of China's economic boom can be explained by its opening its doors to international commerce. At the same time, after 2001, literally tens of thousands of foreign inspectors, NGO personnel, and industry auditors have landed in China and—from the proud nationalist Chinese viewpoint—"snooped" around their nation.

Is Globalization Eroding "National Sovereignty"? Are We Headed for a "Goldfish" Planet?

Once upon a time, in the year 1648 following an exhausting 30-year war, major European powers signed the Treaty of Westphalia, whereby each agreed that they would not interfere in any other nation's affairs. What each government did within its own borders was supposed to concern no one outside that nation. No one else would interfere. Thus, was born the idea of "National Sovereignty," which became a dominant concept of international relations around the world for almost three-and-a-half centuries.

But in a very quiet way, in the last 30 years the concept of National Sovereignty has been eroding, not so much because of politics, but because of International Business. True, there is the occasional military intervention exemplified by Serbia, Iraq, or Crimea. But the more pervasive erosion of national sovereignty stems from economic interdependence, multilateral or bilateral economic treaties, and the Internet. Tens of thousands of "inspectors" employed by governments or accounting firms arrive at foreign factories, checking for compliance with treaties or global industry standards. Thirty years ago, where I placed the sofa in my living room was nobody's business but my own. Today, neighbors have the temerity to approach my house, look through my window, and demand that I place my sofa on the other side of my living room, where they think it would be better placed. Thirty years ago, I would have told them to "go to hell" on the grounds that what I did inside my own dwelling was nobody else's business. Today, however, I have to grudgingly listen to my neighbors because I am dependent on them. It is a mutual interdependence.

Take the case of the proud Chinese, who are entangled with the US to the tune of well over $500 billion in trade (exports plus imports) each year and who own something on the order of $2 trillion in US assets (such as US Treasury bonds). Every few days, the press reports how Washington lectures Beijing on a range of issues from the value of the Chinese yuan, to freeing jailed Chinese dissidents, to clamping down on intellectual property piracy. The pressures are sufficiently great that the Chinese have reluctantly revalued their currency by more than 35 percent since June 2005. The Chinese grit their teeth and bear it, occasionally letting out a low growl, and have retaliated by hacking into the data of American companies.

Foreigners file suit in US courts seeking redress for issues entirely outside US borders. Courts around the world are tackling cases that originate outside their borders. In 2012, an Argentine naval training ship was impounded in Ghana, based on a court injunction issued in that country in favor of a US hedge fund, Elliot Capital Management, that was owed money when the Argentine government defaulted on its bonds in 2001. The energy dependency of Germany and other large European countries on Russian gas and oil imports explained their tepid response to Russia's annexation of Crimea in 2014.

Farok J. Contractor, Ph.D.

A quiet but astonishing transformation has taken place in the last three decades in terms of economic interdependence as well as international scrutiny. Because of the Internet and social media (nearly 3 billion people are now connected), we may be heading toward a "goldfish planet" where individuals and firms are exposed to a degree that was inconceivable 30 years ago – exposed to foreign ideas, business opportunities, pressures, trans-border regulations, and legal liabilities outside the home state of the multinational company

In Conclusion: The Job/s of the International Executive

Borders are increasingly porous to the movements of capital, ideas, and even people, although the "nation-state" with suzerainty over its affairs is still the norm. The planet is still made up of nearly 200 separate fragments (countries and territories). Importantly, for the International Business executive, great differences will continue to prevail across the "fragments" in labor costs, income levels, regulations, and culture. The art of International Business Management and Global Strategy is the ability to sense and arbitrage the differences; to decide on the best method for expansion into foreign markets; to decide for each country on the optimal balance between global standardization and local adaptation; to set optimal prices in each nation; how to transfer "best practices" and good ideas learned from one country to other parts of the firm; and to manage the external regulatory issues and increasingly vocal stakeholders in a "goldfish" environment.

Notes

[1] World Bank Indicators

[2] International Telecommunications Unions (ITU), Geneva, Press Release, 27 February 2013, ITU releases latest global technology development figures.

[3] "Globalization: What the heck is it?" is a piece originally published in 1992, but greatly revised and augmented since then. (See Globalization: What the Heck Is It; Revised May 2013.pdf.)

[4] iPhone 5S Price Index. Prices shown as of November 18, 2013. Official launch of the iPhone5 was in September 2012. The iPhone6 was released in September 2014.

[5] Motheral, Brenda, U.S. drug prices 3- to 6-fold greater than other countries, Rx Outcomes Adviser (December 7, 2011).

[6] A "gray market" is a situation where the multinational has set prices so far apart in two nations that it pays an independent third party to buy quantities in the low-price nation and resell the item in the high-price country, thereby undercutting the large profit margin the firm enjoys in the high-price nation. For most firms, this is no more than a manageable nuisance.

[7] The cost of creating a new drug now $5 billion, pushing Big Pharma to change. (August 11, 2013): *Forbes.com*.

[8] Morgan S., Grootendorst P., Lexchin J., Cunningham C., Greyson D., The cost of drug development: a systematic review, *Health Policy.* April 2011.

[9] Critics allege that because companies do not disclose information, they suspect that an increasingly large fraction of the gross margin ($98 out of $100 in our example) is spent on mass advertising and company overheads, rather than applied to their R&D efforts.

[10] World Bank, Regional aggregation using 2005 PPP and $1.25/day poverty line.

[11] Global AIDS overview: The Global HIV/AIDS crisis today, *AIDS.gov* (the actual figure is likely to be much higher because of underreported cases in developing nations).

[12] Originally started in 1948 under the name "General Agreement on Tariffs and Trade (GATT)," whose mandate was mainly the mutual reduction of tariffs, the organization was renamed "WTO" in 1995, after which it adopted a much more activist, broader mandate—going beyond tariff reduction to other "non-tariff" issues, such as intellectual property.

[13] See Catherine Kolonko, Gilead Signs Deal for Generic Sovaldi in India, *HCPLive®*, September 24, 2014.

CHAPTER 17

Globalization: What the Heck Is It?

The term "globalization" has been a buzzword in the business literature since the 1980s. Once upon a time, "foreign," as in "foreign business," was sufficient. Then came "international," followed by "multinational," and even "transnational," as in "transnational corporations." Starting with Theodore Levitt's 1983 article entitled "The Globalization of Markets," the term "global" became popular in the business lexicon, to be tortured by countless luncheon speakers into so many meanings that one hardly knows its precise significance.

Businesspersons run the risk of creating confusion when they interchange the term "global," which has a specific and distinct meaning, with the words "multinational" and "international." One purpose of this article is to clarify the terminology. But its larger purpose is to discuss investment, marketing, and political trends in the world that are, to some extent, leading to greater integration of national economies (as in the case of the European Union), as well as to growth in foreign investment and trade to unprecedented levels. International trade in the mid-2010s crossed the $22,400 billion mark, while the sales of all multinational company foreign affiliates (i.e., outside their home country) exceeded $35,000 billion. A company may export to foreign customers, or it can invest in production facilities in that nation and sell to customers from factories there. Exports and foreign direct investment are substitutes in that sense. Licensing of knowledge and intellectual property is a third method of reaching foreign markets and international licensing is the fastest growing method of International Business.

Several Companies May Be Closer to Multinational Rather Than Global Strategies

Today, several firms that have direct investments outside their home countries may be described as "multinational" rather than "global" (although this is beginning to change). Take companies such as Unilever. For example, their Magnum ice cream, despite the same brand name, is formulated to taste very different from one European or Asian country to another. The reason is simple. Varying the taste increases local appeal, and such variation in the recipe can be done at very low incremental adaptation costs in the factories. For the most part, the strategy followed by consumer marketing firms tends to be somewhere between adaptive to local conditions in each country (multinational) and extremely standardized (global).

CURRENT TERMINOLOGY

The terms "international," "multinational," and "global" have assumed separate meanings.

INTERNATIONAL — This term generally refers to a company that mainly exports or imports goods and services, or arbitrages between markets in different nations. Companies that reach foreign customers primarily by exports fall into this category. The term is also sometimes used for companies that have just begun their international expansion.

MULTINATIONAL — This word literally means "many nations," but it does not simply imply doing business in many countries. The term refers to a company that has one or more foreign subsidiaries that add value, or produce, in the foreign location, as opposed to merely trading.

In the management-strategy literature, "multinational" also signifies a company whose operations in each nation are somewhat decentralized or autonomous. Each country subsidiary manages its own affairs, focusing mainly on local production, marketing in the country, and other country-specific issues. Such a multinational company may be little more than the sum of its worldwide parts. (Note: This type of organization is also sometimes called "Multi-domestic," "Geographic," or "National").

GLOBAL — This term now often refers to a company that takes advantage of the synergies between its various affiliates, rationalizes activities according to the comparative advantage of each country location, and utilizes the commonalities of production and markets into a standardized larger-scale operation spanning several countries to derive economies of global scale and scope. A global company's strategic purview is a search for global optimization, cost reduction, efficiency, and synergy, as opposed to running several parallel, but separate, multinational operations. (Note: Firms that try and optimize their global operations are also sometimes called "Transnational").

Large producers of household soaps and laundry detergents, such as the US-based Proctor & Gamble (P&G), or Henkels of Germany are constantly torn between the pressure to cut costs by standardizing the design of products and manufacturing across nations, versus the pressure to increase sales by adapting products to local preferences and use conditions. In the European market for laundry detergents, environmental, labeling, and commercial laws forced many of the companies to have different content and packaging. Even today, differences in national laws across the EU nations are not "harmonized" or identical. Local regulatory differences have persisted. Water hardness and mineral content continue to vary, necessitating different chemical formulations for detergent. In Italy, Spain, and other Mediterranean nations, pure cotton garments are more common than in the northern countries, where synthetic fiber content is greater. (This may be a slight difference but R&D chemists in P&G or Unilever have to take fiber content and water quality into account for the best washing experience for the consumer).

The washing machines themselves vary, with different designs, capacities, and washing water temperatures. Considering the average life of a washing machine to be 10 years, it will take a long time before the installation of the machines themselves will converge in design across a region. Distribution methods also vary. Some European nations have large grocery chains that can move large quantities and demand deep discounts. Other regions are characterized by small, independent stores necessitating more costly and fragmented distribution of products. Add to this the variation in advertising practices across nations. Some nations restrict TV commercials to a maximum number of minutes per year. Other channels show advertisements back-to-back between shows (as opposed to the presumably more effective American practice that allows interruption of the program). Finally, advertising costs vary dramatically across countries. Social media data allows customization by consumer profiles.

All of this adds up to a collection of national or even subnational markets rather than to a global or uniform market. So, adapting the product formulation, the advertising, and the distribution to local conditions can still pay off more than a regional uniform policy. That is to say, despite the higher costs of a country-by-country approach, total sales for all countries are also much higher. Thus, a locally adaptive and organizationally fragmented strategy – a "multinational" strategy – can sometimes produce superior overall regional profits. But not always.

The Allure of Global Standardization

The notion of global standardization, however, has continued to increase in allure in recent years. One objective of this chapter is to ask why. What social, political, or economic trends are luring companies to reassess their historical nation-by-nation strategies and go in for a region-wide or global approach?

One can easily think of several examples, from Rolex watches to Benetton clothing, where the products are similar, if not identical, all over the world; where the advertising is standard (except for translations); and, for many retailers, their retail outlets are also similar. Most of these goods are items aimed at upscale customers whose tastes are presumed to transcend national differences. On the other hand, examples that appear superficially to be globally standardized are, in fact, not so. Marlboro cigarettes may be advertised worldwide with the same American cowboy and horse. But the cigarettes themselves vary somewhat in flavor, and the price and methods of distribution are localized. McDonald's restaurants in India have adapted to the local aversion to beef, by substituting chicken in their hamburgers. Drinks such as Coca-Cola or Pepsi are adapted to the local sweet tooth, water conditions, and climate – despite often using similar advertising campaigns in various nations. Thus, products may appear to be global and yet exhibit degrees of variation along different marketing-strategy dimensions.

However, there are enormous pressures that tempt companies to erase the differences and try and standardize. There are three principal reasons:

1. The potential cost savings (moreover, because competing firms may be doing so, our company had better think along these lines as well);
2. The escalating R&D costs that are forcing companies to amortize them over a larger global market, as opposed to a few nations; escalating scale requirements in manufacturing are also providing a push in some industries; and
3. The belief that the world's customers are indeed getting more homogeneous in tastes, and so differences in consumer preferences have narrowed.

Cost Savings from Globalization

When markets are small – and most of the countries of the world are pretty small markets – manufacturing or distribution may not be large enough to reach economic scale. The planet has 193 nations tracked by the IMF. For the year 2019, the 20th-size economy, Turkey, was only 4 percent the size of the biggest, the United States. Below the 40th-ranked economy, not only are countries less than 1 percent the size of the US economy, but they're considered riskier places to do business. Out of 193 nations on the planet, the lower 174 countries **put together** are only 19.3 percent of the world economy. Hence, the world consists of a collection of small, culturally fragmented markets. So, what does this mean for "globalization"?

Of course, it is not just the size of the market from the consumer's perspective, but by combining production in one nation – regardless of its economic size – lower average costs from economies of large scale in manufacturing can be enjoyed. Aluminum production up to the ingot stage requires a huge scale, larger than the demand of most Asian or small European countries; but the rolling operation can be done efficiently at a much smaller scale in each nation. Pharmaceutical research requires centralized expenditures involving hundreds of millions or billions of dollars per drug, but the production of millions of pills in the *final* stage can be done by a few machines, each the size of a desk.

Table 1: Relative Size of Countries' Economies, 2018/19

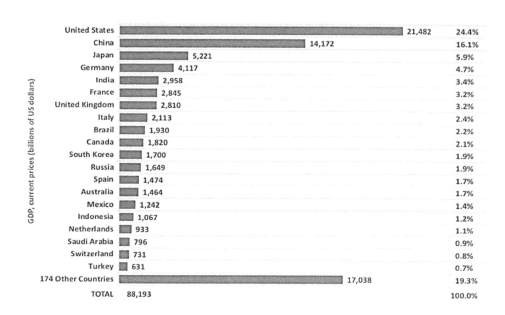

Country	GDP, current prices (billions of US dollars)	Percentage
United States	21,482	24.4%
China	14,172	16.1%
Japan	5,221	5.9%
Germany	4,117	4.7%
India	2,958	3.4%
France	2,845	3.2%
United Kingdom	2,810	3.2%
Italy	2,113	2.4%
Brazil	1,930	2.2%
Canada	1,820	2.1%
South Korea	1,700	1.9%
Russia	1,649	1.9%
Spain	1,474	1.7%
Australia	1,464	1.7%
Mexico	1,242	1.4%
Indonesia	1,067	1.2%
Netherlands	933	1.1%
Saudi Arabia	796	0.9%
Switzerland	731	0.8%
Turkey	631	0.7%
174 Other Countries	17,038	19.3%
TOTAL	88,193	100.0%

For some companies, substantial savings can also be realized by combining advertising. Instead of hiring separate agencies to design separate campaigns, one global agency devises a common theme (and hopes it goes over well with customers of different cultures). The savings can be huge in companies whose annual advertising outlay exceeds $500 million worldwide. In 2019, Unilever spent more than $8 billion in global advertising. For a prime show on American television networks, advertising rates often exceed $1 million per minute, forcing the agency to come up with a common mass-appeal theme for a wide audience. Megastations in Europe or Asia will also force some companies into a region-wide advertising content.[1]

---

[1] Interestingly, the television industry now also offers a countertrend. The economics of cable and other "narrow-casting" technologies offer advertisers the opportunity to target small groups, or market segments, at a cost per viewer not substantially higher than that for the broadcasting channels. This would help perpetuate locally adaptive marketing.

R&D costs in some industries have escalated to the point where firms are forced to look at the entire world market, not just at a few countries, to amortize the expenditures. A new drug may average $800 million to launch, research on a digital telecommunications switch costs more than $2,000 million, and a completely new car design costs more than $4,500 million. With a standard design at the heart of the product, manufacturers may look to adapt some superficial aspects for particular markets. This can extend even to "low-tech" items. Instead of the dozen different shampoo bottles Colgate-Palmolive formerly used in Western Europe, only one or two styles may be used. This will save considerably on the design, tooling, and packaging costs in Europe. However, the labeling and content of the shampoo may vary in different nations. Why? Because the chemical composition of the shampoo is easy (meaning relatively cheap) to adapt. In cosmetics and food preparations, changing the formula or recipe to suit local tastes is sometimes virtually costless, involving nothing more than changing some temperature settings or other process parameters on a standardized automated manufacturing line.

Standardize or Adapt? A Decision Criterion

"You can't sell the same car in different markets. You always have to tune it."
 – Carlos Ghosn, Nissan Motor (*Wall Street Journal*, 12-5, 2004).

What is called "globalization" in many companies, therefore, actually means judiciously combining those stages of production or distribution where efficient scale cannot be obtained by entirely localized operations. The trick, then, in corporate strategy terms, is to make decisions on

- Local adaptation *versus* global standardization, and
- Centralization vs. decentralization

with a mix that varies (within the same firm) depending on the stage of the value chain. For example, in one firm the R&D may be highly centralized and concentrated in just two or three nations because the economics of R&D may dictate clustering of personnel and equipment. Depending on the minimum economic scale of production, there may be several factories in each region, closer to the end customer. Finally, in some firms, marketing may be completely decentralized to the country level.

Global production strategy involves two basic analytical steps: (1) Break down the production process into its constituent parts or slices. (2) For each part or slice of production, or for each adaptation, apply the following decision criterion: "How much will this engineering adaptation cost for this country market – and how much, in turn, will our customers reward us by purchasing that much more of the specifically adapted product?" Undertake the adaptation only if the potential incremental revenues exceed the adaptation costs in that region (such as ASEAN or Europe).

This is illustrated in Figure 1. Consider a laundry detergent company, such as Proctor & Gamble or Henkels, formulating a regional strategy in South East Asia or Western Europe. Focusing on just the issue of how many different formulae for their powdered detergents would be optimal across the region, the analysis reveals (in this hypothetical example) that even though there are fifteen nations in the region, having nine different formulations, or recipes, would be best. The analysis is done by estimating Overall Regional Costs and expected Overall Regional Sales Revenues – a calculation done for each nation, and then added up cumulatively across the region, for one variety, two varieties, three varieties, nine varieties, and so on up to the maximum number of fifteen varieties equal to the number of countries in the region.[2] The horizontal axis in Figure 1 ranges from No. 1 (just one standard variety in the whole region) to No 15 (fifteen varieties, or one variety for each country). There are four aspects to consider as one goes from left to right in Figure 1: (1) Production Costs, (2) Marketing Costs, (3) Transportation Costs totaled across the region, and (4) Regional Overhead and Regional Headquarters Costs as a function of the number of varieties (on the horizontal axis, 1 – 15).

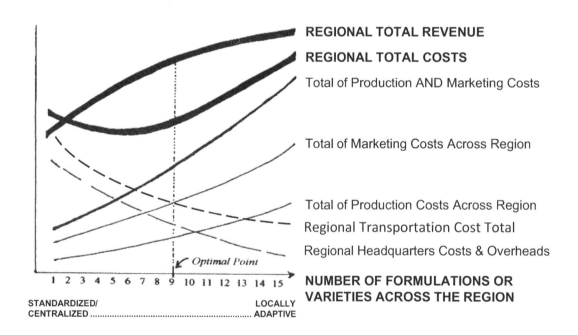

Figure 1: Seeking the Optimum Middle Between Standardization and Local Adaptation

---

[2] Such as ASEAN, or South East Asia, or the EU.

The strategy or analysis in Figure 1 is regional and not based on single nations.

- <u>Regional Total Production Costs Increase from Left to Right</u>: As the number of varieties or formulations increases, more separate batches have to be produced, perhaps in more factories in more countries, and the economies of a giant scale would be diminished. The number of factories in the region overall and their location may increase. Overall total regional production costs hence increase with more varieties.

- <u>Regional Total Marketing Costs Increase from Left to Right</u>: As more varieties of the product are produced – to locally adapt recipes to attract more customers in each nation who better appreciate a locally adapted variety "tuned" to the local taste or culture – the special attributes of each variety have to be communicated to customers in each nation. The marketing message gets fragmented or customized for each cultural or country group. Multiple marketing messages often mean a greater overall marketing budget for the region as a whole. Overall total regional marketing costs increase from left to right.

- <u>Regional Total Logistics and Transportation Costs Decline from Left to Right</u>: As the number of factories increases within the region, having more localized production and inventories inevitably reduces the amount of cross-border shipments. (By comparison, if say one giant factory served the entire fifteen-nation region, in that case there would be fourteen cross-border shipments to the other fourteen nations from the one factory – or much higher transportation and logistics costs overall. Overall total logistics costs are lower on the right.

- <u>Regional Headquarters Overhead Costs May Decline from Left to Right</u>: Going from left to right, the multinational company practices more local adaptation. A locally adaptive strategy does not need as much centralized control and oversight of regional headquarters. On the other hand, toward the left side of the graph, with a higher degree of standardization a greater degree of centralized control is needed from the regional headquarters in order to decide on the optimal location of factories, region-wide inventory, supply chain coordination, pan-regional marketing campaigns, and so forth.

Therefore, this is an analysis that is best performed by a multifunctional team consisting of Production, Supply Chain, Marketing, and Finance persons drawn from different subsidiaries in the region.

It is important to realize that the calculation is done *for the region as a whole*. As we move from left to right in Figure 1, with increasing local adaptation that each national customer group likes, sales in each nation, and therefore Regional Total Sales Revenue, increases. Production, and Marketing Costs also increase, in general – although not in a uniform fashion. But Logistics, Transport, and Regional Headquarters Overheads costs will likely decline from left to right. Hence, the Overall Regional Total Costs is a shallow U-shaped curve. The company's objective *is not to maximize profits country-by-country*, but rather for the region as a whole.

Profit for the region as a whole is simply the vertical gap between Regional Total Revenue and Regional Total Costs. Using Figure 1 as an illustration, the gap or profit is the biggest if the company has nine varieties. Having nine varieties, no more and no less, is optimal in terms of maximizing regional total profits. The company will hence adopt a strategy of having nine varieties of the product across the region.

For most multinational companies, the optimal number of varieties is neither at the left extreme (complete standardization) nor the right extreme (complete adaptation, country-by-country) – i.e., *the optimal degree of adaptation is somewhere in the middle*.

Globalization Does Not Necessarily Mean Standardization: Seeking the Optimum for Each Piece of the Value Chain

Globalization strategy in many companies, therefore, amounts to seeking the best "middle ground" or the optimal position between the extremes of complete standardization and centralization on the one hand *versus* complete local adaptation and local autonomy on the other. Moreover, the optimum number of varieties in a region will be different for different elements of the company's value chain. There will be different optimums for the desired number of product varieties, the number of factories in the region, the number of advertising campaigns across the region, the number of R&D locations, the number of brand names across the region, and so on. For example, some companies, such as Coca-Cola, may have a more or less standardized approach for some elements of the marketing mix, but not for others. They may have an absolutely identical brand image, but they may "tweak" the taste or recipe of their drink from country to country slightly (at virtually little or zero engineering adaptation cost).

Marketing has several elements, some of which can be standardized while others are adapted to suit local cultures and tastes in order to increase local sales. Some companies use a standardized core advertising campaign that is adapted only by using local actors and language. Other elements of the marketing mix, such as price and distribution methods for companies such as Coca-Cola, vary greatly across nations. Others may standardize the product design, but drastically vary the advertising message. Budweiser beer in the US is positioned at the lower end of the mass market. American advertising often features college boys playing (nonthreatening) pranks with animals and often rabid sports fans – decidedly downscale. By contrast, Budweiser ads in China feature tuxedo-clad connoisseurs listening to cool jazz.

In some cases, multinationals are *forced* to adapt products and aspects of marketing because of government regulations or technical standards, such as voltage or mobile phone transmission standards, or because the product is used in a different way in some nations. In Germany or the US, where cars are driven by owners and the occupancy averages from 1.10 – 1.50 persons per vehicle, the back seat is rarely occupied. By comparison, in China or India, BMW and Buick have had to stretch the legroom of the rear seats (or redesign and lengthen the entire car) because affluent owners are driven by chauffeurs. China is already the biggest automobile market in the world, and with Indians joining in car purchases, luxury vehicles are being redesigned accordingly. In Japan, where houses are small and the aesthetic sense places value on the small and beautiful object, appliances and household goods tend to be favored when they are efficient, compact, understated, and elegant. Many nations have varying environmental, packaging, advertising, and data collection regulations that *force* local adaptation. Hence, some degree of local adaptation of some elements of the value chain is necessary, despite the higher costs of such adaptation and the loss of scale efficiencies.

The dangers of a rigid, overly standardized global approach are illustrated by a German chocolate company, Ritter Sport. Some say that Ritter Sport makes some of the tastiest mass-produced chocolate in the world and their product itself does not need adaptation. But despite universally appreciated good taste, their inflexible policy of not adapting their prices,[3] packaging, or slogan has left them with indifferent sales outside of German-speaking countries. For many decades until recently, their globally used slogan was *"Quadratisch, Praktisch, Gut."* Besides the

---

[3] Ritter Sport, in an exhibition of Teutonic rectitude, appears to not only uniformly price in euros, but to add on transportation and foreign distribution costs, with the results that the retail price of a chocolate bar in the US is around $3. By contrast, the German price can be below €1. Unsurprisingly, US sales are negligible.

fact that outside Germany few consumers can read German, the translation of the slogan into other languages is "Square, Practical, Good" – a blurb that is either inscrutable or laughable. The term "square" actually has, or at least had, a negative connotation in American culture. And it hardly excites anyone outside Germany to call a chocolate "practical." On the other hand, the *"Quadratisch, Praktisch, Gut"* slogan resonates with the soul of German culture, which places great importance on lean design and practicality.[4] The failure to adapt their slogan or pricing means that sales outside Germany are meager, considering how tasty the product actually is.

Globalization does not, therefore, mean complete standardization or complete adaptation. For many firms, a strategic overview will, in fact, recommend combining and standardizing *some* particular aspects of manufacturing and marketing that were hitherto fragmented over different countries or adapting others that were overly standardized across nations.

Rather, I would define globalization as the continuous *search* for selective optimization of each stage of the value-added chain, from R&D to distribution.[5] One company may standardize and centralize its research and advertising functions while deciding to adapt and decentralize to the country level its manufacturing, pricing, and distribution practices. Another company may decide to have standardized production in a few, large-scale, rationalized manufacturing centers from which it serves many nations, but have very localized advertising and selling methods in each country. It is a question of finding the optimum balance for each business function.

The optimal balance is affected by the business environment. The next section of this chapter discusses changes in the global environment that are impelling several companies to consider changing their strategies from "multinational" to "global."

Are Changes in the Environment Leading to Globalization?

Were Spain's national identity and culture threatened when the EU committee on computer standards proposed dropping the tilde (~) from computer keyboards? Outside Spain, the tilde is a seldom used or anachronistic diacritical mark. But to the Spanish, it is part of the distinctiveness of their culture, their peninsularity. Indeed, the tilde is part of their country's official name, *España*. However, we should remember that the nation-state as we know it today is not more than about

---

[4] The slogan reflects the firm's excessive engineering pride in designing a square chocolate bar that can be opened with one snap of the wrist. But outside German culture, consumers do not place much emphasis on such attributes.

[5] A firm that tries to globally optimize, and whose strategy also seeks to actively manage cross-border learning and accumulation of knowledge, has been labeled "Transnational" by Bartlett and Beamish (2013).

200 years old. Fixed boundaries, passports, visas, non-overlapping governmental control, and people's identification with large colored splotches on a world map are relatively recent notions in human history. India, Italy, Germany, and the US are all little more than a century old in their present geopolitical state.

There is no guarantee that this national identification will diminish or increase. The identification of a person as "Yugoslavian" has been replaced by "Montenegran" or "Slovenian." Will the cry, "I am a European!" replace the call, "I am a Spaniard!"? Not if I am a Basque, Catalonian, or Corsican nationalist. Everywhere, small groups, from Danes who voted "no" to the Maastricht Treaty, to conservative British Tories, to the Danes and French who voted *"non"* on the EU Constitution in 2005, to right-wing parties increasing their representation in Europe feel greatly threatened by a supranational identification.

Identity in the future can go either way. In the EU, the attempted unification of markets can be seen, by nationalists, as a diminution of local identity. When a country joins a supranational association such as the WTO, or signs a multinational treaty, this signifies a withdrawal or abdication of state power at the national level over tariffs, trade barriers, independent economic policies, and separate national technical standards in favor of the supranational agency. When China joined the WTO, it was with great reluctance and fear on the part of some in the Chinese government. The many benefits of joining the WTO are offset, in the eyes of many, by having "outsiders" determine the country's policies, by having foreign inspectors visit and snoop, and, in general, by seeing local control eroded. Countries that have joined the Eurozone have similarly completely given up their previously independent monetary policy to six old persons in Frankfurt that make up the European Central Bank's Executive Board.

Whether the nation-state in its present form will strengthen, fragment, or wither away is still open to debate. However, current trends make this political question less crucial for business than in the past. To some degree, politics has already loosened its grip on economic matters. First, there has been a virtually global liberalization of policies. Over the past 30 years, virtually every government on the planet has partially deregulated economic affairs and slackened its grip on commerce. Second, the international mobility of capital, information, and even people has rendered less effectual the ability of the state to intervene, even if it were ideologically predisposed to do so. Money and data move across borders virtually costlessly (or at very negligible cost). The growth of world trade and foreign direct investment over the past 50 years, at rates much higher than the growth of domestic economies, means that greater economic interdependence between nations follows, axiomatically. From this followed the need for realistic exchange rates that were best realized by a convertible and floating market exchange rate.[6] But a convertible currency reduces the economic power of a government internally. Even formerly socialist countries such as India, with a relatively small ratio of foreign trade in relation to the gross domestic product, found they could not escape this logic. India made the rupee partially convertible in the 1990s, and the number of permissions needed from the bureaucracy has steadily dropped.

Add to the above the continuing lowering of trade barriers and transport costs, the adoption of supranational technical standards such as ISO 9000 or ISO 14000, and the freer movement of people with so-called international lifestyles, and some pundits are led to propose that markets are converging. Logically, then, business strategies should also converge. But have they?

Factors Preventing Market Convergence

The convergence hypothesis may already be true for some companies (McDonald's, Rolex, or H&M). It may even be true for the majority of items and businesses at some distant time in humanity's future. But at the moment, strong local pressures and differences persist. The persistence of cultural memory among the Spanish Basque, the Montenegrins, the South Moluccans, and a thousand other groups will perpetuate a fragmented marketing strategy for culturally sensitive products such as food preparations (but extending even to the so-called industrial products such as computer keyboards and blood-clot analyzers). For instance, the Spanish, who do not believe in breakfast, consume only around 0.4 pounds of breakfast cereal per capita compared with a whopping 12 pounds or more per capita in Britain and Ireland.

Other "localizing" factors include non-tariff protectionist barriers that WTO negotiators are unsuccessful in removing; resource dependencies on locally grown or locally made raw materials; and the great variation in marketing and promotional practices from one nation to another. In advertising, the availability, cost, and effectiveness of media vary widely. Distribution methods often reflect local tradition. For example, in Japan, the government and business associations often favor small "mom-and-pop" retail establishments over more efficient high-volume outlets—despite the higher price paid by consumers. An unwritten social contract in Japan says that higher prices are paid in return for personalized service (both during the purchase and after sales) and to maintain employment in retail distribution. However, such practices do serve to limit foreign chains such as giant American stores whose executives cannot fathom the cultural and social underpinnings of Japanese distribution.

---

[6] In 1971, the Bretton Woods fixed exchange rate system based on gold values was abandoned.

Local concerns will, to different degrees, always persist in areas such as job creation, military matters, infrastructure projects, and service-intensive endeavors that require local labor.

Summary and Conclusions for Company Strategies

The market and cultural convergence hypothesis is very far from being a reality for all but a few products. The term "globalization" (often confused with the terms "multinational" and "international") does not necessarily mean standardization or centralization of all company practices worldwide. Globalization, in the corporate-strategy literature, merely refers to a worldwide management process, a search for global optimization.

For most companies, "globalization" effectively refers to the attempt to pull together and rationalize only *some* business functions that were hitherto decentralized to the country level. At the same time, it refers to a search for commonalities and combinations of national markets that were hitherto treated separately. As a result of this strategy-planning process, one firm may decide to rationalize its manufacturing globally, while leaving marketing and distribution very different in each country's market. Another firm may find that adapting the product design and content are easy and relatively inexpensive, but that marketing had best be uniform across markets.

This chapter proposes an optimization rule or criterion for each business function or for each market: to assess the costs of adaptation to local conditions against the size of the benefit derived by increased sales, if any, as a result of the adaptation. Conversely, a company may assess the cost reduction or efficiency gain from combining or standardizing certain functions against the drop in revenues, if any, resulting from a less locally tailored approach. Such an analysis should be done incrementally for *each* piece of the value-added chain in order to find the best intermediate optimum point for the region as a whole:

(R&D→manufacturing→distribution→after-sales service) in *each* country market, and then added up for the region as a whole

Globalization, then, is the optimum combination or standardization of *some* functions in some nations and locally adaptive practices in other functions and countries.

REFERENCES

Abdelal, Rawi, and Tedlow, Richard S., (2003). Theodore Levitt's "The Globalization of Markets: An Evaluation after Two Decades." Harvard NOM Working Paper No. 03-20; *Harvard Business School* Working Paper No. 03-082, February 2003.

Bartlett, Christopher, and Beamish, Paul (2013). *Transnational Management*, McGraw Hill.

Bhagwati, Jagdish, (2004). *In Defense of Globalization*, Oxford University Press.

Haier Corp., (2005). "Innovation and Globalization Strategy."

Levitt, Theodore (1983). "The Globalization of Markets," *Harvard Business Review*, May-June 1983.

Rugman, Alan, (2001). *The End of Globalization: Why Global Strategy Is a Myth & How to Profit from the Realities of Regional Markets*, Random House Business Books.

Segal-Horn, Susan and Faulkner, David (2010). *Understanding Global Strategy*, Cengage Learning.

Toshiba, (2005). "Globalization Strategy."

APPENDIX

Organization Structures That Fit Different Strategies

As we have seen above, the strategic mission of firms ranges on a spectrum from being very locally responsive (in the case of products related to the body or sensitive to local culture, such as prepared foods or cosmetics) to rather globally standardized (in the case of technology-driven products, such as telecommunication devices). Unilever products are far more locally adapted compared with Samsung's. But how does each firm's strategic mission determine its organizational structure? We discuss below two archetypes, the multinational versus the global product firm.[7]

A multinational or "multi-domestic" company's emphasis is on customization because customers reward such local adaptation by buying more, while costs per unit may not increase very much because production switch-over or technical modification can be done easily. Minimum efficient scale and experience curve effects may be small. Each national affiliate therefore can run its own show and need not engage in much coordination with other country subsidiaries or central administration.

A global or "transnational" firm's emphasis, on the other hand, is on lowering costs and seeking efficiency by cross-border rationalization. By "rationalization," we mean that not only are various parts of the value chain (R&D→sourcing→manufacturing→distribution→after-sales

---

[7] In classroom teaching, models are necessarily simplified. In realty, few companies conform exactly to the archetypes presented here. In real life, compromises, CEO whims, and organizational history typically make the actual organization structures of firms appear to be hybrids or a hodge-podge. However, models serve to powerfully guide managerial thinking and improvements.

service) spread over different countries, but even within one piece of the chain, e.g., "production," some components may be made in one nation and the assembly in another. The Apple iPhone is said to have components from more than a dozen nations, with assembly done in China and India. Hence a high degree of central coordination and downward direction is needed across the globe or region. Often, such firms are high-technology oriented and have a large R&D overhead that has to be spread and coordinated over all the country units. Why this emphasis on lowering costs? Because many such companies are driven by relentless downward price pressures as each product goes through its product cycle.

According to Bartlett and Beamish's (2013) terminology, firms that seek efficiency and cost reduction through global rationalization and then, in addition, also actively manage learning and knowledge-transfer across affiliates worldwide are called "transnational." (This is only their terminology, and it is not universally used.)

Multinational/Multi-Domestic/Geographic Structures

A typical multinational or multi-domestic organization structure is depicted in Figure 2. Under each region may be found country-level subsidiaries and affiliates operating in a decentralized fashion, with very loose coordination. Such companies develop deep local knowledge, especially in their market, which enables them to fine-tune products to local requirements and maximize sales within each nation (and therefore worldwide). Country manager morale is generally higher than in centralized or globally standardized companies.

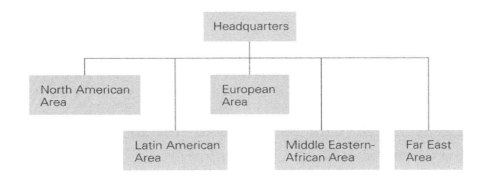

Figure 2: Multinational or Geographic Structure

Source: Charles Hill, International Business, McGraw Hill

Farok J. Contractor, Ph.D.

Table 2

GEOGRAPHIC OR NATIONAL ORGANIZATION

ADVANTAGES	DISADVANTAGES
■ Local/National Expertise	■ Proliferation of Product Designs Worldwide
■ Clear Focus	
■ Low Interference from MNC Homeoffice	■ Small/Inefficient Scale at Country Level
■ Marketing Emphasis	■ Good Ideas May Be Bottled Up in Subs.
■ Low Vulnerability to Political/Foreign Exchange/Logistical Disruptions	■ Duplication of Functions at Each National Organization
■ Local Responsiveness/Adaptation Ensures **High National and Global Total Sales Revenue**	■ R&D and Other Functions Fragmented Worldwide
	■ Parochialism
	■ Weak Headquarters Control -- Power at National Units
	■ **Global Total Costs High**

But there are drawbacks, as shown in Table 2. With only a local focus, products are developed for each nation, and some geographically structured companies may end up with a bloated product line with a proliferation of models across a region or worldwide. With a country-by-country focus, the scale of operations (production or marketing) may sometimes be small and inefficient. Each country unit may act as a fiefdom. Lack of coordination across country units often results in duplication of efforts and functions in each national unit. Good ideas developed in one subsidiary may not be shared with others. As a result, costs per unit, as well as cumulative worldwide total costs in the multinational or geographic firm, tend to be high (compared with a globally organized company).

However, companies that adopt this organizational structure feel that the higher total costs are more than offset by the higher total sales revenue that such an organization type also enables.

Global and Transnational Structures (Global Product Division)

Global, or Global Product Division, structures tend to have a product standardization or convergence strategy, rather than country-market focus. Country distinctions are minimized, if not eliminated. When diversified firms have several disparate product lines, each product division runs its own show, and runs it with a globally centralized mandate. This is illustrated in Figure 3.

Under each product division may be found functionally organized departments such as purchasing, manufacturing, marketing, and other support functions such as finance and global supply-chain coordination. Indeed, global coordination and cost reduction – within each division –

are the main strategic drivers. This mandate results in a continuous search for cross-border rationalization, synergies, and aggregated scale. There is not much emphasis on local adaptation, either because the products in question have a technologically standardized design that is invariant to cultural differences (e.g., aircraft engines or wind turbines) or because the costs of incremental adaptation to a country's requirements are not justified by the resultant increase in local sales.

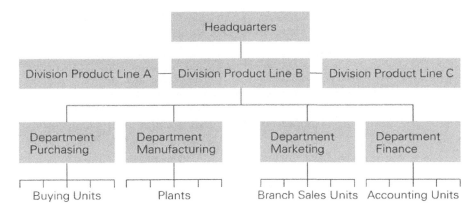

Figure 3: Global Product Division Structure

Source: Charles Hill, International Business, McGraw Hill

The relentless product and efficiency focus leads to lower costs overall. With the high degree of cross-border coordination and transfer of ideas and personnel, there is not much country loyalty. Managers specialize by function, not by country or market, and are willing to be assigned anywhere. Good ideas developed in one location travel quickly through the worldwide system – especially if the company actively manages acquisition of knowledge and promotes the internal transfer of learning.

But there are drawbacks. If there are several independent product divisions of the same company in one country, they may duplicate country-specific functions. The product focus may lead to neglect of, or blindness, to local marketing issues. While the company's product designs may be technology-driven, nevertheless some degree of country adaptation could result in higher sales. As Carlos Ghosn of Nissan Motors observed, *"You can't sell the same car in different markets. You always have to tune it.*[8]*"* Since production and marketing functions tend in such companies to be separate, there are inevitable conflicts over a range of issues, from product design to internal transfer pricing.

---

[8] *Wall Street Journal*, 12-5, 2004.

Moreover, since globally rationalized companies produce parts in different countries from where they are assembled, such firms are far more vulnerable to supply chain risks – from strikes or floods in one component factory affecting the entire system, to increases in fuel and transportation costs, to fluctuations in currency values, to overcapacity and under-capacity.[9]

Table 3

GLOBAL PRODUCT DIVISION ORGANIZATION

ADVANTAGES	DISADVANTAGES
• Product Focus and Specialization	• Possible Duplication at Country Level if Several Product Divisions Present
• Global Rationalization and Standardization Emphasized	• Weaker Understanding of Country Markets
• Economies of Global Scale	• Dampens Country-level Initiative
• Good Ideas Shared Across Nations	• Can Create Production - Marketing Tensions
• Easier to assign best personnel to foreign operations	• System More Vulnerable to - Supply Chain Disruptions - Over-capacity - Under-capacity - Foreign Exch. Risk
• Efficiency in Production and **Low Global Costs Per Unit**	• Global Standardization/Mass Production **Reduces Global Total Sales** (Compared to a Locally-Adaptive Strategy)

Without a doubt, a globally standardized approach lowers costs. It also lowers sales revenue in each nation. However, companies adopt this structure (as more and more are doing) because they feel that the reduction in country and worldwide sales will be more than offset by the reduction in global total costs, thereby increasing global total profits.

---

[9] By comparison, in the multi-domestic firm, relatively autonomous at the country level, a disruption in one location only affects that one nation's operation, and the risk does not spread worldwide.

CASE 3 GUIDELINES AND DISCUSSION QUESTIONS:

FIRE IN A BANGLADESH GARMENT FACTORY

(Case from Harvard Publishing)

TB0335

ANDREW INKPEN

FIRE IN A BANGLADESH GARMENT FACTORY

In November 2012, a fire in a garment factory near the Bangladesh capital of Dhaka killed 112 people and injured several hundred. The factory was owned by Tazreen Fashions Ltd., a subsidiary of The Tuba Group, a large Bangladeshi garment exporter whose clients included Walmart, Carrefour, C&A, Kmart, and Li & Fung. The factory opened in May 2010, employed about 1,500 workers, and had sales of $35 million a year from the production of clothing such as T-shirts, polo shirts, and fleece jackets. The fire started on the ground floor that was used to store yarn, and quickly spread to the upper floors. The yarn was not stored in a fireproof warehouse, as required by law. The building had eight stories, with the top three floors under construction. Most of the workers who died were on the first and second floors, and were killed because there were not enough fire exits or fireproof, smoke-proof staircases. The fire department also had difficulty in getting its equipment close enough to effectively fight the fire.[1]

In the aftermath of the fire, questions were raised as to who should be held accountable. Some people argued that the factory owners and the regulators who establish Bangladesh fire safety standards were responsible. Others said that Western clothing companies and retailers who rely on low-cost clothing manufacturing in Bangladesh should ensure that their suppliers have safe factories. Some assigned the blame to Western consumers' desire for cheap clothing that forced retailers to constantly look for low-cost manufacturing locations.

Readers may obtain the complete text of the above case by Andrew Inkpen from the Harvard Case Collection, https://store.hbr.org/product/fire-in-a-bangladesh-garment-factory/TB0335, or consult Rutgers Libraries.

CASE 3 GUIDELINES AND DISCUSSION QUESTIONS

The case treats ethical issues with the garment export sector in the emerging nation of Bangladesh where around 2.5 million workers are employed in contract factories producing garments for European and North American retail chains. This fire that occurred a few years ago is only one example in a string of annually repeated occurrences. Since the year 2000, over 3,000 workers have been injured and around 1,400 killed in workplace accidents that western critics claim, could have been prevented or lessened with better safety practices similar to those in advanced nations.

Who is to blame? Who should take responsibility? The variety of actors in the global supply chain range from (i) consumers to (ii) the retail chains, to (iii) brokers or agents who find and arrange the contract between the retail chains and the factory in Bangladesh, (iv) the factory owners, and finally (v) the workers. Supposedly supervising the operations are (vi) the government of Bangladesh, (vii) BGMEA – Bangladesh Garment Manufacturers and Exporters Association, and (viii) consumer watchdogs and government agencies in advanced-nation importing countries. How to allocate responsibility across the eight stakeholders listed above?

What can be done to prevent the horrendous continuing injuries and deaths?

Is it appropriate (or not) to apply advanced country standards to an emerging nation? If so, what could be the consequences?

Finally, similar problems in the footwear industry several years ago were tackled successfully by major importing brands such as Nike and Adidas. But this has not yet occurred in the garment import industry, even in 2022. Why did the footwear sector succeed in implementing minimal standards and organizing inspections of foreign factories – and why has the international garment supply chain failed to do so?

CHAPTER 18

Cultural Differences and Their Implications for International Business

In a world of more than 6,000 languages, and even more cultures, how does a multinational company handle the inevitable differences? The fact that cultures are different affects the entire spectrum of business decisions from research to production to marketing and after-sales service.

Take, for example, the color design of a company's packaging or webpage. The color white symbolizes cleanness and purity in many Western nations. But in the Far East, white is the color of funerals and death. When McDonald's first introduced its mascot clown, Ronald McDonald, to Japan, his whitened face scared off many Japanese, especially the children. Red is a favorite color for Chinese, symbolizing holidays, weddings, and the country's flag. But in South Africa and other cultures, red is associated with violence and sorrow.

Much of international business involves dealing with supply-chain and alliance partners from different backgrounds. Just negotiating an agreement with a foreign party can be fraught with misunderstandings and different negotiating styles. The all-important customers in each country need a marketing approach specifically tailored to appeal and resonate with them so they will be induced to buy the product or service. Even within the multinational firm, beyond packaging and website design considerations is the more complex issue of managing multicultural workforces, each with different behaviors, habits, and approaches to work. Foreign subsidiaries are often staffed by expatriate managers deputed from headquarters nations who then have to supervise and understand local subordinates.

The useful contrast between high-context and low-context cultures comes from the field of anthropology.[1] Table 1 summarizes the differences. In simple terms, a "high-context" culture is one in which people pay more attention to the context, relationships, and implicit norms than to explicit procedures and written language. Depending on the "context," behaviors and speech may change. For example, depending on the time of day, the status of accompanying persons, the place where a negotiation is taking place, and the strength of prior relationships, the same individual will express (or not express) differing opinions. In brief, the person's behavior and actions will vary depending on the context.

---

[1] A pioneer in this field was Edward T. Hall, who wrote *Beyond Culture,* New York: Doubleday (1976).

Table 1: High-Context Versus Low-Context Cultures

High/Low Context Cultures

High-context cultures	*Low-context cultures*
• Arab cultures, Brazil, China, Japan, Korea, India, Mexico	• USA, Australia, Canada, Switzerland, New Zealand, Russia, South Africa
• Shared culture & common background	• Diverse cultures & backgrounds
• Long-lasting relationships	• Shorter relationships
• Family	• Family separate from work
• Importance of context	• Less dependent on context
• Spoken agreements	• Written agreements
• Insiders and outsiders clearly distinguished	• Insiders and outsiders less clearly distinguished
• Cultural patterns ingrained, slow change	• Cultural patterns change faster
• Meaning from how something is said; covert & implicit	• Meaning determined by what is said rather than how it is said
• Fewer written words / nonverbal cues	• Many written and explicit words
• Reserved reactions	• Reactions exhibited on surface
• Collectivist: "We" is emphasized over "I"	• Individualist
• Bluntness viewed as rude; patience & indirectness valued	• Try to be "up-front", logical, linear and action-oriented
• Skilled at interpreting non verbal communications	• Straight talk, assertive, honesty valued
	• More likely to miss non verbal cues
• Time is open, less structured, flexible based on needs of the people	• Time highly structured

By contrast, in a "low-context" culture, the context is less important. What matters more is explicit social norms, rules, and the written word in agreements and documents. Past relationships, who one knows, family, place, time of day, etc. matter less than consistent behavior in these settings. Plain talk, honesty, keeping one's word, explicit and long agreements, and a greater attention to time are some aspects of low-context cultures.

The Value of Relationships

Of course, these are overly broad (and dangerous) generalizations. Within each grouping, there could be considerable variation. For example, in low-context nations such as the UK or Switzerland, one does not ask a business associate about spouse or family until long after a relationship is established. But in India, Brazil, and Arab cultures, during introductory conversations it may be appropriate to touch on personal and family matters, and this may actually smooth or facilitate the first meeting or initial negotiation.

The Written Word and Long vs. Short Agreements

Low-context cultures place a greater value and emphasis on the written word, so that plausible emails even from strangers are likely to be answered. However, in some high-context cultures like India, even important-sounding messages will go unanswered unless the recipient knows, or knows about, the sender. This does not suggest that the sender of the email or text should give up. Rather, it means trying to find a third party who will explain to the prospective recipient the genuineness, importance, and status of the sender. Then things will go smoothly. But of course, this adds a layer of complexity and delay to what someone in the US or Europe thinks should elicit a quick reply.

On the other hand, the emphasis on the written word, procedures, and rules in low-context cultures like the US also produces delays, one-hundred-page agreements, fat fees for lawyers (the US has by far the most lawyers in the world), and delayed conclusions. Once relationships have been cemented, for example in Arab nations, some Latin American countries, and certain businesses such as the Jewish diamond trade subculture, a handshake, a verbal agreement, or a six-page memorandum of understanding (MOU) may suffice to seal even a large deal.

To summarize, in high-context cultures understandings are more implicit, nuanced, and based on subconscious cultural cues. Low-context cultures are far more reliant on written language, and spoken words are explicit – sometimes to the point of seeming blunt or aggressive to persons from other nations.

The Role of Hierarchy and Status

The crash of Asiana Airlines Flight 214 in San Francisco in 2013, following a series of crashes by Korea-based carriers, illustrates the degree of hierarchy and status in high-context cultures, where subordinates exhibit deference to superiors to the point where they remain silent even when they should speak up. In the US or Scandinavian nations, on the other hand, even junior managers are encouraged and empowered to voice their opinions. Western executives negotiating a deal with Malaysian or Arab companies are often puzzled by the presence of a large team on the other side of the table; but only one person, the "big boss," speaks.

Flying newer airplanes is a team effort. Cockpits in modern aircraft have so many displays that one captain is often unable to focus simultaneously on all readouts. Investigations of Korean crashes using the aircrafts' voice recorders has shown a repeated pattern in which the co-pilot noticed a problem that was not seen by the captain, but did not dare to speak up, or else used such polite and humble language that the gravity of the message did not get through. For example, in a Korean Air Cargo flight that plunged to the ground in London in 1999, investigators concluded that the co-pilot had noticed that the plane's tilt-angle indicator showed an alarming degree of tilt.[2] In

---

[2] Ashley Halsey, Lack of cockpit communication recalls 1999 Korean Airlines crash near London, *Washington Post*, July 8, 2013: https://www.washingtonpost.com/people/ashley-halsey-iii/

other cultures, the co-pilot would immediately have spoken up or shouted an alarm. Not so in this case. The plane plummeted to the ground. According to observer Malcolm Gladwell, "…Korean Air's problem at the time was not old planes or poor crew training. What they were struggling with was a cultural legacy, that Korean culture is hierarchical…."[3] In cultures like Japan or Korea, hierarchy and status dictate the depth to which the junior bows to the senior manager, the distance apart he stands from or follows the leader, and whether he may, or should not, look the boss in the eye. By comparison, in many Western societies, the failure to look a person in the eye may suggest a weak or shifty character.

Surveys show that the number of hours worked per employee per year is remarkably high in Korea and Japan. But the statistic is a bit misleading because in many companies, subordinates will sit at their desks doing little work until as late as 9 PM, just waiting for the boss to leave his[4] office to go home.

The Inability to Say "No"

In India, I often run into trouble when custom-ordering some material from a shop or asking when something will be completed. The typical answer is, "Do not worry, sir. It will be done." But then I am disappointed when the deadline is not met or the job is not done on time. This used to annoy and frustrate me until I realized that in cultures like India or Japan, the speaker confronted with a higher-status person or a foreigner cannot bring her/himself to utter the words, *"No, it cannot be done because of such and such reason…."* Instead, they politely dissimulate, afraid to "insult" the honored customer or foreigner. The Western manager should know that if a Japanese subordinate uses the phrase "It is difficult," this is a code phrase for "No." And if an employee in a Japanese subsidiary or partner firm says, "We will have to study this carefully," that means "Hell no!"[5]

Collectivism vs. Individualism

High-context societies are more likely to be collectivist. Loyalty to "the group" in Japan is more important than the status of the individual. This attitude is reflected in the greater reluctance

---

[3] Interview by Jennifer Reingold, Secrets of Their Success, November 19, 2008, *CNN Money*: https://money.cnn.com/2008/11/11/news/companies/secretsofsuccess_gladwell.fortune/

[4] Although this is beginning to change, there is a much greater probability that males occupy significant or senior managerial positions in those nations.

[5] "Hell no!" is an American expression that may mystify others. It means "Emphatically NO!"

on the part of Japanese companies to lay off employees during recessions or slumps, such as during the pandemic. This is costly to the company, but may pay off in the long run through employee loyalty and lower stress in society – which then translates into greater productivity and lower national healthcare costs.

Collectivism in Japanese companies is seen, even in 2022, in decision-making involving from three to five times as many managers being consulted, compared to the US focus on leadership-based decisions. Of course, this slows down the process. On the other hand, the quality of the decision may be superior (because more Japanese managers have "signed off" on it) than in low-context cultures, where a lone boss may make a quick determination. Moreover, the implementation of the decision is better executed in Japanese firms because more managers have been consulted.

The above illustrates that, in many cross-cultural comparisons, there is no one "right approach." US-based companies can act more quickly, seize opportunities better, and be more innovative. The greater collectivist involvement and delay in Japan can also be an advantage, as seen in the quality of design and execution in Japanese products and services. Each society finds its own balance between contrasting priorities.

The Perception of Time

Visitors to many European countries and Western nations sometimes remark on the ubiquity of ancient clock towers and church steeples in every village and town. It is no coincidence, in my opinion, that mechanical clocks were first perfected in Europe. These are societies where time is observed more assiduously. Before portable watches, the sound of church bells or towers served to alert individuals of important hours in the day and to synchronize their activities. Modern economies are based not on individual efforts, but on synchronization and sequencing. Time in low-context societies is an indispensable part of economic structure. The time-driven American manager, hinting that he or she is in a hurry, might say under pressure, "I am *running* late" or "My watch is *running* faster than I can keep up with it," as opposed to experiencing time merely moving at a natural pace.

This is another cultural variable where changes are rapidly occurring. Contrary to stereotypes, many managers in Madrid or Medellin may be as driven by their schedules and watches as in London or New York. However, as a (perhaps dangerous) generalization, in high-context cultures people tend to have a more relaxed attitude. If tasks have to wait, there is greater tolerance and a "so be it" attitude.

Implications for Business

Some important implications for doing business in different cultures are highlighted in Table 2. In Low-context cultures such as the UK or the US, the role of lawyers in business and government is significant, both in terms of their numbers and in their participation in deal-making. Since such low-context settings place a great importance on the written word, explicitness, and detail, agreements tend to be long and their language intricate. It is no coincidence that English has the largest vocabulary – the Oxford English Dictionary contains more than 200,000 words. (Paradoxically, despite this, the language most used in the world is English, with an estimated 1.3– 1.7 billion persons deemed capable of composing a basic email in the language.[6])

Table 2 Implications for Doing Business in Different Cultures

Implications in High vs. Low Context Cultures

Practical Implications	High Context	Low Context
Lawyers	Less important	Very important
A person's word	Is his or her bond	Get it in writing
Sanctity of Agreements	Agreements can be changed	Agreements are sacred and enforceable
Responsibility for organizational error	Taken by top level	Pushed to lower levels
Negotiations	Lengthy	Can Proceed quickly

The dependence on and availability of many precise and intricate words and phrases also enable negotiations to proceed more quickly than in cultures where deals are based on cultivating relationships, a process that takes longer in countries like China, where *guanxi* (the Chinese word for relationships) underlies many business dealings. While things are changing, in China and other high-context cultures, disagreements are more likely to be settled through the *guanxi* network than through the courts.

---

[6] Of course, as a "mother tongue," Mandarin has the most native speakers.

The sanctity of agreements is also lower in high-context cultures. To a Chinese businessperson, a written document may be viewed only as an initial step, subject to future modification if conditions change. The Chinese partner asking for a later modification can outrage an American joint venture partner to whom "a deal is a deal," meaning firmly in place, if not forever inviolable.

In many, if not all, high-context cultures, responsibility is assumed at top levels of the organization. It is not unknown for Japanese CEOs to personally contact and express regret to members of the public or customers in the event of a mishap or error.

Hofstede's More Detailed Cross-Cultural Comparisons

Dividing cultures into only two categories is too blunt and imperfect a classification. Prof. Geert Hofstede, a Dutch social psychologist and professor, built his career by enunciating four, and later six, "dimensions" of comparing business behaviors in various countries.[7] In his early career, he worked in IBM Corporation's human resources (HR) department, where he had the opportunity to survey hundreds of IBM employees in different nations. Later, his data covered thousands of respondents in over 70 countries. Figure 1 shows only eight nations for illustration purposes.

Power Distance

"Power distance" is Hofstede's academic language for "degree of hierarchy or social stratification" in a society. China, India, and Mexico (with scores between 77 and 81) show a high emphasis on hierarchy. Scandinavian nations like Sweden (with a score of 31) are far more egalitarian. When Ericsson executives negotiate with Chinese companies or the government, they have to do an advance search to identify and be very conscious of the status of the Chinese individuals they are dealing with. By contrast, a Chinese or Mexican negotiator may be baffled by the Swedish team appearing to have no discipline, with even junior Swedish team members speaking out of turn.

When making appointments in foreign subsidiaries, the multinational firm's HR department needs to think carefully about the implications of nominating a person from a high-power-distance culture to supervise employees from a low-power-distance nation, and *vice versa*.

---

[7] Hofstede, G. (2001). *Culture's Consequences: Comparing Values, Behaviors, Institutions, and Organizations Across Nations*. Second Edition, Thousand Oaks CA: Sage Publications: https://www.hofstede-insights.com/product/compare-countries/

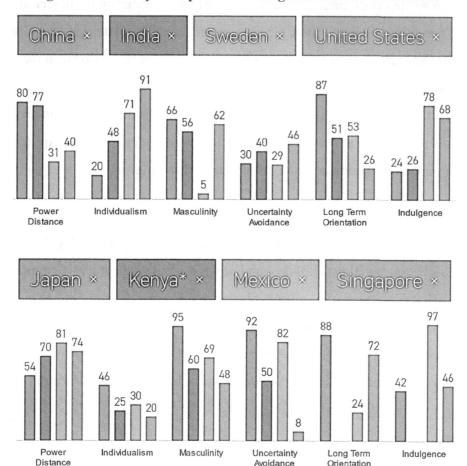

Figure 1: Country Comparisons Using Hofstede's Dimensions

Individualism (vs. Collectivism)

One of the most "individualist" nations is the US (with a score of 91), whose culture glorifies individual achievement, expression, and success. By contrast, China and Singapore, as seen in Figure 1, show a score of only 20 on this scale, suggesting they are conformist societies. Identifying with their group first, Chinese firms often name themselves with the geographic location of their headquarters as the first word in the company's name, as in *Shanghai Automotive Industry Corporation (SAIC)*, China's largest automobile producer, or *Tsingtao Brewery Co. Ltd*, one of its large beer producers, suggesting the primacy of the city (or group) over the individual company. Also, Chinese list their family names before their given names for the same reason.

Indeed, in China, firms have to be completely obedient to their city, provincial, and national governments. Hence, foreign firms operating in China need to be ever conscious of the larger interests of the city or province. Similarly, when dealing with a business conglomerate in India,

Singapore, or Kenya, it is wise to keep in mind the business group perspective, as well as that of the individual company within the group.

Masculinity

This is Hofstede's code word for achievement, heroism, assertiveness, and material success – or in overly simple terms, the degree of "*machismo.*" Mexico and China score high (69 and 66, respectively). Today, this is manifested in literally hundreds of similar movies in China depicting "wolf warriors," a term used for depictions of heroic Chinese fighting invaders from Western nations and Japan, who humiliated the Chinese from 1842 until 1945. (Incidentally, these movies are also an expression of unbridled nationalism, manifested in assertive language recently used by the Chinese government against some Western governments and some Western multinationals. Excessive nationalism is a form of assertiveness.)

For example, in 2021, H&M (Sweden-based Hennes & Mauritz AB), a global clothing company, adopted a seemingly innocuous ethics policy that indicated they would not buy garments from any sources that use forced or bonded labor. This was in response to growing sensitivity on the part of US and European customers regarding "socially responsible" corporate practices. But once some Chinese bloggers discovered this general ethics statement, they associated it with the province of Xinjiang, where Western news sources alleged that cotton harvesting – a mainstay of that province's economy – was done with coerced labor. A storm of boycotts descended on H&M, many store leases were terminated in Chinese cities, the government joined in the general condemnation, and sales of H&M in China declined suddenly.

Interestingly, Hofstede's "masculinity" score for environmentally and socially conscious Sweden itself is a very low 5, as seen in Figure 1.

Uncertainty Avoidance

This dimension tracks the degree to which a culture is averse to uncertainty and ambiguity, traits that are also associated with following rigid codes of behavior, belief, and orthodoxy. Japan's high score of 92 (shown in Figure 1) is consistent with the highly methodical, procedure-driven, collective, and hence drawn-out or delayed decision-making in Japanese corporations. As indicated above, this cultural attitude creates the drawback of delay, resulting in lagging behind more precipitate, risk-taking competitors. But it also means that the final collective and deliberated decision is more sound and the implementation of it more effective.

Long-Term Orientation

Ancient cultures like China and Japan think in terms of centuries, both past and future. The founder of today's Panasonic Corporation, Konosuke Matsushita, charged his top management with developing 250-year strategic plans.[8] In May 2015, the Chinese unveiled a 10-year "China 2025" plan whose unabashed agenda was to identify sectors in which the Chinese wished to catch up technologically with the West. (This also alarmed governments, including the Trump administration, and unleashed a competitive cycle of increasing acrimony between China and the US, as well as some European nations.)

The Chinese hark back millennia to their ancient past. The long-term orientation score for China is a high 87 in the Hofstede measure. These reveries evoke two types of memories: (1) the primacy of the Chinese economy in the world economy until the end of the Ming Dynasty, and (2) the humiliations China suffered at the hands of the British, other Western powers, and the Japanese under the Qing Dynasty. These ancient recollections or dreams are motivating the Chinese drive to surpass the West, as well as the increasingly assertive posture by the Chinese government toward the West and other countries.

In terms of corporate planning, European and other multinationals need to be aware that while their motivation may be to earn quick profits from the huge Chinese market, their Chinese partners are content to patiently bide their time, hungry to learn and absorb the most advanced technology from their foreign partners. There are countless examples. From ordinary combustion-engine automobiles, to solar panels, to wind-generation machines, to electric storage technologies, to high-speed railways, to mobile telephones, to data-mining techniques and artificial intelligence, among many examples, the Chinese have patiently assimilated and improved technologies that originated in Japan and Western countries to the point where their firms today are at the leading edges of knowledge in several fields.

But the US score for long-term orientation is only 26 (shown in Figure 1). The US company CEO, despite knowing all this, may not care. After all, his or her bonus is based on quick, short-term quarterly and annual results, and his/her term in office will be over in a few short years, after which an affluent retirement awaits. There is no loyalty toward the larger group or nation in this behavior.

---

[8] He took this with utmost seriousness, and despite the 250-year planning cycle eliciting chuckles among critics, Matsushita and Panasonic played a signal role in the 20th-century modernization of Japan.

Indulgence

"Indulgence" is Hofstede's summary word for the desire for gratification of basic desires, enjoyment, and fun. Sweden, the US, and Mexico have high scores in Hofstede's surveys in this dimension, whereas China, India, and Singapore are lower.

Such comparisons have important implications for marketing campaigns and advertising. In indulgent societies, advertising would emphasize quick gratification of wants or pleasures, whether it be for food or travel. For example, Swedes love to travel and enjoy their long vacations. The obverse, or concomitant aspect, of pleasurable gratification is freedom from discomfort. In pharmaceutical advertising in the US, the words "fast relief" or "quick relief" are often used for pain-relief medicines. It is no coincidence that the US (a somewhat hypochondriacal society) has, by far, the world's greatest healthcare costs per capita (approximately double that of the UK, France, and other nations with higher longevity), as well as high addiction rates to painkillers.

In nations lower on the "indulgence" scale, marketing messages may emphasize restraint and deferred gratification, such as saving for the long term or retirement. Advertising may emphasize the quality and durability of a product (despite its high price). A marketing campaign may highlight restraint as conforming with social norms and duties toward children, the next generation, parents, or the nation.

The same product sold worldwide can be "positioned" with quite different advertising messages. A kitchen appliance in indulgent cultures can be pitched as a device that helps to quickly prepare a delicious meal. In Germany, its sleek design may be the emphasized feature, whereas in Japan it might be its durability and quality of manufacturing. This is an example of where the product design may be more or less the same globally, but the multinational firm adapts or varies its advertising message to suit each local culture.

American Business Values (and How the Rest of the World Views American Executives)

Measured by the stock of (historical or cumulative) investment, US companies are still the biggest holders of foreign direct investment (FDI) assets. It may therefore be useful to identify some American business values and behaviors and then ask how they appeal to, or repel, employees, partners, or customers in other nations.

Table 3 is a distillation of several values or principles that most Americans would deem as reasonable, worthwhile, and economically efficient. Yet not all of them translate into behaviors that "fit" well in other nations.

How does the US-based executive come across, or impress, persons from other cultures? Typically, the American executive is a woman or man under some pressure to show (quick) results. S/he comes across to the more relaxed cultures in the rest of the world as driven by the clock and schedules. Especially during in-person visits to foreign locations, s/he can be jet-lagged, but despite that plunges immediately into a series of meetings. Moreover, one characteristic of US culture is the value placed on candor and direct, no-nonsense talk, where the speaker quickly gets to the point. Famous aphorisms in the US include, "Don't beat around the bush" and "Let's get down to brass tacks." In contrast, persons from other cultures do not reveal their true feelings for a long time until a relationship has been developed, a process that may take weeks or years in many nations and certainly cannot be achieved in a visit of a few days or a week. Meanwhile, the boss or supervisor at headquarters in the US often wonders why the traveling executive has not delivered results in timely American fashion.

Table 3: American Business Values That May Not All "Fit" Well with Other Cultures

American Business Values

- Informality is acceptable and even desirable (Use of first names)
- My watch is *"running"* / "Time is Money"
- Woman or man in a hurry ("The meter is ticking")
- Firm handshake
- "Look the person in the eye"
- Efficiency
- "Get down to brass tacks"
- "Don't beat around the bush"
- Planning
- Objective criteria, papers, catalogs
- Long contracts – many words
- "A deal is a deal"
- Merit matters (more than seniority)
- Merit matters (more than connections or *guanxi*)
- "Arms-length" relationships
- "The buck stops here"
- Individual decision making
- Individual creativity
- Functional specialization (vs. the generalist manager)

The term "big data" was first pioneered by US companies. Sometimes, the US-based executive comes armed with so much data, facts, and analysis that s/he intimidates foreigners. American business education (and career tracks) emphasize specialization. US employees specialize in just finance, or just marketing, or just analytics and IT for many years, if not for their entire career, which gives them deep expertise in rather narrow slices of overall business operations. On the other hand, in high-context cultures like Japan, the Middle East, or some Latin American countries, and even in Europe where family businesses are more common, the manager is more likely to be a generalist. This contrast may create tension, or cognitive dissonance, between the American who knows a lot about a narrow slice of business and the executive abroad whose experience has covered many of his/her company's departments and functions, but lacks very deep knowledge of any one of them.

US business places much value on efficiency, fast results, and achievement. The US economy is the most productive in the world in terms of output per employee.[9] Other cultures strike a different balance between work, efficiency, and leisure, taking longer lunch breaks and five-week annual holidays (as compared with the brutal 10-working-day vacations most Americans get as personal time off). Moreover, as a generalization, job security is among the lowest in the US, with layoff notices sometimes delivered to employees on a Friday afternoon, a few hours before the end of the week. In other cultures, and even in advanced countries like Germany and Japan, many employees stay with the same firm for life. The result is that the American executive may come across to others in the rest of a world as a person under pressure – tense, arrogant, driven, abrupt, and quick-results-oriented, even though beneath the pressures of American work life is a very charming human being.

US culture places value on informality. Hardly five minutes after meeting someone, executives use their first names. In previous and even current generations in Germany, that will not do. For years after meeting a German counterpart, one is expected to continue to use their family name, accompanied by "Herr" or "Frau" and any other titles they may have received, such as "Dr." or "Prof." This is consistent with the earlier observation that in high-context cultures relationships matter and have to be patiently built over a much longer period of time. In low-context cultures, building a relationship is not as important. What matters more are objective criteria, unambiguous and abundant data, the written word, and long, detailed agreements vetted by lawyers.

---

[9] See the productivity numbers in the textbook chapter "7 Reasons to Expect US Manufacturing Resurgence," also published by Farok J. Contractor at *Yale Global*, August 7, 2012: https://yaleglobal.yale.edu/content/7-reasons-expect-us-manufacturing-resurgence

Low-context cultures also place more emphasis on individual merit, as opposed to family background, status, or seniority. This often creates tension between foreign subsidiary executives in Asia or Latin America, who expect promotion based simply on age or the number of years of service, as opposed to capability or merit. In many cases, a brilliant young American MBA-holder is appointed over the heads of older local employees (who understand their country better), leading to conflicts, lost morale, and plummetting performance by the group as a whole. On the other hand, from the US headquarters perspective, the suggestion that a relative of a current foreign subsidiary employee be hired is met with suspicions of nepotism. Incidentally, in some contexts where relationships and contacts are key to business success, nepotism can *occasionally* produce net benefits if the performance of the subsidiary or team is sufficiently enhanced by a good feeling of group cohesion. There are reports of a few Asian companies actually encouraging relatives to apply for jobs. Such HR policies are also consistent with cultures where key decision-making is done by the group as a whole, rather than by individual managers.

From the above discussion, we can see how the values of American business culture that work well and are considered desirable in the US may, however, clash or be inconsistent with values and practices in other parts of the world.

Conclusion: Some Universally Helpful Tips for Building a Global Civilization

For the last few centuries, humanity has been coming together, a process that has accelerated with globalization – especially in the last 60 years. But for the previous 160,000 years, the story was different. Humankind had fragmented into isolated small tribal groups with little contact with one another. This produced a plethora of languages and cultures. According to current thinking, small groups walked out of Africa around 160 millennia ago then scattered to all continents, "recently" reaching the Americas, some 30 or 40 thousand years ago. Small hunter-gatherer tribes living in isolation eked out a bare living. Out of one source in Africa, there resulted thousands of cultures and languages – as expressed in Latin, "*Ex uno, plures*" (Out of one, many).

The advent of agriculture a mere 10,000 years ago produced the first settled groups of any size, the beginning of humans coming together in larger agglomerations, the formation of cities and nations, the beginning of inter-group trade over distances, and today the genesis of a global civilization. Immigrant nations like the US have adopted mottos such as "*E pluribus unum*" (Out of many, one), which is on the Great Seal of the United States.

Building a global civilization increasingly involves working with people from other cultures and bridging the differences. Table 4 indicates some universally helpful tips for executives, many of which amount to one overall recommendation: to be "other-oriented," as contrasted with "self-referential." This requires a mental adjustment. Some multinational companies already screen employees before posting them abroad to assess the degree to which they are "other-oriented."[10]

The traits described in Table 4 may come naturally to some. For other executives, this is not easy and may take conscious effort or training. The key to understanding the other person or culture is first to be open-minded and wash out, or suppress, presumptions or predilections from one's home culture. Especially for the driven and impatient American executive, great – almost saintly – patience is required in many situations abroad where things can move more slowly. (It helps if the boss back in the US also understands that processes typically take more time outside of the country.) The simple acceptance that people are different, and accepting their different approaches and behaviors goes a long way to building relationships, important in most nations.

Table 4: Universally Helpful Tips

Universally Helpful Tips

- Being open-minded
- Patience
- Acceptance – that people and societies are different
- Build relationships
- Praise and give thanks when deserved (without being obsequious)
- Appreciate the local culture and values
- Look for non-verbal cues (Posture, Facial Expressions, etc.)
- Find local mentors / informants / advisors
- Be *in*direct
- Do not hesitate to ask for help

Even in the poorest of nations, there is much to appreciate, whether it be the local flora and fauna; the town cathedral, temple, or mosque; their art; or simply the country's climate of, perhaps, abundant sunshine. Expressing appreciation (without being obsequious) has smoothed many a negotiation and built successful foreign businesses.

---

[10] Gregg Henriques, Are You "Other-Oriented"? Understanding a common relational style, *Psychology Today*, March 21, 2014: https://www.psychologytoday.com/us/blog/theory-knowledge/201403/are-you-other-oriented

Americans value directness, even outspokenness. But that does not work very well in much of the world. Before having a strong relationship, in most cultures it is better to be indirect and diplomatic. Nonverbal cues such as facial expressions and posture are often more revealing than the spoken word in many nations, especially those where the local culture suggests not revealing thoughts to strangers.

Finally, most humans are fundamentally kindhearted. This is not something that American culture necessarily recommends, especially among males; but the simple act of asking for help (for instance in understanding a spreadsheet, a strategy, or a business situation) often motivates the other parties to go out of their way to help the visitor, more so than they would have done otherwise. Asking for help or clarification is also an expression of humility, an acknowledgment to locals that the visitor recognizes the differences and may be willing to learn and adapt. In longer-term foreign assignments, it is important to cultivate local mentors and informants who can give advice on small and great matters, ranging from finding an apartment or grocery store to offering advice on what strategy best fits the local market.

There is no assurance, or desire, that all humans and all nations will or should become similar. Differences do – and should – remain. Let a hundred flowers bloom. Global economic efficiency is not always dependent on convergence, or mimetic isomorphism. Building a global civilization does not mean that differences should disappear[11] or that there should be supranational governments. What is more important for the near future is bridging the differences across cultures and working together, be it for mutually beneficial international trade, cooperative innovation, climate change, or tackling global pandemics.

---

[11] On the contrary, the theory of comparative advantage that underlies international trade is based on differences existing across nations.

STUDY QUESTIONS

Chapters 16 – 18 (Part V)

1. What pressures drive companies toward either globalized vs. locally responsive practices?

2. What kinds of industries and companies tend towards a greater emphasis on catering to local market and local cultural needs? Which types of firms prefer global standardization?

3. What external environmental factors drive companies towards either locally responsive or globally standardized practices?

4. What strategic planning procedures may be used by a company to seek the appropriate middle ground between local adaptation and cross-country standardization?

5. What are some classic alternative organizational structures for companies operating in many nations?

6. Despite the introduction of a common currency such as the euro for nineteen European nations, which (presumably) makes price comparisons easier, prices for the same item can vary significantly across the "Eurozone." Detail the factors that allow price variations to persist.

7. What is meant by "global rationalization" or seeking the maximum efficiencies from global operations? What exactly is involved? What are the advantages of "global rationalization"? (Hint: See the question below for broad answers.)

8. In the ultimate sense, global rationalization means (i) disaggregating the value chain into smaller and smaller pieces, and then (ii) deciding in which country each piece is best performed. At the same time, (iii) while central control is maintained, the locus of centralized global control for each particular operation, or function may be relocated to other countries and called "Centers of Excellence" for certain operations. Finally (iv) the human resource practices of the globally rationalized company ideally need to recruit and compensate managers without reference to their passport, or country of origin, and at the same time, relocate them to wherever their talents are best utilized in the company's far-flung operations. *However, what disadvantages, costs, and higher risks would such practices also entail?*

APPENDIX:
ADDITIONAL SUGGESTED READINGS

Part I. Overseas Expansion: Strategies to Reach Foreign Markets

European Commission: Anti-dumping: https://ec.europa.eu/trade/policy/accessing-markets/trade-defence/actions-against-imports-into-the-eu/anti-dumping/

Johnston: Economies of Scale – Sending a T Shirt from China to Europe for 2.5 Cents, November 21, 2011: https://econfix.wordpress.com/2011/11/21/economies-of-scale-sending-a-t-shirt-from-china-to-europe-for-2-5-cents/

Kendall: High Court Backs Thai Book Reseller, *Wall Street Journal*, March 20, 2013 (*WSJ* accessible through Rutgers Libraries)

Rubin: Companies Save Billions in Taxes by Shifting Assets Around Globe, *Wall Street Journal*, April 8, 2020

Wikipedia: Grey Market: http://en.wikipedia.org/wiki/Grey_market

Part II. The Economics Basis for International Business

Batabayal: What Is a Tariff: An Economist Explains, *The Conversation*, March 15, 2018: https://theconversation.com/what-is-a-tariff-an-economist-explains-93392

The Economist Explains (A.F.): Why Is Free Trade Good? *The Economist*, March 14, 2018

Part III. Foreign Exchange Rates: Their Impact on International Operations

Section A. Hedging Foreign Currency Receivables and Payables

No Supplemental Readings

Section B. Interest Rates and Foreign Exchange Rates

No Supplemental Readings

Part IV. Foreign Exchange Rates and Pricing in International Markets

Section A. Economic Exposure and Operational Planning

Case 2: *Molto Delizioso*: Pricing and Profits Following Brexit Devaluation; the case must be accessed directly from Harvard Publishing: https://store.hbr.org/product/molto-delizioso-pricing-and-profits-following-brexit-devaluation/W17205; or consult Rutgers Libraries

Part IV. Foreign Exchange Rates and Pricing in International Markets
(Continued…)

Section B. Optimal Pricing as a Function of Exchange Rates

<u>Gallo</u>: A Refresher on Price Elasticity, *Harvard Business Review*, August 21, 2015:

> https://hbr.org/2015/08/a-refresher-on-price-elasticity or consult Rutgers Libraries

Part V. Global Management in a Still-Fragmented World: Local vs. International

<u>Case 3</u>: Fire in a Bangladesh Garment Factory; the case must be accessed directly from Harvard

> Publishing: https://store.hbr.org/product/fire-in-a-bangladesh-garment-factory/TB0335; or

> consult Rutgers Libraries

<u>Earley and Mosakowski</u>: Cultural Intelligence, *Harvard Business Review*, October 2004; from

> Harvard Publishing: https://hbr.org/2004/10/cultural-intelligence; or consult Rutgers Libraries

<u>Huq</u>: The Economics of a $6.75 Shirt, *Wall Street Journal*, May 16, 2013:

> https://www.wsj.com/articles/SB10001424127887323582904578485300080843278

<u>Khan & Rodriguez</u>: Human before the Garment: Bangladesh Tragedy Revisited. Ethical

> Manufacturing or Lack Thereof in Garment Manufacturing Industry, *World Journal of Social*

> *Sciences*, January 2015; consult Rutgers Libraries

<u>Salacuse</u>: The Top Ten Ways Culture Can Affect International Negotiations, *Ivey Business*

> *Journal*, April 2005: https://iveybusinessjournal.com/publication/the-top-ten-ways-that-culture-

> can-affect-international-negotiations/

<u>Trompenaars & Woolliams</u>: Lost in Translation, *Harvard Business Review*, April 2011:

> https://hbr.org/2011/04/lost-in-translation or consult Rutgers Libraries

<u>Yang</u>: Management Styles: American vis-a-vis Japanese, *Columbia Journal of World Business*,

> Fall 1977; consult Rutgers Libraries

<u>Yee</u>: Two years after Bangladesh factory collapse, A struggle to set things right, *Washington Post*,

> April 23, 2015: https://www.washingtonpost.com/world/asia_pacific/bangladesh-garment-

> industry-pushes-to-meet-deadlines-on-safety-standards/2015/04/22/b72ca9f0-e87b-11e4-8581-

> 633c536add4b_story.html

AUTHOR BIO

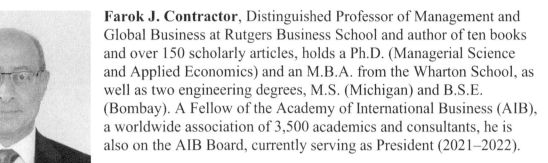

Farok J. Contractor, Distinguished Professor of Management and Global Business at Rutgers Business School and author of ten books and over 150 scholarly articles, holds a Ph.D. (Managerial Science and Applied Economics) and an M.B.A. from the Wharton School, as well as two engineering degrees, M.S. (Michigan) and B.S.E. (Bombay). A Fellow of the Academy of International Business (AIB), a worldwide association of 3,500 academics and consultants, he is also on the AIB Board, currently serving as President (2021–2022).

Professor Contractor's research focuses on key issues in International Business, such as corporate alliances, emerging markets, outsourcing and offshoring, valuation of intangible assets, the technology transfer process, licensing, and foreign direct investment. He is the recipient of a Silver Medal for the number of contributions to the *Journal of International Business Studies*, a leading management journal, and also a Lifetime Achievement Award from the Indian Academy of Management.

He has taught at the Wharton School, Copenhagen Business School, Fletcher School of Law and Diplomacy; Tufts University; Nanyang Technological University; Indian Institutes of Management (IIM – Ahmedabad and Calcutta); Indian Institute of Foreign Trade; XLRI (India); Rutgers business programs in Beijing, Shanghai, and Singapore; and Lubin School of Business, as well as conducted executive seminars on four continents.

Previously, Professor Contractor was a Tata Administrative Service Executive with the international arm of the Tata Group, one of India's largest conglomerates.

He has been a Fulbright Fellow and a Unilever Fellow, and he has worked on projects for UNCTAD.

Professor Contractor's website for managers, students, policymakers, and educated laypeople covering International Business issues has been read over time in 174 countries: https://GlobalBusiness.blog.

For more details on the author's background, see his curriculum vitae on the Rutgers Faculty Page: https://www.business.rutgers.edu/sites/default/files/documents/faculty/cv-farok-contractor-long.pdf.

Made in United States
North Haven, CT
28 October 2023

43291646R00174